Praise for Renting Out Your Property For Dummies

'This book is a comprehensive guide to the process of renting out your property, brim full of sound practical advice based on years of experience. It's an absolute must for the bookshelf of any would-be landlord, novice and experienced alike.'

— Tom Entwistle, Editor of the rental property website, LandlordZONE.co.uk

'The comprehensive guide sheds light on the constantly changing property market and provides the low-down on both the financial and legal aspects of renting. Packed with insider advice, it covers everything from dealing with tenants to dealing with cash flow. Whether you have inherited a home, or are planning to become a property tycoon, it could be your roadmap to success.'

— *The Index* magazine

'A comprehensive guide that covers all aspects of renting a property – and turning a profit.'

— *Personal Finance* magazine

'. . . simple-to-read and understandable pieces of advice . . . could prove to be a sound investment . . .'

— *Western Daily Press*

'. . . an excellent reference source . . .'

— *Junior* magazine

'. . . essential guide . . . one of the best guides on the bookshelves . . .'

— *What House?* magazine

'. . . simple, comprehensive guide . . . packed with insider advice . . .'

— *Oxford Times*

'. . . required reading . . . the amateur's bible . . .'

— *The Herald* (Glasgow)

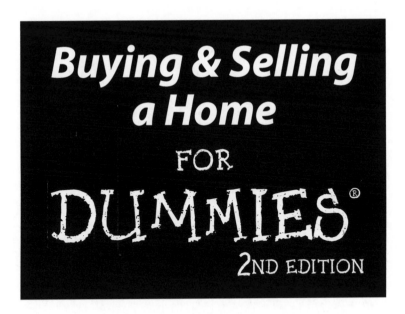

Buying & Selling a Home

FOR DUMMIES®

2ND EDITION

by Melanie Bien

John Wiley & Sons, Ltd

Buying & Selling a Home For Dummies,® 2nd Edition
Published by
John Wiley & Sons, Ltd
The Atrium
Southern Gate
Chichester
West Sussex
PO19 8SQ
England

E-mail (for orders and customer service enquires): cs-books@wiley.co.uk

Visit our Home Page on www.wileyeurope.com

FSC
www.fsc.org
MIX
Paper from
responsible sources
FSC® C013604

About the Author

Melanie Bien is an Associate Director at independent mortgage broker Savills Private Finance. Before joining SPF at the end of 2004, she was personal finance editor and property writer on the *Independent on Sunday*. Melanie has written about buying and selling homes for a variety of national newspapers, magazines, and Web sites, and has written several books and pamphlets to accompany television programmes on property makeovers and design, buying, renovating, and selling property.

Melanie lives in East London.

Dedication

This book is dedicated to Jonathan, JB, Helena, and William.

Author's Acknowledgements

I would like to thank Jason Dunne and Daniel Mersey at John Wiley & Sons for the opportunity to write this book and their help, direction, feedback, and constructive criticism during the process. Also, many thanks to everyone who works behind the scenes at Wiley for their efforts in making this book possible.

Thanks to those friends I had to cancel on at the last minute for being not only understanding but encouraging: it was more to do with deadlines looming than the allure of the Scottish conveyancing process, honest.

And finally, thanks to my husband and family for their untiring support and encouragement.

Publisher's Acknowledgements

We're proud of this book; please send us your comments through our Dummies online registration form located at www.dummies.com/register/.

Some of the people who helped bring this book to market include the following:

Acquisitions, Editorial, and Media Development

Executive Project Editor: Daniel Mersey

Project Editor: Rachael Chilvers

Content Editor: Nicole Burnett

Development Editor: Tracy Barr

Copy Editor: Martin Key

Proofreader: Kim Vernon

Technical Reviewer: Ron Cole

Publisher: Jason Dunne

Executive Editor: Samantha Spickernell

Cover Photos: © Elizabeth Whiting & Associates/CORBIS

Cartoons: Ed McLachlan

Production

Project Coordinator: Erin Smith

Layout and Graphics: Reuben W. Davis, Joyce Haughey, Melissa K. Jester

Proofreaders: David Faust, Caitie Kelly

Indexer: Christina Karpeles

Contents at a Glance

Table of Contents

Introduction

....

*W*elcome to *Buying & Selling a Home For Dummies, 2nd Edition*. You can discover many of life's lessons by trial and error, but because buying a property is one of the most expensive and stressful things you are ever likely to do, the fewer mistakes you make along the way, the better. In this book, you can find loads of information and advice that you might need to make buying or selling your home as smooth, straightforward and pain-free an experience as possible.

About This Book

These pages are overflowing with useful advice and information presented in a light, easy-to-access format. This book helps you decide whether the time is right to get a foot on the property ladder for the first time, how to decide upon the location and type of property you want, what you need to know about arranging the financing, and what happens on the legal side of things. Those selling their homes can also find plenty of help, from setting the price to preparing your property for viewings and haggling with prospective buyers. Just as important, this book can help you maintain your sense of humour – as well as your sanity – as you deal with these challenges and more.

Conventions Used in This Book

To help you navigate through this book, I've set up a few conventions:

- ✔ *Italic* is used for emphasis and to highlight new words or terms that are defined.
- ✔ **Boldfaced** text is used to indicate the action part of numbered steps.
- ✔ Monofont is used for web addresses.

What You're Not to Read

I've written this book so that you can find information easily and easily understand what you find. And although I believe that you want to pore over every last word between the two yellow covers, I actually make it easy for you to identify 'skippable' material. This is the stuff that, although interesting and related to the topic at hand, isn't essential for you to know:

- **Text in sidebars.** The sidebars are the shaded boxes that appear here and there. They share personal stories and observations, but aren't necessary reading.

- **Anything with a Technical Stuff icon attached.** This information is interesting but not critical to your understanding of buying and selling property.

- **The stuff on the copyright page.** Take it from me, there's nothing here of interest unless you are inexplicably enamoured by legal language and reprint information.

Foolish Assumptions

In this book, I make some general assumptions about who you are:

- You may never have bought your own property before but are thinking about it. Perhaps some of your friends have recently got a foot on the first rung of the property ladder, and you're thinking about joining them. Maybe you're sick of renting and are wondering whether buying would actually work out cheaper. Or maybe you've had enough of living with the folks – bless 'em – and are ready to move on.

- You may be a homeowner who's looking to upgrade to a bigger property. Even though you've bought a flat or house before, you may not have sold one and want to know what avenue – selling privately, at auction, or with the help of an estate agent – is best.

- You hope to get information on the best mortgage for your circumstances, whether you are a first-time buyer or moving to a bigger property.

- You want easy-to-understand information that explains just what you need to know about buying or selling property because you've got better things to do (like sleeping, participating in your favourite leisure activity, or even relaxing on holiday) than become an expert on property law. In other words, you want to get it right while you retain control over your life.

How This Book Is Organised

Buying & Selling a Home For Dummies, 2nd Edition is organised into six parts. The chapters within each part cover specific topic areas in more detail. So you can easily and quickly scan a topic that interests you, or you can troubleshoot the source of your latest major headache!

Part I: So You Want to Buy Your First Home?

You may currently be renting a flat or house for good reason – perhaps you aren't in a position to buy your own home. But before you throw in the towel and decide that you simply can't afford to buy your own place, find out for sure whether this is the case or not. You may discover that home-ownership is a possibility for you. This part helps you assess whether you can get your hands on the necessary cash to buy the home of your dreams or whether you need to downscale your ambitions. If you can't afford to raise the money on your own, this part also help you examine what options – like teaming up with family or friends – can help you get your foot on the property ladder. You can also find advice on how to choose the right property and how to research an area, so that when you do finally buy, you're happy with the house and the area you chose. And because you'll probably use the services of an estate agent, this part explains what you need to know about those, too.

Part II: Finding the Right Property

Once you know what you want and have worked out that you can vaguely afford it, the next step is the sometimes hit-and-miss process of actually finding the home of your dreams. Some people are lucky and end up buying the first property they set foot in, while others spend months fruitlessly searching for what they want. In this part, you can find what questions to ask when viewing properties, and I also guide you through the various construction styles and architectural periods you may come across during your search. If you are especially brave, or can't find a property you want to buy, this part also includes information on self-build, including advice on sticking to budget, not falling afoul of planning rules, and getting your home completed on time.

Part III: Making an Offer and Finding the Readies

Buying property is an expensive business, so it's important to get the financing just right. This part takes you from making an offer to signing on the dotted line – and everything in between. Here you can find advice on making an offer that gets you the property you've got your heart set on without paying over the odds. You also get advice on using a mortgage broker and the different types of mortgage available. If finances are tight, you'll find the information on low-cost routes to homeownership helpful. This part also helps you safeguard your money, with advice on the various surveys available to ensure that you don't make an expensive mistake, as well as the insurance cover you need to protect the roof over your head.

Part IV: Selling Your Home

The worst fear of many homeowners is selling their property at the wrong time – and not getting as much for it as they could have done. This part helps you assess whether the time is right to move and helps you ensure that you get the best price for your home. You can find advice on getting your home ready for prospective buyers to view and how to guide them round – especially helpful information if you're selling your home privately. Because many sellers use estate agents, this part also includes information on how to ensure that you get the best services from your agent and what to do if your agent isn't performing as well as you had hoped. Even if you leave the negotiating to your estate agent, the final decision as to whether to accept an offer or not is yours. You can also find advice on whether your response to an offer should be yes or no.

Part V: The Legal Process of Buying and Selling

The legal stuff is usually guaranteed to make most people's eyes glaze over, but if you're buying or selling a home, you must become familiar with the *conveyancing process* – the name for the legal transfer of a property from seller to buyer. Certain things will be expected of you along the way – from signing and returning forms quickly to supplying your solicitor with additional information. By knowing what you need to do and when you should be doing it, you can avoid holding up the entire buying-selling process. This part gives you the low-down of what both parties' solicitors do during conveyancing; it also gives you an idea of the costs involved. And because the property buying and selling process in Scotland differs in many ways from the process used in England, Wales, and Northern Ireland, I give you a full breakdown of that, too.

Part VI: The Part of Tens

Here, in a concise and lively set of condensed chapters, are tips that can make the difference between success and failure. In these chapters I address the things a first-time homeowner should know, offer suggestions on how to sell your home, and provide advice that can help you deal with estate agents.

Icons Used in This Book

Scattered throughout the book are icons to guide you along your way and highlight some of the suggestions, solutions, and cautions of buying or selling your home:

Keep your sights on the target for important advice and critical insights into the best practices in buying and selling property.

Remember these important points of information, and you'll stand a better chance of buying or selling your property successfully.

This icon highlights the landmines that both novice and experienced home-buyers need to avoid.

This icon covers the boring stuff that only anoraks would ever know. You can skip paragraphs marked by this icon without missing the point – or you can read it and impress your friends with what you know.

This icon highlights the real-life anecdotes from years of experience and mistakes, made by friends, who have bought and sold property, and myself. While we should all learn from our own mistakes, it's even better to learn from other people's – and I share some of them with you here.

Where to Go from Here

This book is organised so that you can go wherever you want to find complete information. Want to know what insurance you need to take out to protect your mortgage repayments? Head to Chapter 12. If you're interested in how to get your property ready for prospective purchasers, go to Chapter 15 for that. You can use the table of contents to find broad categories of information or the index to look up more specific things.

If you're not sure where you want to go, you may want to start with Part I. It gives you all the basic information you need to get started in buying and selling your home and points to places where you can find more detailed information.

Part I
So You Want to Buy Your First Home?

'...and another point — this neighbourhood's fine if you want quiet and total privacy.'

In this part . . .

Buying your first home is one of the biggest purchases you will ever make in your life. The chapters in this part guide you through the process of figuring out whether it's the right time for you to take the plunge. I also fill you in on working out whether you can afford to buy your first home, and how you can manage it even without a huge salary or sizeable deposit. I also help you establish where you should buy.

This is the part for you if you've just started to think about purchasing a property, but you're not quite sure whether you are ready, or able, to do so.

Chapter 1

Why Getting Your Foot on the Property Ladder Is a Smart Move

Congratulations! You're thinking about buying your first home and getting a foot on the property ladder. Property is an excellent investment: not only does it enable you to kiss goodbye to grotty rented accommodation and throwing money down the drain – paying the rent – you're also investing in something that's likely to increase in value over a number of years. That has to be a sound move.

But it's a tough environment for first-time buyers, many of whom delay getting on the property ladder because they simply can't afford to buy any earlier. The average age of a first-time buyer in 2006 was 33, according to the Halifax, the UK's biggest mortgage lender. The reason? Many people spend their twenties paying off student debts and struggling on low incomes, which can make drumming up a deposit impossible. Rising house prices, particularly in London and the south-east, have created further problems for first-time buyers, making a place of their own seem an ever-diminishing dream.

Before you go any further you need to determine whether you are ready to buy your own home. In this chapter, I start by giving you the low-down on some of the advantages of owning your own property. Then I help you to assess whether you can afford to do so now or whether you need a bit of help before you are in a position to buy a place of your own.

Recognising the Advantages of Owning Property

Property serves two functions: It provides you with a roof over your head, and it is serves as a wise investment in the longer term. But unless you're buying a rental property, which you do specifically to make a profit (see my book *Renting Out Your Property For Dummies* for detailed information), having adequate shelter is more important than making a huge profit. You need somewhere to live; *that* is the very practical reason behind buying a home. The following sections outline the advantages you'll accrue from making such a practical decision.

Closing the door on the rest of the world

If you live at home with your parents, you may be looking for a bit more independence; if you're renting – with friends or on your own – you may be looking for something you can decorate to your own tastes and make decisions about without anyone else's permission. Buying a home may very well be the answer.

There's nothing quite like walking into your new home – the one you've managed to buy yourself – for the first time. It is the most incredible feeling. But it gets even better. Having your own space means not having to answer to anyone else, not having to do what anyone else wants, and being able to live exactly how you like. If you live alone in your new home, you don't have to queue up for the bathroom anymore. And if you want to stay in bed all day in your one-bed flat, what's to stop you? (Just ignore for a moment the fact that your boss may have something to say about you lounging in bed on a day when you should be in the office!)

The best bit about buying your own place is that it's *your space.* You don't have a landlord to kick you out after six months because he or she's planning on selling the flat or house from under you. And because it's your space, you're more likely to stay in an area for longer (homeowners tend to put down roots), which can be very attractive if you've spent years lugging your belongings between different rental properties.

No more throwing money down the drain

Most tenants complain about paying rent because they don't see any return in the long run. You get a roof over your head for several months, and that's it. If you recognise that property tends to appreciate in value over time, you're likely to feel that you're missing out the longer you delay purchasing your own place.

In addition, decorating rented accommodation is a waste of your time and money. Spending money doing up your home – painting and wallpapering and buying new furniture – makes perfect sense if you own the property. But doing up rental accommodation doesn't make sense. If the landlord supplies the materials and you supply the labour, you may not waste your own money, but you should consider whether you really want to spend your free time adding value to the landlord's property. And if doing up your rented accommodation means paying for the improvements yourself, doing the work on your own, and having the colour scheme approved by the landlord, you may want to think twice about whether it's worth the hassle.

Keeping your own home in good decorative order is a good investment. You will also have less work to do when you come to selling it later on.

Buying When You Don't Have a Huge Deposit or Big Income

With thousands of mortgages available from over 100 lenders, you're bound to find one out there that suits you – even if you haven't got a big deposit or earn hundreds of thousands of pounds every year.

Buying without a deposit (or with a very small one)

Homebuyers used to save up for years for a deposit before they could get on the housing ladder. Without a sizeable deposit, lenders simply wouldn't take you seriously and agree to let you have a mortgage. This is no longer the case. Nowadays, if you haven't got a deposit, you may be able to get a 100 or even 125 per cent mortgage.

If saving up a 5 or 10 per cent deposit would realistically take you several years, it might make sense to borrow a greater proportion of the purchase price now rather than put off buying for a few years. In a rising property market, if you delay your purchase while you save up several thousand pounds for a deposit, you may find that house prices have risen to such an extent that you've been priced out of the market and need an even bigger deposit than the one you've got.

Following are a few points you need to be aware of if you don't have a deposit (or have a very small one):

- ✔ **You won't qualify for the cheapest mortgage rates.** Lower rates are offered to borrowers with bigger deposits because the lender sees them as being lower risk.

- ✔ **A number of lenders impose a higher lending charge (HLC)** – a one-off insurance premium to those borrowing a high loan-to-value (LTV), depending on the lender's terms. The HLC protects the lender, but *you* have to pay for it. The idea is that if you default on your mortgage repayments and the property has to be sold, the HLC will cover any losses incurred by the lender.

- ✔ **You may experience negative equity.** If you borrow 100 per cent or more of the property price and house prices fall, your mortgage may be greater than the value of your home. This means that you're trapped and can't sell until prices rise again.

Coping with a low income

Lenders decide how big a mortgage to let you have by taking your income into account. Four times a borrower's income is the general income multiple, or three times joint income if you are buying with a partner. So, for example, if you earn £30,000 a year, you could borrow up to £120,000 if you are buying a property on your own, or £180,000 if you're buying with a partner who earns the same as you. But a number of lenders are prepared to let you borrow more – up to four, five or even six times your income – in response to rising property prices and the increasing difficulty this poses for first-time buyers.

Lenders increasingly use affordability criteria rather than strict income multiples to determine how much you can borrow. They take into account outgoings and debts as well as income to ensure that you can afford to pay the mortgage.

While you may be tempted to borrow as much as possible in order to purchase a bigger property, keep in mind that doing so isn't always a good idea. You may be able to afford the mortgage repayments initially, but would you still be able to if interest rates were to rise? Even a 1 per cent increase in the base rate could mean a big rise in your mortgage repayments – could you cope with such a scenario? If you can't, your home could end up being repossessed. Overstretching yourself tends to be a bad idea in the long run.

Following are some alternatives to taking a high income multiple and borrowing more money than you can really afford:

- ✔ **Find a *guarantor*.** If you can't meet your mortgage repayment one month, your guarantor (a blood relative, usually a parent) is responsible for doing so. A mortgage lender is more likely to let you have a bigger loan than your salary strictly justifies if a guarantor is prepared to take responsibility for you making these mortgage payments. An increasing number of first-time buyers are finding that having a guarantor is the only way they can get on the property ladder. But if you do use a guarantor, make sure they appreciate the risks involved: the guarantor must pay your mortgage if you default on the repayments, for example.

✔ **See whether your parents can help with the deposit.** If your parents aren't in a position to act as guarantors, they may be able to help with the deposit if they have some savings. With a larger deposit you can borrow less, thereby lowering your monthly mortgage repayments. And if you're really lucky, your folks may not ask for the money back!

✔ **Buy a house with someone else.** An increasing number of friends and siblings are buying property together because it means you can get a bigger mortgage than if you buy on your own. You should also be able to drum up a bigger deposit and the monthly repayments should be more manageable because you won't be the only one contributing to the mortgage. Consider whether you know someone that you could happily buy and share a house with.

If you do go down this route, however, make sure that you get your solicitor to draw up a legal contract stating what share each of you has in the property – how much each of you contributed to the deposit and to the mortgage each month. Then if you do fall out, your investment is protected.

Timing Your Purchase to Avoid Negative Equity

While there are many advantages to getting on the property ladder, there are potential downsides, too. These mainly relate to the value of the property. If you buy at the peak of a housing boom, you could pay well over the odds for your new home. And if a property crash occurs soon after you buy at an inflated price – as happened in the late 1980s – you could end up in *negative equity*. This is when your property is worth less than you paid for it, and it's a very demoralising position to be in. You are effectively trapped until the value of your home recovers, which could take several years. If you can't stay put until then and are forced to sell you are likely to do so at a considerable loss.

Making sure that you don't find yourself in this position is the hard part. To avoid negative equity don't pay over the odds for a property in the first place – and buy as a long-term investment. When property prices are rising, it's easy to get carried away and imagine that they will continue to move upwards forever. But prices don't always go up. Although historically house prices rise over time, they sometimes experience the odd blip or two along the way.

If the worst comes to the worst and property prices do collapse, you'll find the situation more bearable if you didn't pay thousands of pounds more than the property was worth in the first place. Holding off when prices get silly is far wiser than diving in without thinking about the consequences.

Sometimes property prices rise and rise, as they did between the late 1990s and in the 2000s. If you refrain from purchasing until prices fall, you may find yourself 'on hold' for years if the market is particularly buoyant. In this situation, you may have to wait several years until prices have peaked and start falling again before you are in a position to buy. There's no guarantee that prices will fall.

Timing the market is a mug's game: if the experts can't agree on what's going to happen to property prices, how does the ordinary man or woman in the street stand a chance? For peace of mind, don't over-stretch yourself, refuse to pay more for a property than it's worth and be prepared to stay put for a few years. (See Chapter 2 for more information on working out whether it is the right time to buy and ensuring that you don't pay over the odds.)

Determining Whether You're Ready for Homeownership

While being a property owner is a good position to be in, you shouldn't make the decision to buy your first home lightly. Owning a home is a big responsibility: you are committing yourself to monthly repayments for the next 25 years or so.

If you don't keep up your mortgage repayments, you could lose your home. And you'll find getting another mortgage later on more difficult because you'll have demonstrated that you're a bad risk.

You're also responsible for all maintenance and repairs. When the boiler packs up in your new home, you can't phone the landlord to fix things. *You'll* have to call the plumber out yourself and foot the bill. So before you start property hunting, consider whether you've got what it takes to be a homeowner:

   ✔ **Can you afford it?** Property isn't cheap. A mortgage covers most of the purchase price, but you still have to find a deposit (if you can), pay solicitor's fees, the survey, stamp duty, mortgage broker, and lender arrangement fees (if applicable). If you are up to your eyes in debt and struggling to pay it back, you may be better served by clearing the decks a bit before taking on a mortgage.

✔ **Can you manage your finances?** Your mortgage is your most important outgoing every month, so you must ensure that it is paid before anything else. If you run out of cash and can't pay, you're in serious trouble: you will incur penalties, interest charges and the lender may eventually repossess your home.

✔ **Are you creditworthy?** If you've been declared bankrupt or have a County Court Judgment (CCJ) against you, you'll have a hard time getting a mortgage. Obtaining the necessary finance may not be impossible but it will cost you more. Approach a lender who specialises in dealing with borrowers with credit problems but bear in mind that such a lender will charge a higher rate of interest than a mainstream mortgage provider. The smart move may be to wait until you've built up a good credit history before you apply for a mortgage.

✔ **Have you got a steady job?** Lenders prefer borrowers to be in full-time employment. This doesn't mean that if you are self-employed or a freelancer you can't get a mortgage, but it is harder; you usually need proof of earnings in the form of two to three years' audited accounts. Lenders take your income into account when deciding how big a mortgage you can have (see the earlier section 'Coping with a low income' for details); if you don't have an income, you haven't a hope of getting a home loan.

✔ **Are you good at maintenance?** Once you've bought your own place, you won't have a landlord at the end of the phone to call upon in times of emergency. If your washing machine floods the kitchen, would you be able to cope? You don't have to be a skilled builder, plumber, and electrician, but commonsense and knowing who to call upon in case of emergency can help.

✔ **Are you ready to settle down?** I'm not talking about marriage and kids – property itself is a big commitment. If you're planning on travelling around the world in the near future, now may not be the right time to buy a property.

Ideally, you answered 'yes' to each of these questions. Even if you didn't, you may still be ready to become a homeowner as long as you're flexible. Consider these examples of flexibility:

✔ If your credit worthiness is questionable, you may have to pay a higher rate of interest on your mortgage for a couple of years until you have proven to the lender's satisfaction that you can pay your mortgage. After this time, you may qualify for a lower rate from a mainstream lender because you have established a track record of making your payments on time.

✔ If you can't afford a mortgage on your income, you may need to think of other ways of getting the money together – by using a guarantor, buying with friends or siblings or through a housing association, if possible.

Chapter 2

Deciding Whether You Can Afford to Buy and Getting the Timing Right

*W*hen you decide to purchase your first home, it's easy to get carried away with the excitement. But before you start eagerly looking at properties, you need to do a number of mundane, yet ultimately crucial, things.

The first is to consider whether you can afford to buy. Many first-time buyers have been priced out of the market by rising property prices. Those who aren't waiting until they've got a reasonable deposit – at least 5 per cent of the purchase price – may be over-stretching themselves by taking on bigger loans than they can afford. In this chapter I look at the cost of buying your first home and whether you can really afford it or need some help getting started.

Timing is also important: Property prices go up and down; you should avoid buying at the top of the market if possible. In this chapter, I look at how to avoid being caught out by a property market crash.

The Costs of Buying a Home

The property purchase price is undoubtedly going to be your biggest outlay and raising enough cash to cover this will be your main focus. But there are plenty of other costs you need to allow for, most of which must be paid for out of your own pocket – the mortgage only covers the purchase price, less the deposit, unless you've opted for a 100 per cent plus loan-to-value product. Extras include:

✔ The deposit

✔ Stamp duty

✔ Legal fees

✔ Fees for local authority and Land Registry searches (if you're a buying a three or more bedroom house, these are included in the seller's Home Information Pack [HIP])

✔ Survey

✔ Lender's valuation

✔ Mortgage arrangement or application fee

✔ Higher lending charge (HLC) (if applicable)

✔ Mortgage broker fee (if applicable)

Other costs to bear in mind include hiring a removal firm (or van if you're planning on doing it yourself), buying new furniture, and paying for repairs that need doing. Table 2-1 provides a general idea of the costs involved.

Table 2-1	Checklist of Expenses for a £200,000 property purchase
Expenses	**Cost**
Five per cent deposit:	£10,000
Stamp duty:	£2,000
Solicitor's fees (including VAT):	£500 (estimate)
Local searches and Land Registry:	£335 (unless covered in a HIP)
Mortgage arrangement fee:	£1,000
Mortgage lender's valuation:	From £220
Mortgage broker fee:	£1,500 (1 per cent of purchase price)
Survey:	£750–£1,000
TOTAL:	**£16,555**

Insurance may be the last thing on your mind at this stage, but because you're investing so much money in your home, it should be high on the agenda. Buildings insurance is compulsory if you have a mortgage – your lender won't let you borrow the cash otherwise – and you should arrange for your new home to be covered from exchange of contracts. For details of the other types of insurance available, see Chapter 12.

The deposit

How times have changed! First-time buyers used to save up for a deposit of around 10 per cent of the property's purchase price. But with rocketing property prices and the introduction of 100 per cent mortgages and above, this is no longer necessary. Nevertheless, being able to put down a deposit will stand you in good stead for several reasons:

- ✔ If you have a decent deposit (5 per cent or more of the purchase price) you'll get a lower mortgage rate.
- ✔ You won't have to pay a higher lending charge (HLC). This covers the lender if you default on your mortgage repayments. It can cost you thousands of pounds so avoid it if possible.

If you can't raise a deposit on your own, ask family for help. If they are very generous, they may give you the money and not expect it back. But even if they expect it back eventually, you still save money in the long run because of the lower mortgage rate you can get.

Stamp duty

Stamp duty is an unavoidable tax: how much you pay depends on the cost of your property. Duty starts at 1 per cent of the purchase price on properties between £125,000 and £250,000; 3 per cent for properties between £250,000 and £500,000, and 4 per cent on those over £500,000. You don't pay any stamp duty if your property costs less than £125,000 or if it is in a disadvantaged area and costs less than £150,000. Stamp duty is payable to your solicitor upon completion.

Legal fees

You have to pay a solicitor for handling the transfer of the property from the seller to you unless you do your own conveyancing. Fees and charges vary (see Chapter 19 for more details on conveyancing in England, Wales and Northern Ireland, and Chapter 20 for info relating to Scotland). Legal fees are payable on completion.

Survey and lender's valuation

It's worth paying for a survey so you know what state of repair the property is in. If problems are found, you can pull out or use the survey as a negotiating tool to persuade the seller to reduce his price. Two types of survey are available: a Homebuyer's Report, which is suitable for most properties, and a full structural survey, which is often better for very old properties in poor condition (see Chapter 9 for more details and costs). You pay the surveyor once she has completed the survey and reported the findings to you.

If you take out a mortgage, you also have to pay for the lender's valuation, which lets the lender or mortgage broker know whether the property is worth what they are lending to you. The lender or mortgage broker arranges this. The cost depends on the purchase price of the property but expect to pay around £220 for a £200,000 property.

The lender's valuation doesn't reveal anything about the condition of the property. If you want to satisfy yourself on this score, you must pay for a survey.

Miscellaneous fees

If you take out a mortgage, you may also have to pay the following:

- ✔ **Mortgage arrangement or application fee:** Lenders charge a fixed amount of several hundred pounds or a percentage of the mortgage amount for arranging a mortgage. The amount varies between lenders and you usually have the choice of adding it to the mortgage, so you pay it back over the term of the loan.

- ✔ **Mortgage broker fee:** If you use a broker to find your mortgage (and I strongly recommend that you do), you may have to pay a fee. This is usually around 0.4 per cent of the mortgage value. Other brokers don't charge a fee but rely on commission from the lender who receives your business. See Chapter 11 for more about using an independent broker.

Money Talks: Working Out What You Can Afford

Before you start house hunting, work out what you can afford to spend. Unless you're a Lottery winner, you'll need a mortgage, and lenders have an upper limit on how much you can borrow. This is based on your income and credit history and, increasingly, your outgoings. You need to know right from the start how much you can borrow: if you wander into an estate agent's offices with only a vague idea of what you can afford, you won't be taken seriously.

Work out what mortgage repayments you can realistically afford by figuring out how much you have left over once you've subtracted all your outgoings from your monthly income. Make sure that you're not overstretching yourself.

If the mortgage you need for the property you want is more than you can afford, think about where you can economise. Be sensible: you can't skimp on council tax or the gas bill, for example. If you really can't balance the figures, you may have to accept that you're not in a position to buy a property at this time, or you may need to downscale your ambitions.

Buying On Your Own

The number of single households is rising as a result of divorce and people marrying later. As a result, the number of people buying on their own is also increasing. This makes a huge responsibility an even greater one.

Raising enough money if you're buying on your own is harder than buying with another person. Lenders tend to grant mortgages on the basis of income or affordability. If you're buying on your own, expect to borrow around four times income (as opposed to three times joint income if you buy with a partner). If you earn £25,000, for example, you can borrow £100,000. If you buy with a partner who earns the same as you, you can borrow £150,000 – getting you a bigger mortgage.

Some lenders have been criticised for lending buyers more than four times their income. It might be tempting to borrow as much as you can but you will have higher mortgage repayments as a result. And if you fall behind in your repayments, you could lose your home. Don't overstretch yourself. Calculate what you can afford and stick to it.

Pooling Resources

The problem many single first-time buyers face is that they simply can't afford to get on the property ladder. Property prices have risen faster than salaries, so even with a generous income multiple from a lender (refer to Chapter 1 for an explanation of this), you still may not be able to buy alone. You may need to pool resources.

Buying with a partner

The easiest way of buying property is with a partner, whether you're married or cohabiting. You can borrow more cash and are likely to have a bigger deposit if you're drawing from two sets of savings – and you can divide the repayments between you.

However, there are downsides: You could split up, and if you aren't married, the law treats you as separate individuals with no rights or liabilities to each other. To protect your legal rights, ensure that you own the property as joint tenants or tenants in common:

✔ **Joint tenants:** If you're joint tenants and one partner dies, the deceased partner's interest in the property passes to the survivor. Married couples usually buy a property as joint tenants.

✔ **Tenants in common:** If you're tenants in common, each of you has a distinct share in the property; this can be 50:50 or based on how much each partner contributed to the deposit or mortgage repayments. If you die, your share goes to your estate – not to your partner.

If the property is in your partner's name, you have no legal claim to it – even if you paid half the mortgage and lived together for 17 years. Get a solicitor to draw up the documents staking your claim.

Getting by with a little help from your friends

An increasing number of first-time buyers are purchasing with friends. This may sound risky – as you could fall out – but if you choose your friends carefully and get a solicitor to draw up a contract, you've a good chance of making this arrangement a success.

Most lenders allow up to four names on the mortgage deeds, but many restrict the number of salaries they lend on to two. So buying with a group of friends might not enable you to borrow significantly more money.

Make sure that you have a contract stating that you have an equal share to the property so you're covered if you do fall out. It should also state what happens if one of you wants to sell up: for example, you may want to include a clause that says no one can sell within the first five years. Or maybe you want a clause letting the other owners have first refusal to buy them out.

Using a guarantor

Parents can be useful if you're struggling to get on the housing ladder. Even if they can't afford to throw a few grand your way for a deposit, they may be able to act as guarantors (see Chapter 11). This will make them responsible for your mortgage repayments if you fail to meet them.

Your parents must provide your lender with details of their income and financial commitments. If they are mortgaged to the hilt, your lender may not accept them as guarantors þecause they won't be able to meet your repay-ments as well as their own if you default on your loan. And even if they are accepted as guarantors, they should be aware that it might cramp their style. If they later decide to buy a holiday home on the Costa del Sol, they may find they can't get a mortgage because lenders see them as being over-committed.

Knowing When to Buy

Once you've decided to buy, it's worth getting an agreement in principle from your mortgage lender. This gives you an idea of how much you can afford and demonstrates to sellers your seriousness. You have six months until this runs out so there is no need to rush into a property purchase. One of the ques-tions you need to ask is whether it is a good time to buy. If you have to move by a certain date because you're relocating for work, having a baby, or being chucked out of your rented flat, you may have no say in the matter. But if you do have a say, give some thought to the timing.

The property market is busiest in spring and autumn. You can buy in summer or winter but many sellers hold back until the market picks up so they have a greater chance of finding a buyer. The advantage of buying out of season is that estate agents won't be frantic and can spend more time with you. You may also be able to knock the price down if the seller wants a quick sale.

Buying during a property boom

If you can, avoid buying during a property boom. This is when house prices rise at an extremely fast pace, unlike a normal, healthy market where there's a gradual, steadier increase in prices. The danger is that over-inflated prices will come crashing down once the boom-time is over. And if you bought at the peak, you may end up in the worst position any homeowner can find himself or herself – negative equity.

Negative equity is when you owe more on your property than it is worth because the market has crashed (which can happen in a recession). If you're in negative equity, you're stuck in the property until prices recover, which can take several years and be very disheartening. To avoid this, try not to pay over the odds in the first place. If the property feels over-priced and you're stretching yourself, it's not the best of beginnings. You'll really struggle if interest rates rise or property prices fall.

Friends of mine have hung on in the desperate hope that prices will crash only to find that they keep on going up – and they've priced themselves out of the market completely. It's not unknown for property prices to rise year after year. If you're ready and able to get on the housing ladder, I suggest you go for it.

Buying during a slump

The best time to buy is during a property slump when prices have already fallen as much as they are likely to. This means that you won't pay over the odds and you might even be able to get the seller to reduce the price further.

Pay attention to newspaper reports and check out your local estate agents: are prices on several properties being reduced? Are properties taking ages to sell? If so, it's a fairly safe bet that you will be able to get a good deal on a property.

Although you may be tempted to hang on until prices fall even further, they won't fall forever. Property is fairly resilient, and prices eventually rise again after a fall. If you buy in a falling market, and prices plunge even further, don't despair. Prices will eventually rise again.

Chapter 3

Determining What You Want

In This Chapter

▶ Working out what sort of property you are looking for

▶ Researching the locality – before arranging any viewings

*W*hen purchasing your first home is no longer an unrealistic ambition (you've worked out that you can afford it and that now's a good time to buy; refer to Chapter 2 for details), you may think you're ready to rush into the nearest estate agent's office and make appointments to view lots of properties. But before you do, take time to consider exactly what you're looking for. Given that buying a house is one of the biggest and most important purchases you will ever make, it's important to get it right – a vague idea of what you want is not enough.

In this chapter, I focus on all the factors you need to consider when deciding what sort of property you are after. After all, the only way the estate agent will be able to find what you want is if you know yourself.

While you should have an ultimate goal in mind, it's important to remain flexible, or you may dismiss a great property that meets most, but not all, of your requirements.

Establishing Your Criteria

When you first start property hunting, you may have a vague notion of what you are looking for. But you can save yourself a lot of time and energy if you pinpoint your requirements *before* arranging any viewings. Questions to ask yourself include:

✔ **How many bedrooms do I need?** If you're buying on your own and money is tight, you may decide not to opt for a bedroom at all, but choose a studio flat instead. Or maybe, realising that selling a studio can be a problem when you move out (because they appeal to such a limited number of buyers), you decide that a one-bedroom flat (or a two-bedroom flat with a room you can rent out) is more suitable. If you're buying with a partner, you are more likely to require at least two bedrooms – maybe three if you are thinking of starting a family in the near future. If you already have a couple of children, you may need four bedrooms.

✔ **Do I need a garden?** In theory, gardens sound lovely, particularly in summer when you can invite your mates round for barbeques. And if you have children or pets, a garden will be more important to you than if you don't. But gardens are a lot of work. Consider whether you can be bothered with the upkeep. If not, and you buy a property with a garden, you'll have to employ a gardener. Properties with gardens also tend to be more expensive.

✔ **Do I need a garage or off-road parking?** If you have a car, you may prefer to park it off-road rather than struggle to find a space in the street when you get home from work. And if you put your car in a garage at night, you pay lower motor insurance premiums. But remember that in cities you pay a premium for a home with a garage or off-road parking.

✔ **Do I want a flat or a house?** Living in a house is different from living in a flat. Houses tend to be bigger and more expensive to buy, maintain, and insure; flats are cheaper, but noisier, because you are likely to be living in closer proximity to your neighbours. As well as the day-to-day practicalities, in England, Wales, and Northern Ireland, you also have to contend with freehold and leasehold. Flats tend to be leasehold, so you pay rent and service charges to a landlord. Houses tend to be freehold, which means you don't have a landlord to answer to. (See Chapter 19 for more details on freehold and leasehold.)

✔ **Do I want to live in the country, a town, or a city?** This tends to be a matter of personal preference. Some people feel oppressed living in a big city while others are bored by the countryside. The countryside tends to have a slower pace of life, you'll get more property for your money, and the air is cleaner. But the roads can be inaccessible in winter, the shops miles away, and the social life limited. The city is more glamorous with plenty to do, but your money doesn't stretch as far and there's more pollution. The choice is yours.

Working in the city doesn't necessarily mean you have to live there. As long as you are near good transport links you could live in the country-side and commute. The decision comes down to where you and your family feel happiest living.

✔ **Do I want a brand new home or a period home?** The type of home you want is also a matter of personal taste and budget. Some people prefer a property in perfect condition with a brand-new fitted kitchen and bathroom with all the mod cons. Others prefer the history and character of an older building, which may need restoring. (You can find more about period homes in Chapter 6; head to Chapter 7 for info on new-build homes).

Getting the Area Low-down

Even a property that meets all your criteria in terms of size and having a large garden is of little use to if it's in the wrong location. That's why, when deciding what you want from a property, you also need to consider what you want from the locality.

You can find out a lot about an area without traipsing the streets. The Internet is a great place to start. Try www.upmystreet.com, which has details of schools, crime rates, how much council tax you'll be charged, what issues are currently concerning the local council, and restaurants and pubs in the area. Also worth a try is www.yell.com, which provides similar information.

After you get the basic information, check out the area you are interested in for yourself: Don't rely on an Internet search but take the trouble to see first hand. If you travel by car, make sure that you get out and walk around to get a feel for the place.

Location, location, location

It's a bit of a cliché, but location is one of the most important elements when you buy property. Not only do *you* want to live in a nice area with a low crime rate, but most other people do as well. Choosing a nice location means you should have little problem selling your property when you decide to move. It also means you're going to spend more for a property in a good area.

Location costs

A country cottage in the picturesque Cotswolds is going to set you back more than a similar-sized property in Milton Keynes. Properties in city centres tend to cost more than those on the outskirts, while one area in a city may be much more desirable than another: in London. For example, Hampstead is more fashionable (and more expensive) than Lewisham.

Fitting in with the locals

Most people are rather unadventurous when moving house: They tend to go a couple of miles up the road at most, rather than half way across the country to a completely different area. If you're moving round the corner, you already have a good idea about the area. But if you're moving somewhere unfamiliar, you must do your research very carefully first.

Whether you are moving to another town or city, or to the country after living in an urban area, – or vice versa – it can be quite a wrench. And what happens if you don't like it? The only alternative to sticking it out and becoming thoroughly miserable is to go back with your tail between your legs and several thousand pounds poorer. And as well as losing face, you'll have wasted your time.

Such a situation is avoidable, however. One option is to rent a furnished property in the area you are hoping to move to. (The advantage of furnished accommodation is that you don't even have to unpack your belongings.) And if you really don't like it after six months or so, you'll at least know you're not ready to buy there; cross it off your list and look somewhere else.

Even parts of the same city can be wildly different from one another. If you move to another part of the city, you might not like it. Your commute to work, for example, may become impossible. Don't make the mistake of assuming it'll be exactly the same. Check out the new area before you commit yourself.

Postcodes come in and out of fashion. West London has been more expensive than East London for many years but in the past few years prices in the East End have rocketed as artists and media types have moved into the area and London won the Olympics for 2012. If you can spot an up-and-coming area, it could prove to be a very good investment.

Not everyone can afford to live in leafy villages in the middle of nowhere – nor would they want to. The perfect location is one that suits your needs – perhaps because it is within walking distance of the office or a park, for example.

A room with a view

There's something very romantic about looking out onto grass and trees or, even better, water. Sea views always go down well with buyers, so if you buy a property with a sea view – you lucky thing – you should have no trouble selling it on should you ever grow tired of it, which isn't likely. High-rise flats are also blessed with amazing views across cities. Some of London's tower blocks offer superb views that you'd struggle to find on the London Eye.

Spotting up-and-coming areas

When you buy your first property, your main concern should be to find a place you can call a home, where you can live happily for a few years. Making a profit on the property should be a bonus, not your primary aim. Having said that, if you can spot an up-and-coming area – and would be happy living there – you could be on to a winner as your property may considerably appreciate in value.

The trouble is that most people cotton on to such an area long after the trendy types have moved in and pushed up prices. To spot the next hot area before it's boiling, follow these tips:

✔ Look out for plans for new transport links. These always encourage people and businesses to move to an area: Local authority websites should have this information.

✔ Check out cheap areas close to already established areas. Hackney in east London, for example, is the choice of many who can't afford neighbouring Islington.

Once the trendy wine bars and bistros have opened up on the high street, you may have missed the boat. Do your research and get in ahead of the crowd. But be prepared to put up with the boarded-up shops until the restaurants have had a chance to open.

If you're interested in high-rise flats, be aware that they tend to be ex-local authority, and finding a mortgage on anything above the fifth floor is very difficult. Mortgage lenders don't want to take on the extra risk as many of these towers are constructed of reinforced concrete. If you are interested in buying a high-rise flat, contact a mortgage broker for advice as to which lenders you should approach first. (See Chapter 11 for more information on finding a broker).

If you work from home a view may be more important than if you don't. Staring at the council tip isn't likely to provide much inspiration! Of course, as I write this, I'm gazing out over a DIY store – not many people's idea of a room with a view. But then I didn't buy my flat for its view; I bought it because it's also opposite a tube-station, has an intercom system for security, and is a 20-minute walk from work. Not only that, but a good number of my friends live within a mile's radius. The view can be important but it isn't everyone's main concern. If I had to choose between my flat and one overlooking the park, which is a 20-minute walk from the tube, my flat would win every time.

Transport links

If you rely on public transport, you'll regret buying a house in a village where a bus comes through once an hour. And if you buy a property that's miles away from the office, you'll want good train, tube, tram, or bus links nearby.

Try out the journey for yourself at the time of day that you would normally commute to work. Never trust a train timetable!

Local amenities

Depending on your personal interests, certain local amenities may appeal to you more than others. These may include the following:

- ✓ **Sports centre or health club:** If you do a lot of sport or have kids who need occupying at weekends and in the school holidays, you may decide that living close to a sports centre or gym is important.

- ✓ **Public library:** Although these sadly tend to be under-funded in many areas, you can still find some excellent libraries lending CDs and DVDs as well as books.

- ✓ **Place of worship:** If you regularly attend church, mosque or synagogue services, it may be important to live in close proximity to one of these and feel part of a close-knit religious community.

- ✓ **Pubs and restaurants:** This may seem trivial but if you like a drink after work or at weekends, you may prefer a 'local' surrounded by familiar faces than a pub miles away. Likewise, good local eateries or takeaways can be a godsend when you don't feel like cooking.

- ✓ **Shops:** A local newsagent, corner shop, and Post Office are all useful, as are a pharmacy and a large supermarket.

- ✓ **Doctor's surgery and NHS dentist:** A good local NHS doctor and – increasingly rare – dentist are worth having in case of emergency.

Schools

Living in the catchment area of one of the top 50 state schools in the country can add an average of £50,000 on to the value of your home, according to a report from Barclays Bank. This is great news if you live in such an area but not such good news if you want to move to a property near a good school. You may need a bigger budget to enable you to do so.

Research the best schools by checking the school performance tables on the Department for Education and Skills' website (www.dfes.gov.uk). For more information on a school, look at the Office for Standards in Education (OFSTED)'s website (www.ofsted.gov.uk). Contact the schools directly to find out more information, such as the catchment area.

Crime

Many parts of the country have high crime rates. When you are researching an area you should weed these out and cross them off your list, if you want to live happily and securely in your new home – and sell it on easily when you come to move. If you're thinking of buying in the area you rent in, you'll know what the crime statistics are and how safe it feels. But if you're thinking of moving to a new area, do your research carefully first.

In addition to checking www.upmystreet.com, which can give you an idea of the crime rate in an area, spend some time in the area you're considering. I suggest driving round the streets late at night. Are they well lit and do they appear safe? Are gangs of kids hanging around street corners causing trouble? Burnt-out or abandoned cars are also very revealing, suggesting an unloved area with its fair share of troublemakers. If this is what you see, you may want to think about buying somewhere else.

Environmental concerns

An increasing number of people are becoming more aware of the effect the environment they live in has on their health. When considering whether you want to buy in an area, you should look out for the following:

- ✔ **Mobile phone masts:** A lot of negative criticism has surrounded phone masts. Government research shows no general risk to health but says there could be an indirect adverse affect in some cases.

- ✔ **Electricity pylons:** Again, scientists say there is no convincing evidence of a public health risk, but some people are convinced that their health has been affected by living in the shadow of an electricity pylon. If you are concerned, buy somewhere else.

- ✔ **Airports:** Living under a flight path isn't much fun, particularly if it's connected to a very busy airport, such as Heathrow. Properties are cheaper in these areas – and for good reason.

- ✔ **Waste incinerators:** Again, health risks associated with living near waste incinerators aren't clear; if you're concerned, you may want to avoid areas near these incinerators.

- ✔ **Air pollution:** Medical research has indicated that living on a main road results in poorer air quality than living in the countryside. This could have long-term, as well as short-term, effects on your health and that of any children you may have.

- ✔ **Smog:** This air pollution is a growing problem in big cities, particularly in the summer. If you're concerned or don't want to have to put up with it, you may want to cross big cities with smog off your list of prospective locations.

For more information on contaminated land or pollution, go to www. environment-agency.gov.uk. In the *What's In Your Backyard?* section of *Your Environment* you can search by postcode for landfill sites, flood plains, and air pollution.

Let the Search Begin!

Once you've satisfactorily answered all your questions concerning the locality of the property, and haven't been put off by any of the answers, you are ready to proceed. The next step is to register with several estate agents selling in the area and get ready to start viewing properties.

However, if you've come across a few stumbling blocks, such as the local schools not being up to much, you will have to decide whether it's enough to warrant crossing that particular area off your list and starting the search again elsewhere. This is time-consuming so you may be loathe to do it. But in the long run the time you spend searching will pay off, as you'll end up with a property in an area that you are very happy to live in and that suits you down to the ground.

Chapter 4

Dealing with Estate Agents

- -

In This Chapter

▶ Remembering that the estate agent is working for the seller, not the buyer

▶ Finding a good estate agent and getting the best out of him

▶ Pursuing a complaint against an agent

- -

*E*state agents are the butt of many jokes; everyone seems to have a bad word to say about them (unless you happen to have a son or daughter who is one of course!). But while many agents have rightly earned a reputation for being untrustworthy, honest ones who do a good job are out there.

Although an increasing number of people are buying property over the Internet or privately via newspaper adverts, they are in the minority. Most homebuyers end up buying their home through an estate agent. Your local estate agent's window or website is likely to be your first port of call when house hunting, or you might spot an estate agent's 'For Sale' board outside a property and call the advertised number.

In this chapter I discuss your rights, the pitfalls of using an agent, what you can expect from an estate agent, and how to sort out any problems that may occur. Who knows, you could be someone who ends up with a positive story to tell about an estate agent!

What You Need to Know About Estate Agents

Estate agents can seem to be omnipresent. Every high street has at least one branch (and usually many more) full of eager young things driving flash cars and thriving on making the sale. But while estate agents have a bad reputation, they can help you buy your new home – as long as you remember a few things:

✔ **The seller pays the agent and calls the shots.** The estate agent works for the seller because the seller pays the agent commission for successfully selling the property. So the agent's aim is to get the best price possible for the seller to maximise their own commission, which means getting as much money as possible out of you.

✔ **The estate agent must pass all offers for a property on to the seller.** Even if the seller has accepted your offer for his property, that's no guarantee that you will actually end up purchasing the property. *Gazumping* – where the seller accepts another, higher, offer after he has accepted yours – does happen.

The agent is legally bound to pass on all offers to the seller, even after yours has been accepted, and the seller may accept a higher offer. To minimise the chances of this happening, try these suggestions:

• Get your solicitor to help you make an offer on the condition that no other offers will be accepted for a set period.

• Build a relationship with the seller and agent so that the former would feel bad about doing the dirty on you and the latter will at least keep you in the loop as to what's going on.

✔ **The estate agent is legally obliged to treat you fairly.** Although you aren't paying the estate agent, you're entitled to be treated honestly and fairly. If you feel you've been deliberately misled or that the agent has been economical with the truth in the property particulars, you can complain and may be due compensation. See 'Complaining about an Estate Agent' later in this chapter.

✔ **The estate agent is the best source of properties for sale in your area.** Yes, you could try buying privately or hunt the Internet or local paper for private ads for properties for sale. But the quickest and easiest way to house hunt is via an estate agent. Why make life harder for yourself?

Using an agent doesn't have to be an unpleasant or unfruitful experience. There are ways to get what you want out of them – the property of your dreams – while ensuring that they don't play you off against another buyer. As long as you bear in mind that estate agents act for the seller, not the buyer, and simply want to make as much money as possible as quickly as they can, you should minimise the chances of any problems cropping up.

What an Estate Agent Does

The role of the estate agent is to match prospective buyers with properties for sale. They market properties, show prospective buyers around, and help buyer and seller come to an agreement on the purchase price. They get paid commission from the seller for achieving a successful sale.

Basic services

The main role of the agent is to help you find a property you want to buy. To enable him to do this, he will want to know exactly what sort of property you are looking for, where you want to live and how much you're prepared to pay. The agent will then (hopefully) come up with several properties that suit your requirements.

If he has nothing on his books that matches your criteria, he will put you on his mailing list and contact you when he has. Or, if your expectations are unrealistic, given the amount you have to spend, he is likely to try to convince you of this. If you want a three-bedroom flat in the centre of town and have £120,000 to spend when prices are nearer £175,000 for that sort of property, for example, he will try to make you see that this is not a realistic proposition.

If he does have properties you're interested in, the agent will show you around, answer any questions you have and advise you on the price you should offer (he may suggest you can get away with offering less than the asking price). If you make an offer, the agent also acts as go-between with the seller until you both agree on a price.

Other services they offer

Many estate agents offer mortgages, either through an in-house specialist or by referring you to a broker with whom the agent has an agreement. Because the agent's strength is in negotiating sales, not arranging financing, I advise you to steer clear of these. You're unlikely to get the best rate because you'll probably be offered a mortgage from a tiny panel of lenders. Going with the agent-recommended broker may be more convenient than shopping around, but you won't necessarily get the best deal. The best place to find a mortgage is through an independent broker (see Chapter 11 for more details).

You're not obliged to take a mortgage from an agent so don't be pressured into it. Say straightaway that you have already arranged financing (even if you haven't) because this stops agents trying to persuade you to take one of their deals.

Most agents can also recommend surveyors or solicitors. If you haven't already got people to do these tasks, it may be worth finding out what rates they charge. They can be quite competitive because of the volume of business the agent passes on, plus they may be quite good as they have been vetted by the agent. Nevertheless, try not to feel pressured into employing an agent-recommended surveyor or solicitor, and don't commit yourself to anything until you have shopped around for quotes.

Finding a Good Estate Agent

Finding a good agent who has plenty of properties that meet your criteria and who isn't going to mess you about can be hit-and-miss. And if the record number of complaints against agents is anything to go by, more people miss than hit. In 2006, more than 8,000 homebuyers and sellers complained to the industry Ombudsman about the service they received from their agent – a third more complaints than in 2005.

However, a good agent can make all the difference between finding the home of your dreams easily and paying the right price for it, and a far more stressful home-buying experience. To make sure things go more smoothly, do all you can to find a good agent.

Checking out an agent's credentials

Personal recommendation is a good place to start when choosing an agent, so ask friends and family whether they can suggest one (or one you should avoid!). And if an agent you used before did a good job, consider using her again if you're buying in the same area.

To reduce the risk of using an agent who deliberately misleads you, I suggest opting for one who is registered with the Royal Institution of Chartered Surveyors or who is a member of the main professional body – the National Association of Estate Agents (NAEA). The NAEA has 10,000 members (about 60 per cent of the industry). It is a voluntary organisation with a Code of Conduct that members are supposed to follow. If an agent breaches the code, he or she can receive a formal warning or a fine, or be suspended or expelled. For a list of NAEA-registered agents, go to www.naea.co.uk.

For extra protection, opt for an agent who also belongs to the Ombudsman for Estate Agents (OEA) scheme. The OEA has more teeth than the NAEA and can award compensation against agents who breach the rules (see 'Complaining about an Estate Agent' later in this chapter). Membership is also voluntary and many agents, including well-known high street names, haven't signed up. Most complaints are made against estate agents who are not members of the OEA scheme, so it's wise to pick an agent who is. For a list of OEA-registered agents, go to www.oea.co.uk.

Employing a home search agent to do your legwork

If you really can't face dealing with estate agents or you're just too busy to look for a property yourself, you can hire a home search agent to do the work for you. A home search agent will find you a property, deal with estate agents on your behalf, and negotiate the price. Expect to pay between 1 and 1.5 per cent of the purchase price for this.

For more details on hiring a home search agent, contact the Association of Relocation Agents at www.arp-relocation.com.

Getting the Best Out of Your Estate Agent

When you register with an estate agent you will be asked what type of property you're looking for and the all-important question – how much you're prepared to pay. Be as honest as possible on both counts. Once the agent has your details, he may be able to suggest some properties on his books that fit your requirements. As other properties come up, he'll contact you to arrange a viewing.

Be straight about how much you can afford: if the agent laughs when you tell her that you can go as high as £80,000, resist the temptation to say that you can afford more if you can't. You'll get found out in the end, and you'll have wasted everyone's time, including your own.

Finding an agent with properties that you want

The agent(s) you select should offer the type of property you want to buy in the areas you're interested in. If you're looking for an affordable studio flat in Bristol city centre, for example, don't register with an agent who specialises in rural properties in the south-east. Check your local newspaper and estate agents' windows to see what properties they offer. It is also worth looking on the Internet, particularly if you're buying in an area some distance from where you live and visiting the local agent isn't convenient.

Getting the agent on your side

While you're not paying the bill or calling the shots, you can manipulate an agent to make sure you get what you want – the property you desire for the price you want to pay. Here are some ideas:

- **Befriend the estate agent.** You don't have to go for cosy drinks after work, but you do need to make sure that you're his first port of call when a property that meets your requirements comes onto his books.

- **Be serious about buying.** What estate agents like more than anything are buyers who are serious about buying. This means that you're in a position to buy, you've got your finances sorted (if you're a first-time buyer), or you've got a purchaser lined up for your property (if you're already a homeowner). This demonstrates that you can move quickly and won't drag your heels.

- **Be flexible.** Estate agents like people who are prepared to be a bit flexible. If you can cope with a small bedroom as a pay-off for a huge master bedroom or don't insist on buying in a particular street, you'll make the agent's life a lot easier – and he is likely to feel more favourably towards you.

- **Listen to your agent when his advice is sound:** Sometimes buyers have unrealistic expectations about the property they want and how much it will cost them. The agent may suggest you revise your expectations, for example, if you want a two-bedroom house with a garden in central London but only have a budget of £150,000. If your agent suggests that you will only get a one-bedroom flat for your money, listen to him – and then decide whether you want to downsize your demands or pick a cheaper area in order to afford a bigger place.

- **Respond quickly and positively if an agent contacts you to arrange a viewing.** If the property might suit, make yourself available to view it as soon as possible. This shows that you're serious and will make the agent sit up and take notice.

If you follow the suggestions in the preceding list, chances are you'll find that you have edged to the top of the list of buyers your estate agent calls, which means you'll get your pick of the best properties as they come onto the market.

Being specific about your demands

Hundreds of properties come onto the average agent's books every week – and many of them won't suit you in the slightest. If you want to avoid wasting your time (and your agent's), don't be too vague about what you're looking for. If your budget only stretches to a small studio flat, there's little point registering interest in properties with four bedrooms. Not only will you waste time traipsing around properties you'll never be able to afford, but the agent will also quickly work out that you can't afford them – and you won't get the call when a property comes up that is right up your street.

Make sure that you have a clear idea about what you want, what you can live with, and what you can't. See Chapter 3 for more details on establishing your criteria.

Registering with several agents

Because you don't pay the agent anything for his services when you buy a property (unless he is charging you to find a property for you; see the section 'Employing a home search agent to do your legwork' for details), register with as many *suitable* estate agents as possible. If you stick with one, you drastically reduce the number of properties you can consider – so you may miss the perfect one for you.

Try not to lose too much sleep about the agents you use; your choice of agent isn't as important to you as it is to a seller. Buyers should simply register with as many agents as possible. You have no loyalty to any of them, and can view as many properties from as many different agents as you like.

Using Estate Agents' Websites

Most agents have extensive websites listing the details of hundreds of properties for sale. There are several advantages to using the Web:

- ✔ **It saves trawling round estate agents' offices.** You can search the websites of several agents in the time it would take you to visit the estate agent on your high street.

- ✔ **You can take a virtual tour.** As well as property particulars, many sites have several photos of a property rather than just the single bog-standard shot of the front of the property that appears in most estate agents' windows. Many also have virtual tours so you can look around the inside of the property. If the property isn't what you're looking for, you've saved yourself a visit.

- ✔ **Regular e-mail updates save you time.** Once you register your details and requirements, many agents e-mail you an alert as soon as a property that fits your criteria comes onto their books. This means you hear about a property as soon as it becomes available; you save time and effort by not having to trawl through details of hundreds of unsuitable properties.

There are far too many Internet sites to mention here, but a good starting place is www.ukpropertyguide.co.uk, which offers a comprehensive list of the best sales databases in the UK. In Northern Ireland, try www.4ni.co.uk for details of websites of nearly 300 estate agents.

Complaining about an Estate Agent

If you think an agent has treated you unfairly, try to sort things out with him directly, or go to the head office if the company he works for is part of a chain. If the problem isn't resolved, contact your local trading standards service (details in the Yellow Pages). If you live in Northern Ireland, contact the Northern Ireland Executive (www.nics.gov.uk). The Citizens Advice Bureau (again, check the Yellow Pages) is another useful port of call.

If your estate agent is a member of the NAEA or belongs to the OEA Scheme, these organisations may be able to help. But remember that they won't help unless you've tried to resolve the problem directly with the agent first.

If you contact the OEA, you'll receive a complaints form and some guidance notes to help you complete it. You must also sign another form consenting to allow the Ombudsman to gather information about your dealings with the agent. Once these forms have been received, the Ombudsman appoints a case officer to review your complaints. If the Ombudsman supports your complaint, it may award compensation. The estate agent will be informed of this and has 14 days to appeal. Any appeal is considered and the Case Review amended as necessary.

The Case Review is then sent to you, and you have 28 days to accept the decision or make your own appeal. The Ombudsman only reconsiders his decision in exceptional circumstances. Any award of compensation in your favour is binding on the estate agent. And once you accept it, you do so in full and final settlement of your complaint against the estate agent.

If you've no joy after complaining to a NAEA member about her behaviour, you can contact the NAEA. Any breach of the NAEA code is punishable on a scale that begins with a letter of reprimand but could go all the way to a tribunal. If this finds in your favour, the agent could be fined up to £1,000 and expelled from the NAEA.

Contact the NAEA at www.naea.co.uk or on 01926 496800. You can reach the Ombudsman on 01722 333306 or www.oea.co.uk.

Part II
Finding the Right Property

'I did warn you — first appearances
can be deceptive.'

In this part . . .

The chapters in this part guide you through the process of actually finding your property – everything from using an estate agent and handling viewings to buying at auction. I also give you some tips on buying a period or listed home and guide you through the pitfalls of opting for an ex-local authority place.

If you're interested in building your own property from scratch or gutting and completely renovating a house, here you'll find all the tips you need.

Chapter 5

Handling Viewings

In This Chapter

▶ Deciding which properties are worth viewing

▶ Working out the best time to view a property

▶ Knowing the questions to ask and how to interpret the answers

Mike Leigh's film *Career Girls* captures the best bit of the house-buying process – poking around other people's homes. One of the main characters is looking to buy a place in London. Instead of viewing flats within her price range, however, she prefers to look at glamorous pads well beyond her budget. She may not be able to afford them, but seeing how the other half live is far more entertaining.

True, viewing properties can be fun, but, more importantly, it's a vital part of the buying process. You can't make a decision about whether you want to buy a property by only looking at a picture or reading a description. You have to have a good look round and ask the seller various questions. And only once you're inside can you see whether you can imagine yourself living there.

If you're buying your first property, the viewing process can seem daunting. But if you know what to ask, how to interpret the answers, and what else to look for, you'll have a successful viewing. In this chapter, I show you how to do just those things.

Finding Suitable Properties

Before you can view a property, you have to find one that interests you. You can do this in several ways: you may simply come across one you like as you're walking down the street or a friend knows someone who's planning to sell. More likely, you've contacted an estate agent or have been looking at agents' websites (refer to Chapter 4).

While you may want to see as many properties as possible, viewing those that aren't suitable is a waste of time. The trick is to eliminate unsuitable properties *before* arranging a viewing because the house-hunting process is exhausting enough as it is.

Checking out the property particulars: Seeing past the hype

Property particulars are provided by estate agents. These particulars give you details of the property such as how many bedrooms it's got, what size the rooms are and whether there's parking and a garden. It's against the law for an agent to make false or misleading statements about a property. So if the agent says the property has double-glazing, it should have double-glazing.

Even though property particulars mustn't contain false or misleading statements, you still need to take a lot of what is said with a pinch of salt. Agents are well-practised at making something sound much better than it actually is: They have to if they're going to shift some of the properties that come onto their books. Try reading between the lines. 'Traditional' could mean old-fashioned and in need of renovation; 'contemporary' may be too radical for some tastes, and so on.

The property particulars may include terms you don't understand, such as *freehold* or *leasehold*. If you're unsure, ask. Don't worry about looking stupid; if it isn't clear to you, chances are it's confused many buyers. If you don't ask, you could make a costly mistake.

Checking out the property yourself

The best way to see whether a property suits you is to drive or walk past it before arranging a viewing. Often, a picture in an ad doesn't tell the full story. It won't indicate, for example, how much traffic passes by or whether you'll be able to get a parking space in the street if there isn't a garage. A quick drive by, without stopping to go in and look around, gives you a preliminary impression, which might be enough to cross the property off your list. If you like what you see, you can arrange a viewing.

Arranging a Viewing

As soon as you come across a property you like, make an appointment with the estate agent or, if the property is being sold privately, with the seller to view it. Moving quickly is important, particularly if the property has just come onto the market; if it's desirable, you can bet that other buyers will be interested.

Take someone with you on viewings, Not only will this increase your safety (particularly important if you're a woman), but you also get a second opinion, and, if you're inclined to get carried away, someone to stop you. Try not to take the kids along however, as they'll just get in the way and distract you from the task in hand.

Arranging good viewing times

Most people view properties after work, or at weekends (usually a Saturday as most agents don't work Sundays) – which is fine. The key is to arrange to view the house in daylight so that you can see how much natural light it gets: In winter, therefore, viewing on the weekend is better than after work.

Following are some other tips for making the most efficient use of your time:

✔ **Work out how many properties you can comfortably view in one go.** Try not to book in more than a handful or you'll get tired and irritable and be less capable of making the right decision. The maximum I have viewed in one day when house hunting is five, and that was exhausting. Any more than that, and you may find yourself ready to keel over, particularly if you have to travel between properties.

✔ **Consider taking a day off work to view several properties in one go.** This offers a few benefits – the agent will be less busy than at the weekend, you can get a good number of properties out of the way in one hit, and the task won't cut into your leisure time.

✔ **Go as early in the day as you can:** If a flat in a desirable area goes on sale on a Thursday, for example, and you can't see it until Saturday evening, you may have missed the boat. But if you view it first thing Saturday morning, you can beat the prospective buyers lined up to see it during the day. And if you like it you can make an offer, which the seller may accept before anyone else gets the chance to make one.

Once isn't enough: Repeat viewings

If you're interested in a property after the first viewing, revisit it several times. Don't be afraid to make as many repeat appointments as you need to help you make up your mind. The second viewing is useful for measuring up and checking whether your sofa will fit into the lounge. Feel free to take a tape measure and notebook to jot down these details.

On follow-up viewings, ask to look round on your own without the agent or seller watching your every move. This will help you feel less harassed.

Arrange follow-up viewings at different times of the day and night (within reason!) so you can assess how noise and traffic levels affect the property. If, for example, the house is opposite a school, the road will get very busy around 9 a.m. and 3.30 p.m. When you arrange follow-up viewings, try to time them so that you can be at the property during potential problem times.

✔ **If the property is on a major road:** Make sure that your second viewing is during the rush hour. If the noise is incessant, opening the windows on a warm summer evening and still being able to hear the TV may be difficult (if not impossible!). If you have cats or small children, see the road at its busiest to assess whether it's too dangerous for them.

✔ **If the property is close to a train station:** Make an appointment to visit the property during the day to see whether commuters clog up the street with their cars and make it difficult to get in and out of the drive or to park in the street. With a train track nearby you should also be wary of the potential noise (see 'Not forgetting the exterior', later in this chapter).

✔ **If the property is next to a pub or above a shop:** Visit during opening hours. Are the premises noisy or intrusive? Be particularly wary of off-licenses, nightclubs and 24-hour corner shops where people may hang around outside and cause a nuisance.

What to Look for During a Viewing

Before you view any properties, it's important that you're clear about what you're looking for. This may sound blindingly obvious, but until you ask yourself what features a property *must* have and what features you'd quite like but aren't essential, you can't work out whether a property is suitable for you. (If you haven't determined your criteria, refer to Chapter 3.) With your criteria in mind, you can view a property and objectively compare it with your criteria.

Write a list of 'must haves' and 'would likes' before viewing any properties. As long as you can tick off all the 'must haves', the property is suitable. And if you have several ticks next to the 'would likes' as well, consider it a bonus.

Not forgetting the exterior

Your viewing of the property starts before you even set foot inside the front door. Before entering the property, check the exterior and make sure that you're satisfied with the answers to the following questions:

- Do the neighbouring houses appear clean and well cared for? Are the neighbours' drives clear of old bangers and rubbish? The type of neighbours you want are those who take pride in their homes. This can also be an important factor when you come to sell the property.

- Is the road noisy and busy? Is there room for parking (and how easy is it to find) if the property doesn't have a drive? Would it be safe for children (if you have any) to play in the street or for the cat to wander about outside?

- How safe does the street appear? If it is night-time, is it well lit? Would you feel safe walking home late at night? Would you feel happy leaving your car in the street at night?

- Does the roof look sound, or are tiles missing? Don't forget to check the guttering and drains, particularly if it's raining.

- Does the exterior of the property need a lick of paint? If so, you may be able to negotiate with the seller over the purchase price.

- If wood is on the front of the property, is it in good condition or does it need replacing? Again, this may give you room for negotiation over the price. See Chapter 9 for more details on how to do this.

- Have any extensions been added to the property?

Walk round the exterior of the property if possible, and check the garden, if there is one. If you view the property at night, come back during daylight.

Although selling the property is likely to be the last thing on your mind, consider how easy it will be when you do move. Look out for anything that might make this difficult, such as mobile phone masts or electricity pylons in the immediate vicinity, aeroplanes roaring overhead or intercity trains hurtling past at all hours of the day and night. Check train timetables and arrange several viewings at different times to make sure that aircraft noise isn't intrusive.

Poking about in the cupboards

Once inside the property, the agent or seller usually takes the lead and guides you round, pointing out certain features. Go along with them, but don't allow them to rush you no matter how busy they are. Potentially, you're going to spend a lot of money on that property, so take as long as you need. Use the checklist (Form 5-1) to ensure that you don't forget anything.

If you're looking at several properties, make several copies of this checklist – one for each property – and make notes as you go round, otherwise you'll forget which problem belonged to which house. You could also take photos to jog your memory further.

If you want to poke about in the kitchen cupboards, you should be able to do so without feeling that's unreasonable. In fact, opening and shutting kitchen drawers and fitted wardrobes will reveal whether the quality is good. You may find that you'll have to replace them as soon as you move in (which could mean you offer less than the asking price; see Chapter 9 for tips on making an offer). Likewise, have a good look at the boiler and fuse-box; if you need to replace the former or rewire the property, it'll cost thousands of pounds.

Look out for damp patches, mould or cracks in the walls indicating subsidence. Ask the agent or seller what is causing the problem, how long it has been like that and whether any work has been done to rectify it. Be suspicious of new paint or wallpaper as this could hide a problem.

Take a torch and go up into the loft, if possible. Check for any holes, leaks or running water and make sure that the roof is properly insulated.

Property Checklist

Date of viewing: ....

Address of property: ....

....

Type of property and age: ....

Freehold/leasehold? ....

Seller's name: ....

Estate agent: ....

Asking price: ....

Likelihood of negotiation over price: ....

(Put a tick next to room that exists, plus add comments as to general condition or anything that strikes you about it)

Kitchen ....

Lounge ....

Dining room ....

Bedroom one ....

Bedroom two ....

Bedroom three ....

Bathroom ....

Downstairs toilet ....

Car parking ....

Garden ....

Central heating ....

Double glazing ....

Fixtures and fittings included? ....

....

Has seller made any structural changes? ....

....

Running costs

Gas ....

Electricity ....

Water rates ....

Council Tax ....

Cable? ....

Form 5-1:
Property
Checklist
(Page 1 of 2).

Give the following a score out of 10 (10 is excellent; 0 is poor)

Traffic: ....

Noise: ....

Condition of paintwork: ....

Guttering: ....

Roof: ....

Wiring: ....

Windows: ....

Any repairs needed? ....

Does the area feel safe? ....

How long will it take to commute to work? ....

Local amenities

Schools: ....

Pubs, restaurants, and takeaways: ....

....

Cinema/theatre: ....

Swimming pool/sports centre: ....

Shops/newsagent: ....

Parks: ....

Is seller part of a chain? ....

Comments: ....

....

....

Date of second viewing: ....

Form 5-1:
Property
Checklist
(Page 2 of 2).

Asking All the Right Questions

You probably have a hundred and one questions to ask. I suggest jotting them down before the viewing so you don't forget them. And remember to make a note of the answers, particularly if you're viewing several properties. Questions you might want to ask the seller include:

✔ **Why are you moving?** People move for many reasons: usually because they've outgrown the property with the arrival of children, or it's now too big for them because the children have left. But if the seller is moving because the noisy neighbours are making her life hell, you need to know about it.

✔ **What are the neighbours like?** If he's made a formal complaint about the neighbours to the council or the police in the past, the seller has to inform you of these problems. (Your solicitor will also ask the seller this question via the seller's questionnaire that he sends to the seller's solicitor during the conveyancing process.)

If the seller doesn't tell you about difficulties with the neighbours and you experience problems after you move in, you can take the seller to court for withholding information. Remember, however, that the seller doesn't have to tell you that the neighbours are noisy or disruptive if he hasn't formally complained about them.

✔ **How long have you lived here?** Moving house is so stressful that if the seller has only been in the property for six months and can't give a good reason why she's moving, alarm bells should ring.

Be wary, too, of sellers who have lived in a property for 20 or 30 years. The chances are that a lot of work is needed to update the property. Many people put up with problems over the years and learn to live with them. You may not be able to.

✔ **How long has the property been on the market?** If the property has been for sale for only a couple of weeks, you may have to make a decision quickly in case someone else snaps it up. But if the property has been on the market for months (or years!), there could be a problem. The price may be too high, there may be major structural problems, or the property may be at severe risk of flooding – all making it difficult for a buyer to get a mortgage. Or maybe the problem is that the seller is difficult and messes people around. If the problem is with the property – and not an uncooperative seller – think carefully before you buy. You, too, may experience problems when you come to sell.

✔ **Have many people viewed the property and has anyone else made an offer?** The answer to these questions gives you an indication of how much competition there is and how quickly you have to move if you want to purchase the property. But be wary that sellers and agents may exaggerate interest from other prospective buyers, although it is difficult to find out whether this is the case or not.

✔ **Is the property freehold or leasehold?** If it is freehold, as many houses in the UK are, there is no problem as you will own the property outright. But many flats are *leasehold,* which means you simply purchase the right to live there for a certain number of years. You must pay service charge and ground rent every year to the freeholder, or landlord, and abide by certain rules. The landlord is also responsible for repairs to the communal areas (see Chapter 19 for more details on the differences between leasehold and freehold). If the property is leasehold, ask the seller for evidence of the service charges and what the landlord is like. Is he reasonable or has the seller had problems with him?

✔ **Are you in a chain and when do you want to move?** Most sellers are also buyers. If your seller is buying another property, there's a strong chance that the seller of that property is also a buyer. This is known as a *chain,* and the longer and more complicated it is the greater the chance of something going wrong. A hiccup with one property can break the entire chain. What's more, resolving the problem could take months. Don't get caught up in a complicated chain if you can help it.

✔ **How much are the utility bills and council tax?** Ask to look at the sellers' gas, electricity, and water bills. Ask what council tax band the property comes under and look at a bill, if possible.

✔ **Has any work been carried out on the property?** If so, when and how extensive was it? Ask to see receipts or guarantees. Also mention the work to your solicitor so that she can check that any necessary permission was obtained beforehand.

✔ **What fixtures and fittings are included?** Some sellers leave the carpets or curtains because they're buying new or can't face the hassle of taking them: Others strip the property to the bare bones. Find out what the seller's intentions are so that you don't get a nasty shock when you move in. If there's anything you'd like, negotiate with the seller to leave the items for an extra sum. Make sure what you agree is stated in the contract; otherwise, if the seller takes items she agreed to leave, it will be difficult to prove this after you have bought the property.

✔ **Has the property ever been burgled or the seller's car stolen from outside?** If the answer is 'yes, several times', you may rethink buying the property. But if an isolated incident occurred, the seller may have tightened up security since then, so you'll benefit from secure locks and maybe a burglar alarm. Also ask whether the property is situated in a Neighbourhood Watch area; if so, you'll know that the neighbours look out for each other's homes, which can act as a deterrent to burglars. Being in a Neighbourhood Watch area also means lower insurance premiums.

✔ **How easy is finding a parking space?** This is a concern if you have a car and the property doesn't have a garage or off-road parking. Ask the seller how much you have to pay for a permit (if required). Glance at the other cars parked in the street. If they're valuable and their owners are happy to park them there, it should be fairly safe for you to park your car there, too. But if only old bangers are in sight and a couple of burnt out cars for good measure, ask yourself whether you'd be comfortable parking your car in that road (unless you drive an old banger yourself!)

✔ **Where are the nearest schools/hospitals/shops?** This depends on what's important and relevant to you and your family. If you have children of school age, a decent primary or secondary school is important, for example. Most people feel comforted by the presence of a good hospital in the vicinity. Local shops and newsagents, plus a big supermarket, also make life easier, particularly if you rely on public transport. You can ask about the frequency of local buses and trains, too.

Decision Time

After you view the property several times and don't think you'd gain anything else in viewing it again, you're ready to make a decision. Do you like the property enough to make an offer? If you decide to make an offer, keep these tips in mind:

✔ Make sure that you don't decide to buy the property just because you've had enough of house hunting and want to buy *anywhere*. You'll regret it in years to come.

✔ Don't rush into making an offer. Even if you're really excited, curb your excitement in front of the seller or agent. If they can see how thrilled you are, they'll be delighted because it means you're more than likely to offer the asking price.

✔ If you can get away with offering less than the asking price, try. Mask your excitement; show interest by all means, but remain guarded. Once you've saved a few thousand pounds on the asking price you can celebrate with an even bigger bottle of champagne. Carefully assess whether this is a good strategy first, however. See Chapter 9 for more details on making an offer.

✔ While you can save yourself money by containing your excitement and haggling over the price, you should still make an effort to convince the seller of your seriousness.

✔ If you're a first-time buyer, mention that you're not tied up in a chain. And if you're already a homeowner, find a buyer for your property before looking for a property to buy. This will convince the seller that you're not a time-waster, and they're likely to feel more favourably towards you than someone in a complicated chain who has yet to find a buyer for their own property.

✔ Whatever you do, be friendly towards the seller. It doesn't cost you anything and may act in your favour if you and another buyer are competing for the property. If you created a favourable impression, the seller may decide to go with you – even if your offer isn't as high as the other buyer's.

After you've made an offer, you have to instruct a solicitor and arrange a survey. See Chapter 9 for more on this.

Chapter 6

Looks Are Everything: Period Homes

*I*f you think that newly-constructed flats and houses are soulless and lack character, you don't necessarily have to opt for one. A glance around the average UK city reveals an eclectic mix of styles to choose from: Georgian houses (if you're lucky), early-to-late-Victorian terraces, and more commonly Edwardian semis. The seventies tower block may dominate the landscape in some cities, but even high-rise flats are being tarted up as owner-occupiers move in.

Period homes have a unique appeal: There's nothing quite like living in a property steeped in history and character. Being able to say that Charles I once stayed the night in your master bedroom is more likely to hold your dinner-party guests in thrall than if you live in a 1930s three-bed semi. But while period houses are charming, they also have their problems and can be very expensive to restore. In this chapter, I show you what you need to consider before purchasing one.

Of course, old properties don't have a monopoly on character: Some ex-local authority high-rises have their own charm and attraction for buyers. But mortgage lenders aren't always so keen. In this chapter, I also discuss the problems you may face when trying to buy a high-rise and what you should watch out for.

Homebuyers can be spoilt for choice, no matter what their budget, where they want to buy, or what their personal tastes. And if you can't find anything you like, you can always have a go at building your own. See Chapter 7 for more details on self-build properties.

Architectural Periods and Construction Styles

If you have decided that a modern property is not for you and you prefer to buy a period home, you're almost spoilt for choice. Architectural styles are ever changing and from the 1800s to modern times, there has been a series of different styles in house building. Many of the better-built older style properties are still around today. If you're really lucky, you may come across even older properties for sale, such as a fine example of a Jacobean or Elizabethan house. In Table 6-1, I list the main architectural periods to choose from:

Table 6-1	Architectural Periods	
Period	*Date*	*Monarch*
Elizabethan	1558–1603	Elizabeth I
Jacobean	1603–1625	James I
Carolean	1625–1649	Charles I
Cromwellian	1649–1660	Commonwealth
Restoration	1685–1689	James II
William & Mary	1689–1694	William & Mary
Queen Anne*	1702–1714	Anne
Early Georgian	1714–1727	George I
Georgian	1727–1760	George II
Late Georgian	1760–1812	George III
Regency	1812–1820	George III
Late Regency	1820–1830	George IV
William IV	1830–1837	William IV
Early Victorian	1837–1860	Victoria
Late Victorian	1860–1901	Victoria
Edwardian**	1901–1910	Edward VII

*In architectural style usually refers to 1860–1900 and has little to do with Queen Anne's reign
**In architectural style usually means 1901–1918.
Source: www.bricksandbrass.co.uk

A change in monarch didn't necessarily result in a shift in architectural style. As you may expect, architects, designers, and builders often drew their influences from several different periods and earlier styles as well as the one they happened to be living in. As a result, a number of styles reappear years after a monarch has died or straddle the reigns of several monarchs (see Table 6-2):

Table 6-2	Architectural Periods	
Period	*From*	*To*
Gothic Revival	c1750	1900s
Neoclassical	1750s	1830s
Greek Revival	c1819	1840s
Arts and Crafts	1880s	1914
Art Nouveau	1890s	1920s

Source: www.bricksandbrass.co.uk

In the following sections, I explain in more detail some of the more popular styles you're likely to come across.

Georgian

If you find an affordable Georgian house for sale, count yourself lucky and snap it up immediately! This period boasts some of the most handsome buildings in the world. Georgian houses (see Figure 6-1) are usually easy to spot:

 ✔ Simple, yet elegant design

 ✔ Perfectly proportioned

 ✔ Sash windows, panelled front doors, carved wood, and stonework

 ✔ Wrought- or cast-iron railings at the front of the property

 ✔ Pillars or pilasters – square columns

The influence of Classical architecture on Georgian style is very apparent. The Georgians were great admirers of Ancient Greece and Rome. The rich travelled to Greece and made sketches of the ancient monuments there, which they brought back home with them. Two distinctive styles emerged during the Georgian era: Palladianism and Regency style, both of which are explained in more detail in the following sections.

Figure 6-1:
This
Georgian
terrace
demon-
strates the
period's
symmetry,
perfect
proportions,
carved
wood, and
stonework.

Palladianism

Early Georgian houses were heavily influenced by the sixteenth-century Venetian architect Andrea Palladio. Known as Palladianism, this style came with strict guidelines and rules that helped builders set out the proportions of buildings in the image of a Graeco-Roman façade. Hence, the buildings of this era are very distinctive.

The brick or stone walls tend to be plain and simple, with detail restricted to door surrounds, such as the decorative semi-circular fanlight – a common feature of Georgian doorways (see Figure 6-2).

Palladianism was a backlash against Baroque style, which was popular during the late sixteenth and mid-eighteenth centuries. Baroque architecture was over-decorative and associated with Catholicism, so it's little wonder that the Protestant Hanoverians preferred the strict lines and rows of columns or pilasters associated with Palladianism.

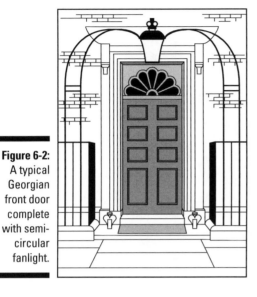

Figure 6-2:
A typical
Georgian
front door
complete
with semi-
circular
fanlight.

Regency

The architectural style of the first 30 years of the nineteenth century is known as the Regency period, even though the future George IV was only actually Prince Regent between 1811 and 1820.

Regency style was much grander and more extravagant and exotic than Palladianism (see Figure 6-3). Balconies put in an appearance, often with a hint of oriental style or with canopies over porches. And plain window openings came with double-hung sash windows.

Victorian

If you live in London, you're probably familiar with Victorian houses whether you know it or not. A quarter of all the homes in the city were built during the reign of Queen Victoria. But that doesn't mean they all look the same – far from it. With a reign spanning more than half a century, there was bound to be a shift in architectural style during the period.

Early Victorian architecture was greatly influenced by Georgian architecture (see Figure 6-4). This influence isn't really surprising: There is no reason why a change in monarch should bring about an overnight shift in architectural style. But the reference to the Georgians diminished as the economic confidence of the Victorian era grew and the machine age dawned. It wouldn't be long before the Victorians wanted to stamp their own style on their buildings, rather than rely on the Georgians for inspiration.

The industrial revolution meant that an increasing number of people moved from the countryside to the towns to work in the factories, which had sprung up. During Queen Victoria's reign, back-to-back dwellings of the industrial towns made their first appearance (see Figure 6-5). These terraces were high density and predominated in the industrial north.

During Queen Victoria's reign, three main styles predominated:

- Gothic Revival
- Arts and Crafts
- Queen Anne Revival

I look at these in more detail in the following sections.

Figure 6-4:
Early to mid-
Victorian
style, still
betraying a
Georgian
influence.

Figure 6-5:
Late
Victorian
houses
appear
much more
'modern'
than those
built during
the early
part of
Queen
Victoria's
reign and
are still
quite
common in
London
today.

Gothic revival

Gothic architecture first appeared in the thirteenth and fourteenth centuries but it became popular once again between 1855 and 1885. The rather grand Gothic style was used particularly in the construction of important public buildings, such as the Houses of Parliament and many churches. Of course, such grand designs weren't really suitable for small Victorian houses, so many builders took certain elements – such as stained glass, Gothic porches (see Figure 6-6), bay windows with elegant pillars, and battened oak doors – and adapted them. The result was a grand Gothic feel without going the whole hog.

As a result, the Gothic Revival often appears as a mis-match of eclectic styles (see Figure 6-7). Plenty of surviving houses of this style appear around the country, although they aren't to everyone's taste.

Figure 6-6: Gothic porches can appear rather grand.

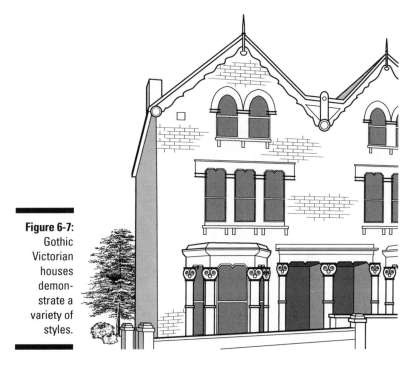

Figure 6-7:
Gothic
Victorian
houses
demon-
strate a
variety of
styles.

Arts and Crafts

With so much emphasis on mass, machine-produced goods in the Victorian era – culminating in the 1851 Great Exhibition at the Crystal Palace – a back-lash to the industrial revolution was almost inevitable. The move away from such excesses with a return to high-quality yet simple traditional hand-made building techniques using skilled craftsmen and local materials was known as the Arts and Crafts movement.

Predominant between 1860 and 1910, the Arts and Crafts movement (see Figure 6-8) was founded by a group of writers and designers, including William Morris. But while the style represented a return to simpler times, such goods and architecture tended to be very expensive and so only afford-able to the wealthier middle classes. A few examples of asymmetrical Arts and Crafts houses with rustic tiles appear around the country, and the advantage of buying one of these properties is that they tend to be well-built and of sturdy construction. Many also came with a large garden.

Figure 6-8:
An example of a large yet simple house built in the Arts and Crafts style.

Queen Anne Revival

This style, which predominated during the second half of the nineteenth century, had no real connection with the reign of Queen Anne herself (1702–14). A Classical influence was once again apparent although the strict rules of proportion were absent. Instead, it was mixed with some original Queen Anne, as well as Flemish and Dutch styles. The result was informal and irregular. In fact, the style was so eclectic that it attracted plenty of critics.

During the Queen Anne Revival period, simple red-brick buildings became popular once again, as were sash windows with small panes of glass. Queen Anne Revival buildings (such as the one in Figure 6-9) were common in parts of London and seaside towns.

Twentieth Century Architecture

Early twentieth-century houses were similar in style to their Victorian counterparts but smaller in scale – as servants became less common – and simpler. As new railway lines letting people commute to work were built, houses could be constructed outside towns and cities for the first time. A number of influences made a mark, particularly Art Nouveau and Art Deco.

Art Nouveau

Originating in France in the 1880s, Art Nouveau had very little influence in the UK until the turn of the century. It was the first style to really stop looking backwards for inspiration and drew instead on the present for ideas. Two types of style are classed as Art Nouveau: those with curvy lines or those with a more austere linear look.

Figure 6-9:
A classic
Queen Anne
house.

Art Nouveau proved to be a rather difficult style to demonstrate in architecture, which explains why it was more commonly used for interiors, such as Parquet floors, detailed floral wallpaper, stained glass windows, and cast-iron fire surrounds.

Art Deco

As with any style, Art Nouveau had its sell-by date. Art Deco replaced the flowery shapes and pastel colours of Art Nouveau with bolder, intense colours, and a lot of chrome and black. The emphasis was on modern, clean lines and sleek, dramatic, geometric shapes, producing a futuristic look.

Art Deco may have originated in France, but it was enthusiastically adopted in the UK and US. The big advantage of the simple cubic forms that characterised this architectural style was that it was mass-produced and cheap and as a result most people could afford it.

Nowadays, Art Deco buildings are tremendously sought after. If you do come across a purpose-built 1930s flat or revamped former factory divided into apartments, you're unlikely to have much trouble selling it on again.

Edwardian

As with most period styles, Edwardian style tends to be rather eclectic, taking ideas from the mediaeval, Georgian, and Victorian eras, and combining them with more modern influences. The Victorian terrace evolved (see Figure 6-10) with Art Nouveau influences in fireplaces and stained glass. Some Edwardian properties show a return to leaded windows with small panes, last seen in the Arts and Crafts movement.

Large sash bay windows, columns, and pilasters also reappeared, while walls were lighter. In addition, Edwardian houses are less cluttered than those of the Victorian period.

Figure 6-10:
A typical Edwardian terraced house.

The suburban semi

In the 1930s, in an effort to get people out of Victorian slums (an unfortunate feature of crowded cities), the suburban semi (see Figure 6-11) sprang up around existing towns and cities. Some four million new homes were built between 1919 and 1939 – their solid construction still makes them a popular choice of homeowners today.

Figure 6-11:
A typical
1930s semi.

Problems with Period Homes

It's a fairly safe bet that a period home will cost you a lot of money. A Victorian house is bound to set you back more than a modern three-bed semi, even before you've budgeted for any restoration that needs doing.

Shoddy modernisation by the previous owners

If you buy a badly modernised period home – for example, the previous owners replaced the original grand Georgian front door with a modern glass one and concealed the original brickwork with stone cladding – the bill for restoring the property to its former glory could be substantial. Repairing the damage to a poorly modernised house could cost even more than doing up an unmodernised property. At least the latter is likely to still have its original features; in the former, they may have been ripped up, in which case you'll be spending your time traipsing round salvage yards trying to find as close a likeness to the originals as possible.

Think carefully before committing yourself to a big modernisation project. Getting specialists in to replace the roof with original tiles or restore period features is expensive. Get an estimate for the work from two or three builders before committing yourself. And while you're about it, consider where you and your family will live while the work is being carried out. Living with builders and their dust isn't easy and may not be practical.

The cost of restoring original features

If you buy a period house in need of restoration, you will save a lot of money if the property still has its original features. If you're very lucky, these features will be hiding behind several coats of modern paint or under a tatty carpet. When restoring a period home you need to consider the following:

- ✔ **Making structural repairs:** If the structure of the building isn't sound, your first task will be to rectify this, particularly if you're planning to live in the property while the rest of the work is completed.

- ✔ **Re-doing the roof:** If lots of tiles are missing or the wrong tiles have been used in a modernised period home, you have to source original tiles if you're serious about restoring your home to its former glory.

- ✔ **Replacing windows:** If a shoddy modernisation left you with uPVC windows, you need to replace them with wooden ones in the original style. You'll also need to refit broken sash cords on sash windows, and repair or replace damaged stained glass windows. You may be able to find something suitable at salvage yards, or you could commission a new panel to be made in a similar style.

- ✔ **Restoring the doors:** If you have the original doors, you can bring them back to their glory days: Strip off the old paint, repair the wood if necessary, and repaint the door with a colour as close to the original colour as possible. Also polish any metalwork.

In the 1950s and 1960s, it was the fashion to cover original doors with a sheet of hardboard. So before you toss out a door, check whether you have a gem hidden underneath.

- ✔ **Cleaning up the woodwork:** If the original woodwork has been painted over, you need to strip all paint from original features, particularly panelling. You also need to replace or repair any faulty woodwork.

- ✔ **Refurbishing the floors:** Original tiles, wood, or flagstones are often hidden underneath a modern floor, so first check to see whether this is the case. Varnishing or painting is relatively inexpensive and can revive old floorboards.

- ✔ **Updating the drainage:** If the original drains are still in place, they will most likely struggle to cope with modern sewage demands. If you have to replace your drains, expect to spend a lot of money, as this task is likely to prove expensive.

✓ **Incorporating modern conveniences:** Period homes can be charming but most homeowners want their creature comforts. This means installing modern appliances: The Victorians may not have had central heating, but that doesn't mean you'll want to do the same in order to give your Victorian conversion an authentic feel. You have to find the right balance between old and modern.

Although there may be a lot of work that needs doing, you won't have to pay for all of it to be done straightaway. Some work will need attending to urgently, such as a big hole in the roof. But I imagine you could live with the 'wrong' window frames or a modern door where the original one should be until any urgent work is completed – particularly if you can't afford to have it all done at once.

As you renovate your period home, you may baulk at the cost of replacing windows with materials as close to the original as possible, or decide that a modern door on a Victorian home will look just fine. These types of decisions may save you money in the short term, but they cost you in the long run. If the day comes when you want to sell your home, prospective buyers may well be unimpressed by your cost cutting.

For information on restoring period property in a thoughtful and responsible way, contact the Society for the Protection of Ancient Buildings (SPAB) on 020 7377 1644 or go to www.spab.org.uk.

Skimping on a survey

Some homebuyers cut corners to save money by not commissioning a survey. But if you're buying a very old property, it is vital that you commission a specialist structural survey. You must establish the condition of the property. A specialist structural survey looks at the property's structural integrity; the quality of the roof and walls; the damp management; the state of the brickwork; the windows and doors; and the drains. If you don't know exactly what you're taking on right from the beginning, a lot of extremely nasty and expensive surprises are likely to be lying in store for you.

For the survey on a period home, use a surveyor who specialises in properties of that period. For more information on what different surveys cover and how to find a good surveyor who is a member of the Royal Institution of Chartered Surveyors (RICS), see Chapter 9.

Ensure that you have enough surplus cash to deal with the most urgent of repairs after you purchase the property. You may be able to knock the seller down a bit if a lot of work needs to be done, but bear in mind that the price is already likely to reflect the cost of necessary repairs.

Dealing with rules about listed buildings

If the property you're interested in buying is a listed building – that is, it is on a statutory list of buildings demonstrating special architectural or historic interest – you should discuss the survey's findings with your local conservation officer (you can find the number in the Yellow Pages). If a lot of work is needed, you must ensure that you will be able to do this without encountering too many planning problems – even if you're going to re-instate original features. See Chapter 8 for more details on listed buildings and restrictions on maintenance and repairs.

Buying an Ex-Local Authority Property

Say 'council flat' and many people immediately think of grim tower blocks with broken-down lifts, drug taking, and muggings on problem estates. But local authority housing has come a long way, and many buyers snap up ex-local authority flats and houses because of the following:

- ✔ They're often solidly constructed.
- ✔ Many are in decent low-rise blocks with working lifts as opposed to high-rises with lifts that never work.
- ✔ Some have architectural cachet.
- ✔ They tend to be a lot cheaper than other period homes, like Victorian conversions, for example.
- ✔ High-rise flats often have amazing views across cities and let in plenty of light.
- ✔ They are often close to major transport links and located in fashionable locations in the centre of cities.
- ✔ Finding such properties for sale is becoming easier and less stigma is attached to buying one.

Some of the 1960s and 1970s tower blocks have become highly desirable for their views across major cities. But mortgage lenders may not be as keen as you are: many lenders aren't interested in any flat higher than the fifth floor. The build quality is also a major consideration – reinforced concrete is not acceptable to lenders. The number of owner-occupiers (as opposed to Council tenants) the building has will also be taken into account – the more, the better, from the lender's point of view.

Mortgage lenders usually make their decisions on a case-by-case basis, so if your initial application is turned down, shop around to see whether another lender will let you have the money you need. Use a mortgage broker to make your life easier. Brokers will know which lenders are more likely to lend on ex-local authority properties and which ones to avoid. See Chapter 11 for more information on finding an independent mortgage broker.

For more information on ex-local authority properties for sale, try www.ex-localauthority.com. For a fee of £80, you can register for four months' access to the database with thousands of ex-council properties for sale.

Chapter 7

New and Self-Build: No Previous Owners

*H*ave you ever despaired of getting your property exactly how you'd like it? Sometimes there's only so far you can go with interior design. You can paint and decorate as much as you like, and even build an extension, but if you really want a detached bungalow in a rural setting, you're not going to be able to turn your two-up two-down terrace into one. The only way to realise your dream is to move.

But for some people even moving isn't enough. They are so keen to get their home just right that they're prepared to build it from scratch. While in theory this sounds like a fine idea, you need to research such a project carefully and get an accurate idea of the costs involved. And then you need to think about whether you can spare the time – and put up with the hassle. After all, buying a property is stressful enough without all the added problems that building a house can bring. Before you commit yourself to such a project, think it through very carefully.

If self-build (that's building your own property) is a step too far but you still want some say in your home as it's being built, buying off-plan – before the property is finished – is another option. Developers often let buyers choose different kitchen cabinets or let them influence the layout. But this isn't without its risks, either: I explore these in this chapter. I also look at the hoops you need to jump through when building your own home and problems to avoid, and I help you assess whether all that hard work is really worth it.

Is a Brand New Home Right up Your Street?

Brand new homes don't appeal to everyone. Homeowners can generally be divided into two types: those who like period, character properties complete with creaking floorboards, and those who like spanking new, modern spaces with the latest mod-cons. For the former, dark wooden furniture and antique leather sofas are in keeping with the cosy feel. The latter tend to prefer streamlined fittings, lighter wood, and more modern materials such as steel and laminate flooring.

A brand new home is for those who not only want a property that nobody else has lived in before but also want it exactly how they like it. There are two main types of new property to go for – new-build or self-build.

- ✔ **New-build,** as the name suggests, is a property newly built. Many home-buyers who opt for a new-build home buy at the *off-plan stage;* this means the property isn't actually finished, in fact, they may have little more than a series of drawings to go on when they put down their deposit. Properties sold off-plan may be in great demand – buyers know that if they don't put their cash down there and then, they could miss out.

- ✔ **Self-build** is much more involved. Instead of buying a property someone else has built (or is building), you plan and execute the project yourself. Although only 5 per cent of self-builders do all the actual work them-selves – the vast majority hire contractors to do it for them – the princi-ple is the same. You buy a plot of land, ideally with outline planning permission, before commissioning an architect or surveyor to draw up the plans for your home, which you submit to the planning authority (the local council). Once these are approved, construction begins.

Whether you do the work yourself or hire experts depends on your personal skills and what you're happy doing. But be prepared to do a lot of the donkey-work in order to keep costs down.

Whether you opt for a new- or self-build property there are pros and cons in choosing a new home. The positives include these things:

- ✔ **You don't have to cover up anybody else's ghastly decorating mis-takes.** When you move in, you should have very little to do to the prop-erty because you were so involved in the design and decoration of it in the first place.

- ✔ **You get a modern, fitted kitchen.** Appliances are often cleverly con-cealed in a minimalist home. Or if you want a country feel in fitting with your home's rural setting, you can opt for a rustic kitchen complete with Aga.

✔ **You get a clean white bathroom suite.** You don't have to spend your time ripping out the old-fashioned 1970s pistachio green bathroom suite that is all too frequent in older properties. And you're also likely to end up with a modern power shower rather than a feeble shower attachment providing a dribble of water.

✔ **Everything is exactly where you wanted it:** With self-build, this is a given, allowing for planning regulations. For a new-build, you usually have some say in the finished article as long as you buy the property off-plan long before it's completed.

✔ **You don't have to worry about subsidence, damp, a dodgy old boiler, or ancient wiring.** Everything will be brand new and up-to-date.

✔ **Warranties come on all kitchen appliances, such as fridge, freezer, dishwasher and oven.** New properties also come with an NHBC warranty (see 'What Buildmark Cover does – and doesn't – insure you for' later in this chapter), which covers your home for ten years.

New- and self-build properties also have disadvantages, including the following:

✔ **Possible lack of character.** Clean lines and modern fittings that appeal to one homebuyer may appear cold and featureless to another. Whether a brand new property is for you depends on your personal taste. Some people prefer a new feel while others hate it. Decide which camp you fall into.

✔ **Lack of solidity.** Old houses tend to feel sturdy with thicker walls, heavier doors, and general all-round solidness than new-builds. Be careful when viewing a new-build apartment or house: check the quality of the workmanship, knock on walls and doors, and don't agree to hand over the remainder of the cash until the home is finished to your satisfaction.

✔ **Quality can be an issue.** This is particularly the case when it comes to the fixtures and fittings in new-build properties. Developers cut corners. Unless you keep a close eye during the building work, you could end up with inferior materials to those you were expecting. (But if you really hate the kitchen cabinets, you should be able to choose different ones.)

✔ **The sheer scale of the work involved.** With new-build, you'll end up chasing the developer to get the plans altered to your satisfaction, chasing the builder to ensure he uses the bathroom tiles you want, and making sure that teething problems are ironed out once you move in. Self-build is even more time-consuming and a lot more work than you think. Even if you aren't doing much of the building work yourself, you'll feel like you're chasing everyone all the time – builders, carpenters, suppliers, the list goes on.

While there are disadvantages to brand new properties, if you want a blank canvas on which you can make your mark, self-build in particular is the only one way to go. As long as you're aware of the potential problems, you can go a long way to minimising them.

Buying Off-Plan

A new-build property is far less work than self-build because someone does all the graft for you. The best way of buying new-build is at the off-plan stage, that is before building work has started. You may be able to influence proceedings so that the finished product is more to your own taste. The downside is that you may need to wait many months before building work is finished. Buying off-plan can significantly reduce the amount of work you have to do once you move into the property, saving you time, effort, and money.

When buying off-plan, all you're likely to have to go on is the developer's plans, knowledge of where the property is to be built (the plot), and the show home that you may have looked around. But, unusually for a property purchase, you won't be able to see the property you're buying until you have committed yourself to paying for it.

The big advantage of buying off-plan is that there is still time to make changes to the plans. Of course, you can't change the actual structure (and make the property bigger than it is meant to be, for example), but some developers do let you change the layout or opt for different kitchen cabinets or other amenities.

Being prepared to act quickly

During the property boom of the late 1990s, buying off-plan was all the rage. But even without a property boom, people still buy off-plan if the development is particularly desirable. A fantastic location, for example, does a lot to fuel demand and drives fear into buyers' hearts: If they don't stake a claim there and then, even to an unfinished or barely started property, they might miss out.

If you spot the beginnings of a new development in a location where you would love to live, or see show houses or flats that spark your interest advertised in the paper, get round there and take a look as soon as you can. There's no point waiting until the development is complete; if it is highly desirable, by then, you may be too late.

Many developers organise open days, evenings or weekends to drum up interest among prospective buyers. Attending these events is a great opportunity to take a look round the show home and gauge the level of interest in the development. If the open evening is well attended, you'll have to move more quickly than you would if only two people turn up. You'll also have an opportunity to talk to the agent handling the sale and should be able to get a pretty good idea from her as to the amount of interest that has been shown in the development.

Taking advantage of incentives

With so many new-build flats and houses coming onto the market, developers are desperate for your business. To encourage you to choose their development, most offer 'incentives' such as paying your deposit, stamp duty, or even your mortgage for a period of time. These are all perfectly legal but must be declared to your mortgage lender when applying for a loan so that the lender has a transparent picture of the transaction.

Viewing the show home: Beware the tricks of the trade

The show home is a useful tool for the developer because it allows him to illustrate the likely quality and scale of the new flat or house to prospective buyers. And it's much easier for a buyer to see – and imagine herself living in – the finished product with her own eyes than try to visualise it from a set of plans.

Don't let yourself be taken in by the show home. It's not usually the property you're actually buying. Developers pick show homes for a reason. They're likely to be situated on the best plot in the development and will be finished to the highest specification because they'll be scrutinised so carefully by prospective buyers. More time and effort goes into the show home than other properties in the development because this is the property that makes up buyers' minds.

The fact that the show home doesn't represent what your home will be like doesn't mean that it isn't worth looking at or that your finished property will be sub-standard. But you need to remember that you're looking at a home that's been designed to appeal to you. So that you don't find yourself surprised by the way your own less-polished house looks, make sure that your contract states that you're getting the materials and fittings you think you're getting.

A front door isn't just for Christmas

When you view the show home, don't forget to test the strength of the front door and ask whether it conforms to safety standards. So dazzled was I by my new flat that I didn't ask these questions. It was only after we had all moved into our homes and several flats in the block were broken into that it transpired that our 'front' doors were the same doors the builders had used on the bedrooms. In other words, they offered little protection from thieves who simply kicked them down.

As I'd just bought a new flat, I was a bit short of cash and the quote for a new metal door with all the bells and whistles – a five-lever mortice deadlock to British Standard BS 3621, for example – was £450, including fitting. Luckily it was the week before Christmas, so when my mother asked what I wanted, the door was top of the list. I got my new door and the flat was as safe and secure as it should have been if the developer hadn't cut corners in the first place.

Check the build quality before signing up to anything. If you're not sure, ask the developer what locks and type of door are set to be used.

View the show home with a healthy dose of scepticism. Keep these things in mind when you look at show homes:

- ✔ Ignore the view unless it is the same as the one you will get from the flat or house you're actually purchasing.

- ✔ Ask the agent to confirm the dimensions of your property. Is the show home bigger, smaller, or the exact same size as your property is likely to be?

- ✔ Try not to be distracted by furnishings, such as the sofa or bed – items that won't be included in the sale – unless of course, you're picking up tips on how to furnish your own property (or not!)

- ✔ Ask to see samples of any finishes that will be used in your property that are different to those in the show house. If the developer is planning on using different kitchen worktops or bedroom carpets, demand to see a sample first so that you know what you will end up with – and request an alternative if you don't like the look of them.

Putting down a deposit

If you like what you see, the next step is to secure it. Some developers require a non-refundable reservation fee as soon as you have seen the plans or show home to demonstrate that you're serious. You may be expected to exchange contracts within 28 days, at which stage you pay a 10 per cent deposit. Then you have to sit back and wait for your property to be built, which could take months or even years, depending on how advanced the project is when you pay your deposit. After your home is finished, you pay the balance, get the keys, and move in.

The danger is that if the property market collapses in between putting down a deposit and completing on the property, you may find that you're committed to buying a house that is worth less than you agreed to pay. But if you're buying a home to live in rather than as an investment opportunity, you'll just have to stay put and wait for the market to recover. Don't forget, the opposite could happen: Prices could rise, in which case you'll end up paying less than the property is worth.

Choosing the kitchen cabinets and beyond

One of the great advantages of buying off-plan is that you usually get a big say in your property. If you buy early enough, you may be able to pick one of the best plots, and the developer may be happy to give you free rein, perhaps agreeing to omit non-load bearing walls if you prefer a more open-plan look. You should also have a say in the materials used. If you think the wood being used on the floors is too light, you should be able to request a darker colour.

In fact, if you're buying off-plan, ask the developer for the full specification detailing what materials are to be used in your property. That way you won't have any nasty shocks when you move in – and if the developer tries to cut corners with cheaper materials, you'll have some comeback.

The earlier you request something be changed, the more likely the developer is to agree to it.

While some developers are happy to let you make a number of changes, others aren't so keen. The most common reason is that the fittings you've asked for cost more (the builder can't buy them in bulk and you've probably requested a more expensive fitting than the original plans included). Your request may also delay the project, especially if the fitting is out of stock and has to be ordered. If you're determined to get the materials you want, you have to negotiate carefully with the developer and may have to pay extra for them.

What to do if you aren't happy with the finished article

The danger in relying on a set of plans when purchasing a property is that you may not end up with what you expected. The fixtures and fittings may be sub-standard or the work slapdash. Sometimes, things just aren't finished properly, and you end up having to call the builder back to make good. The one advantage of moving into your property before other properties in your development are finished is that the builders will still be on site; if you come across any faults, they should be able to rectify them fairly quickly.

To give yourself the greatest protection in case something goes wrong – such as the developer going bust or the build quality being poor – ensure that your developer is registered with the National House-Building Council (NHBC), the regulatory body for the industry. The advantage of using an NHBC-registered builder is that NHBC inspectors carry out checks during the building process to satisfy themselves that the property conforms to NHBC standards. Double check whether your developer is NHBC-registered by calling the NHBC on 0870 241 4329 or check the register on its Web site (www.nhbc.co.uk).

New homes must come with Buildmark Cover – an insurance policy that covers you against specified risks. This insurance isn't a complete guarantee against all defects, however. It doesn't' cover general wear and tear, condensation, damage arising from failure to maintain the property, or minor faults that appear after the second year. If the developer isn't registered with the NHBC, he should have some other form of insurance (such as Zurich) from a reputable firm that guarantees you get your deposit back if the developer goes bust.

Building Your Home from Scratch: What's Involved in Self-Build

Building your own home from scratch takes time, money, and effort. Yet an estimated 20,000 people opt for self-build projects in Britian each year, so why don't these considerations put more people off?

Apart from getting your home just the way you want it (allowing for local planning regulations), self-build works out a lot cheaper than buying a ready-built house. By the time the property is built, the average self-build house is worth up to 50 per cent more than you paid for it. Before you jump on the self-build bandwagon, however, be sure that you're up to the job.

A number of excellent websites are very helpful in helping you decide whether self-build is for you in the first place and then guiding you through once you've committed yourself to a project. Check out Self Build ABC (www.selfbuildabc.co.uk) or Buildstore (www.buildstore.co.uk) for more details.

TECHNICAL STUFF

What Buildmark Cover does – and doesn't – insure you for

New homes, both new-build and self-build, should come with a ten-year insurance policy, known as Buildmark Cover. This is issued by NHBC-registered developers and builders and is essential if you want to sell your property on because new buyers will demand it on recently-built homes. The cost is included in the purchase price of your home – your builder pays a premium to the NHBC.

Buildmark Cover ensures that if the builder goes bust before starting to build your home or finishing it, NHBC reimburses the money you have paid to him if the amount can't be recovered from the builder. If the property is unfinished, NHBC can arrange for it to be completed.

Once you've moved in, you're covered for any defects caused by the builder not meeting NHBC standards. For the first two years, the builder is responsible for necessary repairs. Report faults to him in writing and keep a copy of the letter. If he doesn't rectify the fault, you can contact the NHBC. If the builder still fails to address the problem, the NHBC will arrange for the remedial work to be carried out.

After two years, certain things aren't covered by Buildmark, such as gutters, central heating, and fixtures and fittings.

Things to think about before you decide

Although more than 20,000 people build their own homes every year, self-build isn't for everyone. If your idea of hell after a hard day in the office is to spend an evening digging the foundations of your new home, think twice about self-build. Although many self-builders carry out no building work themselves whatsoever, you must at least oversee the project and have certain qualities – and lots of contacts – to make it work, otherwise you'll find yourself constantly getting stressed out and will hate the experience.

Do you have what it takes?

Self-build best suits these people:

- **Builders:** The more work you can do yourself, the cheaper the project will be. People who commit themselves to self-build should prepare to at least do the donkey-work: fetching and carrying, digging foundations, piling up bricks, painting, and decorating. Of course, if you're also competent enough to do the wiring or plastering (don't attempt if you aren't), you can save yourself a lot of cash.

- **Those with great contacts in the building trade:** You don't have to be a builder or electrician, but it helps if you know good people who are. If you don't, your job will be that much harder.

✔ **Those with great organisational skills:** If you plan your project down to the smallest detail before you get started, you can significantly reduce the likelihood of anything going wrong.

✔ **Those who enthusiastically roll their sleeves up and get stuck in:** People who take a keen interest in their self-build project have a far greater chance of success than someone who leaves all the work and detail to the experts. As long as you don't interfere in things you don't understand and simply offer your services where required, you're more likely to have a successful self-build experience.

✔ **The financially astute:** Working to a budget is crucial in a self-build project. If you're the type of person who lives within their means, you'll be at a great advantage. Few things are worse than accidentally over-spending on one aspect of the project and then having to scrimp on something else. If you blow your budget on much pricier bricks or roof tiles, for example, you won't have the funds you need when it is time to pay for your kitchen fittings. Before you start, know what each stage in the construction is going to cost; if you can't calculate this yourself, ask a surveyor or builder to help.

Housing options in the interim

Building a new home can take months or years, depending on the scale of the project and the funds available. During this time, you need somewhere to live.

Fortunately, you don't necessarily have to sell your home to raise the money for your self-build and live in a caravan on-site for months on end while you wait for your new home to be finished. An increasing number of lenders are prepared to let self-builders have a mortgage. In these situations, you can stay in your existing home until the new one is built before selling up. See 'Arranging the financing' later in this chapter for more details on self-build mortgages.

Time and hassle – guaranteed

Although it is vital that you set a timetable before starting a self-build project, whenever builders are involved, expect things to run over schedule. Even the best-laid plans can go awry. Do your research, plan carefully, and seek expert advice where necessary. You reduce the chance of things going wrong, but you may not be able to eliminate problems entirely.

The other guarantee with self-build is the hassle factor. If you're someone who'd do anything for a quiet life, think twice about taking on such a project. Even if you aren't hands-on when it comes to the building work, you still have to make the financial arrangements and manage the build, making sure the various steps of the project are carried out smoothly and on time. Unless you have a project manager to supervise the work, you'll spend a lot of your time chasing tradespeople, deliveries of materials, surveyors, and inspectors from the council.

If you have a stressful, full-time job and work long hours, you probably won't want to spend your precious free time chasing builders. And it won't be enough to do these tasks just at evenings and weekends: a lot of ordering and chasing needs to be done during working hours. If you can't devote time to the project, can't be on site, but still want to pursue self-build, appoint a project manager to do the necessary coordination and overseeing for you.

Finding the right plot of land

Location is particularly important with self-build because any old plot simply won't do. You must find a location in which you'd be happy to live. And ideally, the plot should already have outline planning permission (OPP) because obtaining this can be hard work (see 'Applying for Planning Permission' later).

A real shortage of suitable land for self-build exists in certain parts of the country, particularly the south-east of England. When searching for land, try the usual sources: estate agents, auction houses, local and national newspapers, and the Internet. For a fee, you can also register with PlotSearch, which has details of more than 20,000 plots for sale (www.buildstore.co.uk). Annual membership costs £39: with this, you get details of self-build plots for sale in one county of your choice.

Be sure that you have the land valued to make sure you're paying a fair price for it. Unlike buying a house, when you're likely to have a good idea about what similar properties in the area cost, you may not be so sure about land. A surveyor can provide an idea of how much the plot is worth. She will also be able to give you an idea of the cost of building the property you want and an idea of its final value. Mortgage lenders demand this information before they agree to finance a self-build.

Applying for planning permission

Your local planning authority wants to ensure that your plans for a new home and the materials you intend to use comply with *Building Regulations*. These are requirements that must be met during construction, and your council's Building Control Surveyor will assess your proposals. You can get a copy of the Building Regulations from your local council, download them from the Internet or view them at your local library.

For this reason, if you buy a plot of land without planning permission (or a building warrant in Scotland), you have to apply to the local planning authority for consent to build your home. In Northern Ireland you must apply to the Building Control Department of your District Council. This is much cheaper than buying land with planning consent, but obtaining permission isn't straightforward – and is by no means guaranteed.

Types of permission

Outline planning permission (OPP) means that the local planning authority has agreed in principle to the building of a house. Restrictions and conditions may be attached relating to access, boundaries, and types of material to be used in the construction and the style of house allowed. If your plot has OPP, examine the documents carefully so that you know what these conditions are.

A plot may also be sold with *detailed planning permission* (DPP), which means detailed plans outlining a specific type and size of house have been approved by the local planning authority. You must examine DPP documents carefully because the type of property in the DPP may not be what you want. To change something, you must reapply for planning permission. This act doesn't cancel the existing permission, and there's no guarantee that the planning authority will agree to your plans and grant you permission.

Some plots are sold with *full planning permission:* a combination of OPP and DPP. This is used when the proposed development is contentious because the plot is in a conservation area or next to a listed building. Conditions will be attached, so check the small print. Such permission is valid for five years from when consent is granted.

If your plot has outline permission, the next step is to apply for DPP. This involves submitting plans for your house to the planning authority for approval. If accepted, you will be given the green light to start building (see 'Applying for Planning Permission' later for more details on this.) You must work with your local planning officer to get the necessary permission, and you may have to compromise. Being flexible makes the whole process a lot easier.

Important deadlines

OPP is valid for five years from the date it was granted but you must apply for DPP within three years of that date. DPP must then commence within two years of being granted. If a plot has *lapsed planning permission,* this means work wasn't started within the stated time frame. Getting planning permission again is by no means a foregone conclusion.

The process

Obtaining planning permission can be a long drawn-out process, so it often pays to call in the experts – architects or surveyors – to ensure that you have a good stab at your application being approved the first time around. You must be patient and prepared to cooperate with the local planning authority.

Town planners can also be helpful in preparing your application for planning consent. Planning Consultants UK has an excellent website full of hints on ensuring that your application is successful (www.planning-consultants-uk.co.uk).

When you apply for planning consent, your application form should be accompanied by the following:

- **A plan fee:** The amount depends on your local authority.
- **Two sets of drawings:** These should be detailed, drawn-to-scale and include relevant notes and the site location.

The local authority will confirm receipt of your application. It has five weeks (or two months, if you agree) to respond in one of the following ways:

- **Your plans are accepted.** You're issued an approval notice and can start building.
- **Your plans are rejected.** You receive a refusal notice, along with the reasons for rejection. You can apply for a review, submit a new application, or give up.
- **Conditional approval is granted.** This happens if your plan has certain defects that need to be put right. With conditional approval, you also receive a schedule of amendments that you must comply with.

If your plans are refused outright, you can appeal to the local authority. If it stands firm, you can appeal to the Secretary of State. Your Building Control Surveyor can provide you with more details of how to do this.

Dealing with the authorities

Approving the plans is just the first stage of your local authority's involvement in your self-build. The Building Control Surveyor will make at least nine visits to your property during the building process to ensure that you're meeting Building Regulations. You'll be given a set of inspection request cards detailing at what stage an inspection is compulsory and how much notice you need to give. The stages are as follows:

- Commencement of work
- Foundations dug
- Concrete foundations
- Damp proof course
- Hardcore laid over the site
- Drain connection with sewer
- Drains inspection
- Drain backfilled and ready for test
- Final completion or occupation before completion

If the inspector believes that you aren't complying with Building Regulations, the Building Control Officer can force you to amend the work. If you refuse, you can be prosecuted and will have to pay costs.

You can't move onto the next stage in the building process until the Building Control Surveyor has given the previous one the okay. His advice and guidance can be helpful so be sure to listen to it – you may even save some money.

Once the local authority is convinced that the work meets all the Building Regulations, you'll receive a Certificate of Completion. This is a valuable document so store it carefully as you will need to produce it when you come to sell your property.

Who ya gonna call? Tradespeople and professionals

If you're new to self-build, you probably don't have a clue as to who does what. Below, I list some of the tradespeople and professionals you may need. Remember, though, if you can do the work yourself, you can save quite a bit of cash:

- **Architect:** A good idea unless you know about design. A Chartered Architect will produce detailed planning and construction drawings. Get quotes from two or three architects and check client references before commissioning one. The Royal Institute of British Architects (RIBA) has a database of architects in the UK and can put you in contact with one near you. Contact RIBA on 020 7580 5533.

- **Project manager:** Many self-builders save themselves thousands of pounds by being their own project manager. A project manager supervises the building work, hires labourers, and orders materials. If you haven't the time or inclination to do this, you can get a builder or architect to project manage for you.

- **Bricklayers:** These must be good, as the end result can't exactly be covered up. They can lay blocks as well as bricks.

- **Electricians and plumbers:** Both these have first and second fixes, which means they have to visit twice during the building work. Check that electricians are registered with the National Inspection Council for Electrical Installation Contracting (NICEIC), and the plumbers with the Institute of Plumbing or the Council for Registered Gas Installers (CORGI), before taking them on.

- **Groundworkers:** These are responsible for digging foundations, setting them out, and installing drains.

- ✔ **Joiners:** Again, first and second fixes are required to install the floor joists and construct the roof timbers, and later to do the flooring, hang the doors, and do the skirting boards.

- ✔ **Plasterers:** You need plasterers for installing the plasterboard and then bonding and skimming.

- ✔ **Roofers:** You may need to employ a specialist, depending on the roofing material you use.

- ✔ **Scaffolders:** At some stage in the building process you need scaffolding, and it's important that you use a certified scaffolder to supply, erect, and maintain it. Scaffolding must meet with Health and Safety requirements.

Whichever tradespeople or professionals you hire, ensure that you check references and agree on a quote for the work, in writing, beforehand.

Money matters with self-build

Self-build may work out cheaper than buying a ready-built home, but that doesn't mean it's cheap. If you're a first-time buyer, remember that self-build is not a short cut to getting a foot onto the housing ladder: You need cash to get started and to pay tradespeople up front. The average self-build costs £150,000.

Costing the project

Before you get started on any building work, you must set a budget and divide it up so that you know how much each stage of the work is likely to cost. This prevents you from exceeding your budget in the early stages and running out of cash long before you finish.

If you have never budgeted for a self-build project before and have limited knowledge of the building trade, it's almost impossible to set a budget on your own. Consult a surveyor for help in drawing up a budget. Do this before you do anything else.

Things to budget for include:

- ✔ Cost of purchasing the land: This can be as much as a third of your entire budget if it already has planning permission.

- ✔ Architect or surveyor fees (if you use them).

- ✔ Application fees to the local planning authority.

- ✔ Connection to water drainage, electricity, and gas. Expect to pay upwards of £2,000. If the plot is particularly remote, expect to pay more.

- ✔ Valuation fees for surveys required by your lender.

- ✔ Labour costs and materials.

Steering clear of the cowboys

My father built our family home during the mid-1980s, so I've seen at first-hand how easy it is to run into problems. But apart from the difficulty in getting planning permission in the first place, one of the biggest problems he faced was the useless plasterer who ordered the wrong type of plasterboard and then put it up anyway and started plastering over it.

It was only when the plasterer did a runner before the job was finished – with my father's money – and another one was hired to replace him that my father realised the mistake the first plasterer had made. The whole lot had to be ripped off and replaced with the correct plasterboard, delaying the project by several weeks.

There are plenty of cowboys out there (certainly bad and ugly, but never good!). Hire tradespeople on the basis of recommendation and check client references before taking them on.

No matter how much planning you do beforehand, the actual cost of building work can be much higher than the projected cost. Be sure that you have a contingency fund of around 10 per cent of your entire budget to cover any shortfall so that the project isn't held up.

Saving on stamp duty and VAT

While stamp duty is the bane of homebuyers' lives, the advantage of self-build is that you don't pay stamp duty on the property no matter how much it is worth when finished. You only pay stamp duty on the purchase of the plot. So if your plot costs less than £125,000, you pay no stamp duty at all. Stamp duty is charged at 1 per cent on purchases costing £125,000 to £250,000, rising to 4 per cent on purchases of more than £500,000. This is a real opportunity to save some money: If you purchased the land for £200,000 and the final value of the property is £600,000, you pay stamp duty of £2,000 (1 per cent of £200,000). Somebody buying the property after it was built would pay £24,000 in stamp duty (4 per cent of £600,000) – £22,000 more!

In addition, you can claim back value-added tax (VAT) on new housing, so you'll be able to claim back the VAT you pay on construction materials bought from a VAT-registered supplier. VAT is charged at 17.5 per cent of the purchase price, so you could save hundreds of pounds.

You can only put in one claim for a VAT refund, which must be done within three months of the project being completed. Ensure that you keep detailed proof of the VAT you have paid to enable you to make a claim.

If you employed VAT-registered subcontractors on your project, they should not charge you VAT. But you *will* have to pay VAT on professional fees, such as those of architects or surveyors. Claims cannot be made for furniture, carpets, curtains, white goods, or transport of materials and tools. For more details, contact your local HM Revenue and Customs office (check your Yellow Pages for details).

Buying the right insurance

Make sure that you have the right cover for your new home during the build. Third party liability insurance is strongly advised and mortgage lenders often require a Contractor's All-Risk policy before lending you the money.

If your builder is unable to produce evidence that he is insured, you must take this cover out yourself. If you're employing contractors, you need an Employer's Liability policy and it may also be worth taking out a Self-Build policy to cover your unfinished home from subsidence, storm, impact, vandalism, or fire. As soon as contracts are exchanged, you need to have buildings insurance in place.

You should also ensure that your home has a guarantee, such as that offered by NHBC or Zurich. Without this, you won't be able to sell your property on because you won't be able to prove that it has been built properly (see 'What Buildmark Cover does – and doesn't insure you for' earlier in this chapter).

Arranging the financing

If you don't have the cash to pay for the project – and let's face it, most people don't – you will have to borrow it. Thankfully, obtaining finance is much easier than in the past. If you've already got a property, the easiest way is to release equity (funds) and then sell your home when the project is finished. But if you've got a big mortgage, this may not be possible because you won't be able to release enough cash.

If you're mortgaged to the hilt, you have to take out another loan to finance the self-build. Only a limited number of lenders will fund self-build projects as they prefer to grant mortgages on finished properties; getting money before a brick has been laid is a lot harder.

You have to supply your lender with detailed information about the project before you will get finance, including:

- House plans and specification
- Planning permission approval with at least two years before it runs out
- Estimate of the cost from a quantity surveyor
- Construction timetable

✓ Site and plans approved by the local authority

✓ Builder's details (if you're employing one)

✓ Architect or surveyor's details

Remember that lenders usually charge their standard variable rate while you complete the building work, but once it is finished, you can usually switch to a cheaper standard fixed or discounted deal.

Arrears stage payment mortgages

Most self-build mortgages stage payments in arrears so that funds are released to you after a certain stage of the work has been completed and valued to the lender's satisfaction. These stages are usually the foundations, roofing, plastering, and at completion.

Lenders worth approaching for such a mortgage are the Ecology, Nationwide, Britannia, Norwich & Peterborough, Skipton, Bradford & Bingley, and Stroud & Swindon building societies.

Because money is released in stages *after* the work is complete, you need the cash on hand in the first place to pay for it. The best way to raise this money is from savings, but you may need to take out a loan or pay for the work on your credit card. These solutions aren't ideal, but if you opt for the cheapest credit and pay it back as soon as the lender releases the funds, you'll minimise the cost. In determining how much cash you need, keep in mind that these mortgages typically let you borrow only 75 per cent of the cost of the land and the building work. You'll have to find the remaining 25 per cent elsewhere – ideally your savings.

You may also have to pay for the plot out of your own pocket, although some lenders agree a separate loan for this, as long as the property has OPP. The lender then lets you borrow between 25 and 95 per cent of the cost of the land. But if there's no OPP or there is less than a couple of years before it expires, you have to raise the funds to buy the land yourself – at the risk that you don't get planning permission at all and won't be able to build on it.

Advance stage payment mortgages

These loans let you have the cash *before* carrying out the work – no money is held back until work is completed. The Accelerator Self-Build mortgage is the most popular form of advance stage payment loan. You can borrow up to 95 per cent of the cost of the land and 95 per cent of the cost of each stage of the build – payable in advance. This means work doesn't have stop at any stage while money is raised for the next step. Accelerator mortgages are also available as self-certification loans, so they're ideal for the self-employed.

Lenders offering Accelerator mortgages include Accord Mortgages (part of Yorkshire Building Society), Intelligent Finance, Skipton Building Society, Lloyds TSB Scotland, and The Mortgage Business (part of HBOS).

You'll still need to raise some cash of your own with an Accelerator mortgage; a 5 per cent deposit for the land and then 5 per cent of the cost of each stage of the building work. So ensure that you have enough cash saved before starting the work. If not, you have to borrow as you go along, which is an added financial strain, even if you choose the cheapest loan on the market.

Chapter 8

Renovating Wrecks: Property in Need of Work

A property that is perfect in every way, needs no work doing to it, and is ready to move straight in to is many buyers idea of hell. Instead, they want a blank canvas, something they can make their mark on and do up to their own taste. For these people, the ideal is often a derelict property in need of extensive renovation. Two bonuses: Property that needs gutting often costs less than property in pristine condition, and a renovated property can increase its value by thousands of pounds if you get the renovations right.

Not everyone is cut out for property renovation. TV home makeover shows are fuelling interest, but the reality is that renovation is time and labour intensive and mistakes can be costly. A nicely done renovation is rewarding, true, but you need to think carefully before taking the plunge. In this chapter, I help you figure out whether buying and renovating a dilapidated house is for you. I also look at the pitfalls to watch out for when buying a listed or thatched property and how to make sure that you don't fall foul of any building regulations. And because getting a full structural survey is vitally important when you buy a house to renovate, I explain why you can't afford to scrimp on the survey and examine the false economy of cutting corners and trying to get by without one.

Many people see property renovation purely as a business proposition – a way of making money – rather than getting a home exactly right for their family to live in. Others see property renovation as a way to scoop up a house for a great price and then put heart and soul into turning it into the home they've always wanted. This chapter is aimed at the latter group – those who are buying a wreck with the aim of doing it up so that they can live in it, rather than property developers whose aim is to sell for a profit as soon as the work is completed.

Can You Stomach Renovation?

The first thing you need to do is assess whether doing up a property is a job you feel comfortable with. Property renovation and development may be booming, but many of the people who've made a killing are experienced. Those who aren't trained architects, surveyors, or builders know of architects, surveyors, or builders they can call upon. And as you discover with property renovation, having good contacts is vitally important to the success of your project.

Calculating the amount of work you're comfortable with

No two renovations are the same. When you choose a property, carefully assess whether the work required is realistically something you can handle or out of your league. Because nothing is worse than feeling out of your depth, you must be really honest with yourself. Ask yourself these questions:

✔ **How skilled are you at DIY jobs?** If your own property has the scars of several botched DIY jobs – the result of your own handiwork – thinking that you can renovate an entire property on your own is madness.

   If you lack the skills and time to do the work yourself but find your heart still set on property development, I recommend that you resign yourself to calling in the experts and stick to a consulting role. See the section 'Knowing when to call in the building experts – and where to find them' for the people you'll need to contact.

✔ **How much time do you have to devote to the project?** And if you also have a busy, stressful job with long hours, it's unrealistic to think that you can do all the work at weekends and during the evenings. Be critical of your personal skills and the amount of time you have to devote to the project. A good self-assessment can make the difference between a successful renovation and a costly disaster.

✔ **How much cash is the project likely to cost you?** You may be getting the property on the cheap because it needs a lot of work doing but the renovations could work out to be very costly. Work out your budget *before* buying a property and be wary of committing yourself to a project that you simply can't afford. Otherwise you'll be stuck with a half-finished property for months (or even years!) while you try to raise the necessary cash.

If you have a little building experience or DIY expertise and have time on your hands, a less extensive renovation project – such as a property that needs interior refurbishment rather than a new roof and completely gutting – may be more realistic. Taking on a smaller project may be a better place to start for these reasons:

- You can save a lot of money by doing some of the 'easier' work – such as chipping old plaster off the walls or grouting tiles in the bathroom or kitchen – yourself.

- You can develop and become more confident in your skills. Building up your own experience and knowledge is invaluable even if you plan to hire experts to do the work for you. After all, you still need to make sure that they don't pull the wool over your eyes and that they do a good job.

Figuring out how extensive the renovation is

Once you know how much work you're comfortable with, you need to be able to judge whether a particular property requires just what you can provide – or more. In other words, you need to be able to determine how much work – and what type – needs to be done in the property you're considering. Make sure that you have a survey done and if you don't have the necessary experience to judge what work is needed from this, ask a builder or surveyor for advice.

Something that looks like a straightforward renovation may not be. You may think the crack in the living room wall is simply a bad plaster job only to discover that the cause is bad subsidence and that the foundations need extensive underpinning. Don't buy any property – particularly one that needs a lot of work – without a full structural survey.

Knowing when to call in the building experts – and where to find them

If you lack the skill and time to do a renovation yourself, you're going to need skilled professionals to do the job for you. Even if you have some building experience, you may need to hire help for the areas you don't have experience in. The following sections explain who some of these pros are that you're likely to be working with.

Project managers

Renovating a property is a full-time job because you need to be on site several hours a day to ensure that everything is running as it should be. If you haven't got the time or inclination to do this, you need to hire a project manager to oversee the renovation.

The project manager is responsible for hiring all the necessary people to complete the job – the contractors, see the following section – ordering the materials, and generally running the site to ensure that the project finishes on time and to budget. She needs to be on the site six or sometimes seven days a week to ensure that everything is getting done. As a result, a project manager doesn't come cheap and could cost you up to 10 per cent of your total budget, depending on the work involved.

Personal recommendation is the best way to find a project manager. Ask friends, relatives, neighbours, and builders or other contractors you trust whether they can suggest someone suitable.

To save costs, you can be your own project manager. Many people who are new to property development give this a go – and are actually very good at it. Keep these things in mind:

- ✔ If you don't have the time and don't have an eye for it, leave the project management to the experts. Otherwise, it's false economy.

- ✔ If you've never done any property renovation before, you're unlikely to have a full contacts book of builders, plumbers, and electricians suitable for the job you need done. You'll have to build one up quickly if you aren't using a project manager.

Contractors

Unless you're an experienced builder, electrician, and plumber yourself, you'll need to call in such experts. These are known as *contractors*, because you contract them to do a certain job.

Following are some ideas on locating reputable contractors:

- ✔ Personal recommendation is the best way of finding contractors. Ask family, friends, and neighbours who've had similar work done whether they can recommend a builder or plumber. Then inspect his work yourself and take up other references.

- ✔ Don't take on a contractor just because he is a friend of a friend. If anything goes wrong with the job, seeking redress and treating the situation as a business transaction can be a lot harder. In addition, you risk falling out with your friend. Make it a rule to work only with qualified contractors personally unconnected with your friends or family.

✔ If possible, choose a builder who belongs to the Federation of Master Builders (FMB) or Guild of Master Craftsmen. These people are vetted before joining and follow a code of practice. Also, if you're unhappy with a member's work, you can follow a complaints procedure to address the issue. To find a member, look out for the FMB or Guild logo on builders' vans, stationery, and advertising.

✔ Check out www.homeservepropertyrepairs.com, which enables you to search for contractors working in your area. The listed contractors are recommended by members of the public and have been screened for their credit and legal history and number of years in the business.

✔ The Yellow Pages also lists contractors, but use this as your last resort because you'll have no idea from the entry whether a contractor is good or bad. If you do rely on this source, go and see a couple of past projects and then check out references.

As you narrow your list of contractors, do the following:

✔ Get at least three quotes for the job – and don't necessarily go for the cheapest. Make sure the quote clearly states whether materials are included and what, if any, you're expected to supply. Once you reach agreement, make sure that you get the quote and any conditions in writing.

✔ Check out the contractor's last job and ask the employer whether the contractor's work was satisfactory.

✔ Talk through what you want and try to gauge how helpful and cooperative a builder is. If he is at all dismissive or patronising, you may find working with him difficult and might be better off looking for someone else to take on the job.

✔ Ensure that your builder has clear instructions about what you want, in writing, *before* starting the job. This should make renovation go much smoother.

Although you can find many reputable contractors who wouldn't dream of conning you, there are also plenty of cowboys – builders who don't do a good job, run over schedule, and try to charge you more than you agreed for the work in the first place. Spotting when you're being taken for a ride is crucial to the success of your project so be on the lookout for shoddy workmanship. With some careful research and management, however, dealing with contractors needn't be a disaster.

Architects

If the property requires a lot of extensive changes, you may decide to hire an architect to draw up plans for these and to call on their technical know-how. Architects can also work as project managers, seeking planning and technical approvals, managing site inspections and generally sorting out the whole job. It's worth consulting an architect as early as possible and certainly before you start renovating a property.

A consultation can cost between £55 and £95 an hour, depending on how specialised or complex the project is.

When commissioning an architect, opt for one who is a member of the Royal Institute of British Architects (RIBA). Via RIBA'S website (www.architecture.com), you can search for an architect by location, size of project, sector of expertise, or type of service. Members are subject to a code of professional conduct, and while RIBA has no statutory powers to seek compensation if you feel your architect has let you down, it does offer practical assistance.

Considering where you'll live during the renovation

Because it's likely that you will have sold your own property to finance the purchase and renovation of the new one, you'll have to think about where you're going to live. The two options: in your new house or elsewhere.

If your property is going to be without a roof for any length of time, you won't be able to live there while the work is being done. And even if replacing the roof isn't one of the renovation tasks that need doing, ask yourself whether you really want to live in a property full of builder's dust, noise, rubbish, and strangers coming and going.

Living elsewhere may be the easier solution, but it's also more expensive, especially if you rent. Here are some ideas that may save you money:

- ✔ **Try to rely on the good nature of friends and relatives who may have room to put you up.** This can dramatically reduce your costs, which may be essential if the renovation is likely to swallow up all your spare cash and take many weeks, if not months, to complete.

- ✔ **Live in a caravan on-site.** This option has is plusses and minuses. While you're living on-the-job you're ever-present to keep an eye on things, make sure that work is getting done when it needs to be and ensure that the site is safe (such as preventing anyone from stealing the roof tiles or other building materials during the night). But living in a caravan can be cramped so it is not the best long-term solution. It might also make you feel like you're Alan Partridge. Weigh up the pros and cons before taking the plunge.

Finding Your Wreck

As with any property purchase, start with estate agents. Register with several and let them know what you want. For tips on working with an agent, refer to Chapter 4. Here are other ideas of finding your wreck:

- ✔ **Go to an auction.** An auction is another great source of properties in need of extensive renovation because vendors know they'll get a quick sale albeit for a knockdown price.

  Although the salesroom can be a great source of bargains, always be sceptical about properties for sale at auction. Why does the seller want to get rid of his property so quickly? What is the condition of the property? If you're not careful, you could find yourself buying something that needs a lot more work than you'd bargained or budgeted for. For guidelines to buying a property at auction, head to Chapter 10.

- ✔ **Get online.** The Internet is another good source of properties for sale in need of renovation. Register with a number of property sites and take potluck.

- ✔ **Look at local papers.** Local newspapers are another good source of properties for sale, so make a note of what day they come out. Many often have their own Internet sites as well, which are updated more regularly so check these daily.

- ✔ **Stumble across one and inquire.** Sometimes, you can find your ideal property simply by stumbling across it, quite literally, while you're going about your daily business. There are several virtually derelict properties within half an hour's walk of my flat, for example, all in need of some tender loving care. If you do come across an old wreck, and it has an agent's board outside, you're in luck – call the number and arrange a viewing. If no board is outside, ask the neighbours who owns the property and what her plans are. It may be that the current owner would be delighted if someone took it off her hands, especially as she won't have to pay commission to an agent for arranging the sale.

Calculating Costs and Setting a Budget

One of the biggest mistakes people make when renovating property is to go wildly over budget. If you have got plenty of spare cash, getting carried away may not be a problem. But if money is tight, blowing your budget could have a catastrophic effect and put the project months behind schedule.

Estimating how much you need to spend

The first step to setting a budget for the project is knowing how much work needs to be done. If you're new to property development, you have to rely on the experts to guide you. Get three quotes for each job (see the earlier section 'Contractors' for details on what to look for and remember that the cheapest isn't necessarily the best). Although estimates will vary from property to property, the following prices give you a very general idea of cost when fully refurbishing a three-bedroom semi-detached house:

Work	Estimated Amount
New roof (tiled)	Around £45 per square metre
Rewiring	£3,000
Plumbing	£3,000 to £5,000
New kitchen	£3,000
New bathroom	£1,500
Loft conversion	£8,000

Figuring out your budget and sticking to it

When you buy a house in need of renovation, not only do you have to pay for the property itself, you also need to budget for the following:

- **The contractors' fees:** These include wages, materials, fixtures, and fittings. To figure out how much you need to allow for these, add up the quotes you've accepted from the contractors who'll be doing your work.

- **Your contingency fund:** You use this fund to cover any unexpected expenses or as an emergency fund should something go wrong, which can easily happen, particularly if you're new to renovating property. The contingency fund should amount to 10 per cent of your total budget.

The contingency fund is not an optional extra. Rather, it's as integral a part of your budget as the money you have earmarked for building materials. If something unexpected crops up, this fund ensures that your project is completed during the time allotted and is not held up – or abandoned – while you try to find the extra cash.

The purpose of the budget is to ensure that you don't get carried away, and you must be ruthless with it. If you opt for marble flooring in the bathroom, for example, when you budgeted for lino, you're likely to run out of cash and end up skimping on the kitchen with cheap cabinets that fall apart within 18 months.

Nearly everyone goes a little crazy in one area or another when developing property. This can be a problem if you're renovating the house only to sell it on for a profit. Even when you plan to live in the property, you still don't want to run out of cash and end up living in an unfinished house while you try to save up to complete the job.

If you do run out of cash, your project will fall behind schedule while you try to find the extra money you need. Tradesmen you've lined up will go on to the other jobs they have lined up, and you may have to wait before they can come back and complete your job. To save yourself the stress and hassle that inevitably comes when a job falls behind because of lack of funds, work out your budget carefully in the first instance – and then stick to it.

Using a Surveyor

The best way of calculating how much work is needed is to get a surveyor to assess the job. She will know what is likely to be causing cracks in the walls, for example, and what remedial work is needed. Cutting corners at this stage in order to save a few hundred pounds is a very risky strategy and strongly inadvisable in the long run.

Locating a surveyor

Personal recommendation once again comes top of the list when choosing a surveyor. But don't forget other sources, such as estate agents and mortgage lenders, who deal with surveyors every day. Keep in mind, however, that the surveyors that mortgage lenders use are more adept at providing basic valuations, which are fine if your renovation is straightforward. But if your project is more complicated, hiring a surveyor who specialises in renovations and can provide an in-depth survey is usually money well spent.

As with builders, not all surveyors are used to working with all types of property. Try to find one who has experience of working on properties similar to yours, especially if it has unusual features. Follow up references and check previous projects to ensure that employers are satisfied with the surveyor's work.

Credentials are important; ensure that your surveyor is a member of the Royal Institution of Chartered Surveyors (RICS), the main professional trade association. Members are easy to spot because the letters *MRICS, FRICS,* or *TechRICS* appear after their names. For extra peace of mind, check with the RICS whether the surveyor's qualifications are genuine by phoning 0870 333 1600.

Full structural survey required

There are two types of survey available when you buy a property (as well as the lender's valuation). Of these, the full structural survey is best when you buy a property in need of renovation (for more detail about surveys, go to Chapter 9).

The full structural survey is the most expensive (anything from £700 to £1,500, depending on your requirements and the size of the property). It is also the most comprehensive, running to many pages. It will uncover any hidden problems and give you a full picture as to what you're committing yourself to. This information is vital in establishing whether you can afford to do all the work required. You can also use the findings as a bargaining tool when making an offer: If there is a lot more work than you envisaged, try haggling with the vendor to reduce the asking price.

Many buyers are put off by the cost of full structural surveys, but it's money well spent, particularly if you're buying a house that needs a lot of work. And given that you could be spending hundreds of thousands of pounds buying and renovating the property, the cost of the survey is small fry in comparison.

When you hire a surveyor, you should receive a full outline of the job in writing, detailing his qualifications, what he will do, and how much the survey will cost. Insist on this before commissioning him.

Although your surveyor won't tell you whether or not you should buy the wreck you have set your heart on, the survey can give you a clear idea as to whether it's a good idea or not. Quite often, the surveyor will recommend that more specialist surveys be carried out: for example, if a tree is situated close to the porch, she may suggest another survey to discover whether its position will affect the foundations and cause problems in the future. You can use this information to determine whether you want to have the tree removed.

The surveyor can also help you understand how serious the survey's discoveries are. If the survey uncovers subsidence, for example, it might not be as bad as it sounds, particularly if the property is in the southeast of England where many houses are built on clay soil. In that situation, the surveyor may feel that underpinning, which is relatively straightforward, will be enough to rectify the problem. If your survey does uncover subsidence or damp, take advice from the surveyor as to what work is needed and how much it will cost.

Buying a Listed Property

Many listed properties fall into disrepair because they tend to be fairly old and more expensive to maintain than a relatively modern property. Because of their listed status, owners of these properties have to get permission for any changes they make. Obtaining this permission can be time-consuming and off-putting. Although listed properties are often charming, they can present all kinds of problems, which you should be aware of before buying one.

Listing bands: What they mean

Listed buildings don't necessarily have to be old, although most buildings constructed before 1840 tend to be listed. Buildings illustrating technical innovation or associated with a famous person or event can also make it onto the register. And we're not talking just about pretty Cotswold cottages either – power stations, football stadia, and barns can all be listed.

English Heritage is responsible for the administration of the listing system in England. In Wales, this is the responsibility of Cadw; in Scotland, Historic Scotland; and in Northern Ireland, the Environment and Heritage Service.

There are several different types of listed building. In England and Wales, these are Graded I, II*, and II. In Scotland, grades A, B, and C are used, while in Northern Ireland, where just 2 per cent of properties are listed, it's A, B+, B1, and B2, all of which roughly signify the same thing. In England, 90 per cent of listed buildings are Grade II, and in Scotland, Grade B is the most popular (60 per cent of properties). These grades roughly translate as:

- **Grade I/A:** Buildings of exceptional interest.
- **Grade II*/B:** Particularly important buildings of more than special interest.
- **Grade II/C:** Buildings of special interest that warrant every effort to preserve them.

Finding listed properties

With around 500,000 listed buildings in the UK, there is a strong chance that you'll come across one that you want to buy if you're looking for a property in need of renovation. For information on listed buildings and advice on conservation and renovation work, contact the relevant authority:

✔ English Heritage (www.english-heritage.org.uk)

✔ Cadw in Wales (www.cadw.wales.gov.uk)

✔ Scottish Heritage (www.historic-scotland.gov.uk)

✔ Environment and Heritage Service in Northern Ireland
(www.ehsni.gov.uk)

For a selection of listed properties for sale, try the Society for the Protection of Ancient Buildings (www.spab.org.uk) or Pavilions of Splendour, an estate agent specialising in listed properties (www.heritage.co.uk)

Ensuring that you don't fall foul of the law

While you can't install modern double-glazing into a Grade I listed seventeenth-century period cottage, you don't necessarily have to live with something you don't like. Alterations can be possible as long as you get Listed Building Consent from your local planning authority first. This is a bit like applying for Planning Permission and is often granted if your request is reasonable.

Demolishing, altering, or extending a listed building without Listed Building Consent is a very serious offence: The penalty can be an unlimited fine or up to 12 months imprisonment. It is essential that you familiarise yourself with what is and isn't allowed. In addition to extensions, alterations needing consent include the following:

✔ Painting over brickwork

✔ Replacing doors and windows

✔ Removing external surfaces

✔ Installing a satellite dish, TV aerial, or burglar alarm

✔ Changing roofing materials

✔ Moving or removing interior walls

✔ Building new doorways

✔ Removing or altering fireplaces, panelling, and staircases

If you're in any doubt about what you can and can't change, contact your local planning office. It's better to be safe than sorry.

To stay on the right side of the law, you must look after your listed building properly. If you don't, your local authority can serve a 'repairs notice' specifying the work it considers necessary for the preservation of the building. If you don't comply with this notice within two months, it may make a compulsory purchase order on the property.

Maintenance costs and insurance

The cost of materials for listed properties tends to be greater than with 'regular' renovations because you may need to source specialist materials, such as reclaimed bricks or tiles, in keeping with the style of the original building. Some grants are available to assist with urgent major repairs on Grade I, Grade II*, or Grade A or B buildings. It is extremely unlikely that you'll be able to get any sort of grant for a Grade II or C listed building, however. To apply for a grant, contact your Conservation Officer via the local council.

VAT (value-added tax) is not payable on alterations – as long as a VAT-registered builder carries out the work and you have Listed Building Consent. But remember that VAT remains payable on repairs and other work not requiring consent

When it comes to insuring a listed building, a specialist insurer is likely to be your best bet. Buildings insurance covers the cost of rebuilding the property should it be destroyed in a fire, for example, so take professional advice from a surveyor on the rebuilding figures. And listen to recommendations made by your insurer as to ways in which you can reduce the risks, such as fire precautions. For more information on insuring your property, head to Chapter 12.

Thatcher's Britain

Many thatched cottages are centuries old, approximately 60,000 of them are still around in the UK, proving their hardiness. And you can't beat them for character, history, and general prettiness. If a straw-roofed country idyll is your idea of heaven, however, beware. Not only do thatched cottages come with higher maintenance and insurance costs than your average modern semi, three-quarters of them are also listed, so woe betide you if you use the wrong type of straw to thatch the roof.

If you're tempted, think carefully about what you're getting into. The Thatched Owners Group produces a fact sheet for prospective buyers of thatched properties. This sheet explains the different types of thatched roof available, what questions to ask before you buy, and advice on maintenance and insurance. Contact the Thatched Owners Group on 01767 600707 or visit www. thatched-group.com.

Cost of maintaining a thatched roof

As an owner of a thatched cottage, your biggest expense is likely to be the roof. How often it needs replacing depends on the material, the weather it's exposed to, and the presence of rodents. As a general guide, the Thatched

Owners Group reckons that Water or Norfolk Reed lasts 50 to 60 years; Combined Wheat (sometimes called Devon Reed) 25 to 40 years; and Long Straw just 15 to 25 years. And don't forget the Ridges on the top of the roof, which last between 10 and 15 years. While you may be tempted to opt for the longest-lasting roof, doing so could cause problems because regional styles are encouraged. Check with your local Conservation Officer to see what is required in your area.

When viewing a thatched property, ask the agent when the roof was last thatched and surveyed, whether any coatings are applied to it, and whether it has needed any repair work in the past decade. If you do buy the property, find out who the thatcher was; you may be able to use him again.

Insurance required for thatched cottages

A number of companies specialise in insurance for thatched homes, so prices aren't as high as you might think. The Thatched Owners Group also runs an insurance scheme, with discounts for members.

Fire is one of the greatest insurance risks to a property with a thatched roof, but you can reduce this risk by doing the following:

- Apply fire retardant treatments to the thatch and internal timber.
- Test the wiring every few years to minimise the risk of electrical fire.
- Have the chimneys swept on an annual basis.

Making an Offer

Once you have found a wreck you like the look of, the survey's been done, and you've set a budget as to how much it is going to cost to do up, you're ready to put in an offer. This is similar to making an offer on any other property – although the advantage is that you can try using the necessary renovations to get the vendor to knock down the price.

Dilapidated properties are often priced with a quick sale in mind, so you should be getting a reasonable deal in the first place. But if your survey uncovers the need for extensive work, which perhaps wasn't apparent at first and is going to add several thousand pounds to your budget, try to get the vendor to reduce the price. Tell him what the survey reveals and offer below the asking price on the back of this. The vendor may stick to his guns in the hope of getting the asking price, but if the property has serious structural problems another buyer is unlikely to pay as much as he wants either.

If an agent is handling the sale, try to get him on your side. Although he is answerable to the vendor, who pays his commission, he'll want to get a sale as soon as possible. If you point out the structural faults found in the survey and that other prospective buyers are likely to take the same view, he may be able to talk the vendor round.

In some cases, the property may be so keenly priced and have such development potential that it is likely to spark lots of interest. In such a situation, haggling with the vendor over the price is strongly inadvisable. You could end up missing out if another buyer is prepared to pay the asking price. Assess the situation, with guidance from the agent if necessary, very carefully.

For more information on how to make an offer, go to Chapter 9.

Arranging the Financing

Once the vendor accepts your offer, the next step is to contact your mortgage lender and arrange the financing (if you haven't done so already. Getting pre-approved for a mortgage has a lot of advantages. Go to Chapter 9 for details.)

The mortgage process is slightly different for a dilapidated or run-down property than it is for one in a good state of repair. The reason is that a run-down property is likely to be worth much more than the asking price once you have done it up. Yet if you're like many buyers, you have to borrow the money to do the necessary work. Unfortunately, lenders rarely let you have more money than the property is currently worth in case they have to repossess it and sell it to cover their costs. If the property is worth less than they lent in the first place (because they let you borrow the renovation money, too) and you default before you finish repairs, the lenders can't recoup their money.

When you buy a house in need of repairs, the ease with which you get a mortgage largely depends on the state of the property. The surveyor's valuation plays a crucial part in this; if the property is thought to be habitable, lenders generally agree to let you have a mortgage on it. A property that has a kitchen and bathroom, no matter how basic, should pass the habitable test.

Sometimes, the surveyor suggests that the property is only worth what you want to borrow after certain work has been completed, such as treating damp. In such a situation, the lender may agree to let you have a mortgage to buy the property but retains say, £5,000, which you get after the work has been completed and the surveyor has agreed that it has been done satisfactorily. The trouble is that you're likely to need the funds to pay for the work in the first place.

If you don't have the cash, find the cheapest way of raising it: Extend your overdraft, take out a personal loan, or use a credit card. If you use any of these strategies, make sure that you shop around to find the cheapest deal. The Internet is a good place to start: Try www.moneysupermarket.com. On this site, you can compare thousands of loans, overdrafts, and credit cards. After you complete the work and the funds are released from the lender, make sure that you clear this extra debt so that you don't pay more interest than you need to.

Contact your bank manager to see whether he will lend you the money to fund the refurbishment until your lender releases the funds. Take along proof of the mortgage offer: This may convince him to lend you the money at a more competitive rate than a bank or building society you don't have a relationship with.

Your lender will require detailed plans of what you intend to do with the property. If planning permission is needed, you should already have it, because the lender will require proof. If the lender is agreeable, the money will be released in stages, the number of which depends on how much work is needed. Different lenders have different requirements, so make sure that you're clear what your lender is offering.

Part III
Making an Offer and Finding the Readies

'I'm afraid stamp duty is an unfortunate inevitability but if it will make you feel better, you can punch Alistair for five minutes.'

In this part . . .

Getting the price right is one of the most important aspects of buying a property. You don't want to pay over the odds and you certainly don't want to offer more than you can afford. So the chapters in this part take you through making an offer, negotiating with the seller, and getting a mortgage.

Here you'll find the answer to any question you may have about the cost of purchasing a property – from survey fees to mortgage charges, insurance, and stamp duty. And if money is tight, I provide information on schemes aimed at helping those on low incomes onto the housing ladder.

Chapter 9

Making an Offer: What Happens Next?

In This Chapter

▶ Making an offer

▶ Reducing the chances of being gazumped

▶ Choosing the right survey

▶ Exchanging contracts and completing your purchase

*A*fter you've found the property of your dreams and the seller has accepted your offer, it's all too easy to get carried away fantasising about the new furniture you're going to buy and the big housewarming party you will throw. While such thoughts are understandable, you still have a long way to go before you realise your dream.

Even if the seller does accept your offer, there's no legal guarantee of ownership or that you'll eventually be successful in purchasing the property. Consider this sobering statistic: One in three agreed sales don't make it to exchange of contracts, according to the National Association of Estate Agents. No wonder buying a property is one of the most stressful things you will ever do.

Although the buyer's offer is binding in Scotland (see Chapter 20), in England, Northern Ireland, and Wales, which I look at in this chapter, this isn't the case. Either side – the buyer or the seller – can pull out up until the time that contracts are exchanged, resulting in financial losses, time wasted, and much inconvenience. One of the main reasons for agreements falling through is when the seller accepts a higher offer from a buyer even though he has already accepted another offer – a practice called *gazumping*. It's up to you to protect yourself. In this chapter, I look at how you can reduce the chances of being gazumped.

And because finding the right solicitor to oversee the purchase and commissioning a survey (rather than relying on the lender's valuation), are crucial parts of the house-buying process, I look at how to go about both of these.

Making an Offer

Buying a property is a nerve-wracking experience: It's no wonder it's rated as one of the most stressful things you're ever likely to do. And making an offer on a property is no exception.

Once you've found the home of your dreams and have worked out that you can afford it, the next step is to put in an offer on the property. An offer is not legally binding but demonstrates your interest in buying the property. You usually make the offer verbally to the estate agent, if one is handling the sale, or directly to the vendor if the house is being sold privately. You may prefer to make the offer in writing although doing so isn't strictly necessary.

The offer should be subject to survey and contracts – you're not obliged to proceed with the purchase until you're happy with the findings of the survey and contracts have been exchanged.

If an estate agent is involved, he will put your offer to the seller and act as go-between, letting you know whether the seller is prepared to accept it or not. In an ideal world, your offer would be accepted straightaway but in a *sellers' market* – where there are more buyers than there are properties for sale – there's a strong possibility that another buyer will have her eye on the same property as you. If this is the case, you could get caught up in a bidding war. If you have your heart set on the property, upping your offer to outbid the other potential buyer means that it will cost you more in the long run.

Remember that the estate agent is working for the seller, not you. The seller pays the agent commission for achieving a sale; therefore, the more you pay for the property, the bigger the agent's commission. For this reason, treat everything the estate agent says with a healthy dose of scepticism. Refer to Chapter 4 for advice on how to deal with estate agents.

Offering below the asking price

It always used to be the case that buyers would try to knock a bit off the asking price, and sellers, expecting lower offers, would add a few thousand pounds on in the first place to allow for it. But in recent years demand for property – and the price of houses – has rocketed.

The housing market is governed by supply and demand. At times, there are more buyers than sellers; at other times, the reverse is the case. Assess carefully what sort of market it is before you make an offer, or you could face losing out on the property of your dreams – or paying well over the odds for no reason. The best way to find out whether the market is favouring buyers or sellers is to do some research. Chat to estate agents to find out how long properties hang about before being sold and whether they achieve the asking price. And keep up to date with house price movements by reading the national newspapers, which are always full of tales about the British obsession – the housing market!

When to offer less

Even if the property is fairly priced, you don't want to pay more for it than is absolutely necessary. In some situations, you may want to offer below the asking price:

- ✔ **If you're purchasing in a *buyers' market*.** In a buyers' market, where there are more properties for sale than people willing to purchase them, it is often worth offering below the asking price. If properties are taking a while to shift, the seller runs the risk of having to wait weeks, or even months, for another buyer to come along if he rejects your offer.

  In a sellers' market, where there are more buyers than properties for sale, the reverse is the case. And if several buyers are interested in one property a bidding war could break out – a seller's dream but every buyer's nightmare.

- ✔ **If the property has hung around on the market for several weeks or the vendor is keen to sell immediately.** Either of these situations could be a good opportunity to offer a few thousand pounds below the asking price. Ask the estate agent how long the property has been advertised and keep an eye on the estate agent's window and local 'For Sale' signs when a property goes on the market to see how long it's been up for sale.

- ✔ **If the property needs a lot of work.** If the property is in need of repairs that are not reflected in the price, obtain estimates as to how much the work will cost and then use these as a bargaining tool to get the seller to reduce the price. You may well have a strong case for doing this, particularly if you're buying a dilapidated property in need of a lot of work. Head to Chapter 8 for information on buying property requiring renovation.

If the seller calls your bluff and refuses to reduce the price, you have to decide how much you want the property. If you firmly believe it is overpriced and you're not really bothered about buying it, stick to your guns. There'll be another property around the corner. And chances are the seller may well decide to lower the price anyway once he realises that you aren't going to budge.

If you have your heart set on a property and don't begrudge paying a little over the odds to get what you want, you may decide to go back to the seller and agree to pay the asking price. Otherwise, if both of you refuse to budge, another buyer may snatch your dream home from under your nose.

> # Calling the seller's bluff
>
> My father recently made an offer on a property in Guildford, Surrey, which he was interested in purchasing with the aim of renting it out to tenants. The house had been on the market at £285,000 for four weeks, with no viewers. My father viewed it and realised it was perfect for his purposes: In a good location with the right number of reasonably sized rooms and in excellent condition with very little work needing doing.
>
> He offered £265,000, reflecting the slowdown in the property market and the fact that nobody else had been round to view it. He was also aware that the estate agent was busy reducing other, similar-sized properties on his books. The agent said that he didn't think the seller would accept less than £280,000. Indeed, after the agent had spoken to the seller, he told my father that he had been right; the seller would only accept £280,000. It is likely that he had advised the seller that he
>
> might be able to get this amount out of my father, demonstrating his importance in the negotiating purpose, no doubt. Of course, the added incentive was that the extra £15,000 would have boosted the agent's commission.
>
> My father stuck to his guns. While he liked the property, he saw it as a hard-headed business purchase and although it suited his needs, he was prepared to go elsewhere if it meant paying the correct price. He told the agent that £265,000 was his final offer so did the agent have anything else on his books for this amount? Later that day, the seller accepted my father's offer of £265,000.
>
> Sometimes it pays to stand your ground. But you need the confidence to make sure you're doing the right thing and aren't going to regret it. Research the market carefully and get a good feel for what you can get away with – and what you can't.

Holding your nerve

If you're haggling with the vendor and have offered below the asking price, some time may pass before you hear the verdict, especially if the seller is prepared to accept some reduction but doesn't want to appear too desperate. Once you've decided to offer less than the asking price, try not to panic and bombard the agent with calls, saying you've changed your mind and will pay the asking price after all. Wait for the agent to report back to you: If he sees your desperation, you'll be playing right into his hands, and you can kiss goodbye to any bargaining tool you thought you had.

Assess the situation rationally. If you have thought about your offer carefully, believe the property to be over-priced, and are not prepared to pay more than it's worth, stick by your decision. A rational decision is often the right one. If you aren't sure you did the right thing because you didn't really think your decision through in the first place and you subsequently think you may have made a mistake, you won't be able to hold your nerve.

When it's wise to meet the asking price

If the property is fairly priced, you've decided you want to buy it, and the agent has several other potential buyers lined up, trying to haggle over the price is foolish. It is likely that another buyer is prepared to pay what the seller wants, and by the time the estate agent has got back to you, the seller may have accepted the other offer. If you like the property and can afford to buy it, don't start messing about. My advice is to offer the asking price – and quickly.

My first property purchase was a one-bedroom flat in a new development in the East End of London. I arrived for the viewing having psyched myself up to offer £5,000 below the asking price, not because I felt it was over-priced but because that's what everyone told me you did when buying a property. I instantly fell in love with the flat and decided to make an offer. The agent told me that only four flats were left for sale in the block (out of 42), so if I didn't put a non-refundable £500 deposit down within 24 hours to demonstrate my interest, chances are by the weekend they'd all have gone. I realised there wasn't much point trying to haggle considering the situation and had to make a quick decision: Was I prepared not only to pay the asking price but also to stump up a deposit? The answer was yes, and I visited the agent's office the next day to pay the deposit to secure my flat. I also discovered that the remaining flats had already been sold. My decision turned out to be the right one, particularly as the property doubled in value over the next five years.

Instinct can be a useful tool when purchasing a property. If you go with your gut feeling, you'll make the right decision a lot of the time.

Sealed bids

When several buyers are after the same property, it may go to sealed bids, which are standard in Scotland and becoming increasingly popular elsewhere during sellers' markets. With sealed bids, the seller's solicitor or estate agent will fix a closing date and time by which all prospective buyers must make an offer for the property, in writing. As well as the price you're prepared to pay, you should include details of when you want to move and whether you would like any carpets or curtains included in the sale.

Once the deadline has passed, it is too late to submit a bid. The seller's solicitor or agent will open all the bids and inform the seller what they are. The seller than gets to choose the winning bid, which isn't always the highest. If she wants to sell her curtains, for example, and one buyer is prepared to pay extra for them, this may swing it in his favour.

Sealed bids speed up the process. The seller knows that by a certain date she will have a number of serious offers on the table to choose between.

If you can move quickly because you're either a first-time buyer and not part of a chain or you have a buyer for your home and your finances arranged, this will count in your favour. If the seller has two identical bids from buyers but one of them can move quicker than the other, she is likely to opt for the buyer who can complete first.

Once the seller has made her decision, it's final. You can't negotiate so make sure you bid high enough if you have your heart set on the property. Instead of bidding a round number, try to go just above this in order to see off any competitors who are also bidding around this mark. For example, instead of bidding £180,000, try £180,101.

Avoiding Being Gazumped

Once your offer has been accepted, there is still no binding commitment on either side, except in Scotland (see Chapter 20). To make matters worse, under the Estate Agency Act, agents are obliged to pass on *all* offers received on a property to the seller, even if an offer has already been accepted. So if the property has been taken off the market because the seller has accepted your offer, there is still a risk that someone else, perhaps someone who viewed the property before you, will make a bid which the agent has to pass onto the seller. In some cases, buyers bypass the agent and go straight to the seller anyway. If the seller accepts the later offer, this is known as *gazumping*.

Gazumping can be quite common in England, Northern Ireland, and Wales, when the housing market is buoyant. The dragged-out process of buying a property in these areas – the process can take as long as 10 to 12 weeks, sometimes even longer – is a prime reason why gazumping happens. And in a buoyant housing market, where prices increase at an incredible rate, the property could well fetch several thousand pounds more by the time the sale comes to completion. So if a desperate buyer offers more than you, the seller may well be tempted to take their cash.

Gazumping can be heartbreaking for a buyer. The financial cost tends to be high because you may have forked out hundreds of pounds for a survey, instructed a solicitor, and paid a mortgage application fee. You will also have to decide whether you're prepared to get involved in a bidding war for a property you thought was practically yours. The trouble is that many buyers feel they have to stick with the purchase because they have already invested so much money – and end up paying over the odds so that they don't lose that cash.

Although gazumping is frowned upon, it isn't illegal. And a higher offer can be very tempting to a seller, particularly if the sale is dragging on. You can reduce the likelihood of being gazumped by pushing the sale through as quickly as possible. Follow these tips:

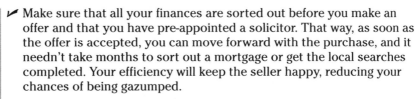

✔ Make sure that all your finances are sorted out before you make an offer and that you have pre-appointed a solicitor. That way, as soon as the offer is accepted, you can move forward with the purchase, and it needn't take months to sort out a mortgage or get the local searches completed. Your efficiency will keep the seller happy, reducing your chances of being gazumped.

✔ If you drag your heels over the property purchase and seem to be delaying things unnecessarily, the seller may lose patience and accept another offer. Don't let your actions leave you open to being gazumped.

Lock-out agreements

One of the best ways of ensuring that another buyer doesn't outbid you at the last minute is to ask the seller to take the property off the market for a certain period of time after a price has been agreed. You then agree to adhere to a strict timetable to complete the purchase.

If you have offered the asking price and the seller accepts it, this is not an unreasonable request. If the seller does agree, an 'Under Offer' sign should replace the 'For Sale' board outside the property or in the estate agent's window. Check that this has been done and if it hasn't, get the situation rectified.

If the property is advertised with more than one agent, make sure that all of them know that it is 'under offer' and no longer on the market.

Pre-contract deposit agreements

One way of minimising the chances of either party pulling out once an offer has been accepted is to establish a pre-contract deposit agreement. You can ask the agent to arrange this: Buyer and seller each hand over a small percentage of the agreed purchase price – typically 1.5 per cent – to a third party such as a solicitor. Either party that subsequently pulls out of the deal forfeits this sum to the other party, unless there is a very good reason behind it, such as the survey indicating that the property is not worth what the buyer offered for it. As part of the agreement, you also arrange to exchange contracts within a set period of time.

Both buyer and seller benefit from a pre-contract deposit agreement. As a buyer, you know that the seller isn't going to accept a higher offer after you've shelled out hundreds of pounds on a survey and legal fees. And the seller knows that you're serious and not about to change your mind on a whim after her property has been off the market for several weeks.

Buyer and seller insurance

If you're really worried about being gazumped, you can buy insurance to protect you in the event of this happening to you. A number of insurance schemes are available; these pay out if the purchase falls through after your offer has been accepted. For a one-off premium of around £70, buyers and sellers can take out a protection policy, which provides around £1,500-worth of cover for legal and valuation costs if the other party causes the deal to fall through.

Several insurers, mortgage lenders, and brokers offer buyer and seller protection policies. If you're interested, ask your lender or broker for more details. But remember: To ensure that your legal fees are covered if the sale does fall through, you must take the policy out before you instruct your solicitor.

In a strong housing market, buyer and seller protection policies can be very attractive because they offer a lot of cover for a relatively small premium. But if money is too tight to mention and the market is sluggish or the property you're buying has languished on the market for several months, you may come to the conclusion that such a policy is an unnecessary extra.

Making the seller your new best friend

The best way to ensure that you don't get gazumped is to get the seller on your side. There are several ways of doing this:

- ✓ **Offer the full asking price and prove you have the cash *and* that you can move quickly.** That way you won't look like a timewaster.

- ✓ **Be easy going and don't fuss over minor points.** If the seller won't leave you the curtains, for example, let it go and buy your own.

- ✓ **Listen to the seller.** Instead of imposing your timeframe on her, make it clear you will complete on her timescale. If this means kipping in your brother's spare room for a couple of weeks because you have to move out of your current accommodation ahead of moving into your new home, it's a small price to pay in the long run.

- ✓ **Don't underestimate guilt.** Establish a friendly relationship with the seller so that she would feel bad about doing the dirty on you and accepting an offer from a rival buyer.

- ✓ **Stay in regular contact with the seller or the estate agent.** You want to know exactly what is going on and whether other buyers are sniffing around. Establish a regular flow of information so that they know when your survey is completed or you've received a formal mortgage offer.

After Your Offer Is Accepted: Let the Conveyancing Begin!

Once the seller has accepted your offer, you receive a letter confirming the agreed price, address of the property, and the name, address and contact number of the agent handling the sale. The letter also includes details of your solicitor and the seller's, so you must have a solicitor lined up in advance. Now it's time for the whole conveyancing process to begin.

Conveyancing is the legal process of transferring ownership of a property or land from one person (the seller) to another (the buyer). During conveyancing, all the legal documents such as title deeds need to be checked and the signing of documents and filling in of forms needs to be organised. Land registry and local searches are also vital to find out whether any long-term plans exist that could affect the value of the property – in England and Wales, these are all included in the Home Information Pack (HIP), supplied by the seller.

Conveyancing can take a frustratingly long time, which is why the Government introduced HIPs. Originally, the HIP was supposed to include a survey, giving the buyer the full picture as to the condition of the property. But this was dropped and now the HIP contains details of searches and an energy performance certificate. (Head to Chapter 16 for details on HIPs and Chapter 19 for more on conveyancing.)

Instructing a solicitor

Although you may already have a perfectly good solicitor, he may not be suitable to handle your house purchase unless he is also experienced in conveyancing. If you don't know a conveyancing specialist, ask friends and family for recommendations. And if all you hear is bad reports about various solicitors, at least you'll be able to cross them off your list.

Hundreds of solicitors are listed in the Yellow Pages, but this gives you no idea of their quality. Rather than go down this route, ask your agent or mortgage broker to suggest one if you don't have a personal recommendation to go on. They deal with solicitors every day, so they're likely to know someone who may be suitable. And you may even get a discount on the fees if you use one recommended by an agent or your broker.

If you're really stuck, try the Law Society (www.lawsociety.org.uk) or call 0870 606 2555, for a database of solicitors in England and Wales. In Northern Ireland, try the Law Society of Northern Ireland (www.lawsoc-ni.org) or call 028 90 231 614. A licensed conveyancer doesn't have to be a solicitor, however. Try the Council for Licensed Conveyancers (CLC) on 01245 349599 or www.theclc.gov.uk, for a list of specialist conveyancers.

Many lenders won't accept a solicitor who is a sole practitioner – that is they don't have any partners in their firm – so bear this in mind when choosing a solicitor.

You don't have to opt for a local solicitor. In most instances, you won't have to go to the solicitor's offices at all; in this day and age, everything can be sorted out over the telephone, by fax and post, and your passport is taken as proof of identification. If you live in London, for example, you're bound to find a cheaper solicitor if you look beyond the City.

All solicitors in England and Wales have to be registered with the Law Society. In Northern Ireland, they must be registered with the Law Society of Northern Ireland. This means there is an established complaints system if something goes wrong. The CLC also has a complaints system and will refer you to the Legal Services Ombudsman if it can't deal with your complaint itself. If your complaint is upheld, you could be in line for compensation.

Understanding the costs

Solicitors' charges vary, so be sure to get a couple of quotes in writing before instructing one. As a general rule, expect to pay around £700 plus VAT (value-added tax) in solicitor's fees if you're purchasing a £200,000 property, for example. If the property is leasehold, where a third party owns the freehold of the building, add on another £75 plus VAT to cover the extra work involved in checking the lease.

As well as the solicitor's fee, which is payable on completion, you may have to pay for disbursements. These are local authority and Land Registry searches. In England and Wales, this information is provided in the Home Information Pack (HIP). (For more on HIPs, go to Chapter 16.) In Northern Ireland your solicitor will instruct local authority and Land Registry searches to ensure that the property has planning permission in the first place and for discovering whether any buildings are planned nearby, such as a supermarket, which could affect the property's value. The cost of these searches varies depending on the size of the property, but for a £200,000 house expect to pay in the region of the following:

- ✔ Local authority search fee: £100
- ✔ Land Registry fees: £200
- ✔ Water authority search fee: £35

A number of Internet sites offer a fixed price for conveyancing. This may well work out cheaper than using a high street solicitor, but remember that this is a bit like sticking a pin in the list of solicitors specialising in conveyancing who are listed in the Yellow Pages. Stick to recommendations to minimise the chance of problems further down the line.

We have ways of getting round a solicitor

Jane, a friend of mine, got very frustrated because the purchase of her flat was taking so long, so she called the seller to find out what the hold-up was. The seller revealed that my friend's solicitor was waiting for Jane to sign some documents and return them to him, although these hadn't even been passed onto Jane by the solicitor. Convinced of her solicitor's incompetence and fed up with not being able to speak to him personally, Jane took matters into her own hands and befriended the solicitor's secretary.

This tactic worked brilliantly as the secretary always answered the solicitor's phone and seemed to know more about what was going on in that office – what documents were lying in the in-tray, for example – than the solicitor himself. The secretary also wasn't used to clients being polite to her, so she was happy to chat with Jane. As a result, the hold-ups vanished, everything was done promptly, and Jane grew to enjoy her daily chat with the secretary who lacked the patronising, hurried air of her boss.

If you're selling a property at the same time as buying, you'll save money by using the same solicitor to do the conveyancing on both properties.

Chasing up your solicitor

Solicitors can get very busy. But you probably want to move as quickly as possible, especially if you want to avoid being gazumped. The only way to make sure that your solicitor does get his finger out is by applying the pressure and keeping your finger on the pulse. Although nobody wants to be a pest, call or e-mail your solicitor on a regular basis, particularly as you approach exchange of contracts, to ensure that you aren't holding up the purchase without realising it.

Arranging Your Finances

Make sure that your finances are arranged in principle before you have made an offer, doing so ensures that you can move quickly. Chapter 11 deals with the ins and outs of mortgages, but if you haven't arranged anything by the time you've made an offer on a property, you'll have to move really quickly if you don't want to annoy the seller and delay the process.

Getting a mortgage application approved can take a couple of weeks, sometimes longer if yours is not a straightforward case. But many lenders will supply you with a certificate saying they are prepared to lend you a certain amount of money in principle, and you can get one of these certificates before you even step foot inside a potential property.

Once you've made an offer and it's been accepted, you can fill out the mortgage application form and return it to your lender. You'll be asked for details of your address, job, income, and any outstanding debts. If you're buying the property with another person, that person also has to supply this information. Depending on the lender's particular requirements, you have to supply pay slips for the last three months, six months' worth of bank statements, and your P60, revealing how much you earned in the last tax year.

You can save time and hassle by having all this information ready before your offer is accepted. If you haven't kept your bank statements and have to order replacements, do this before you find a property you want to buy. Likewise, if you have lost your P60, contact HM Revenue and Customs to order a replacement. If you leave all this until you need to send off your application, you could hold the purchase up by several weeks.

Arranging a Survey: The Full Monty or the Bare Minimum

Before your lender agrees to let you have a mortgage, it will insist on a valuation of the property. At this stage, you must decide whether you're happy with just this valuation or want a survey, and if so, what type. What you decide depends on the condition of the property, your own buildings knowledge, and the amount you can afford to spend.

Opt for the most extensive survey you can afford. When the cost of the survey is compared with the amount you're spending on the property, it looks like money very well spent.

Basic: Lender's valuation

The valuation report is compulsory, and the lender arranges a local surveyor to carry it out. You have to pay for it – the cost depends on the value of the property but expect to pay £300 on a £200,000 property. The valuation only benefits the lender. It doesn't tell you anything about the condition of the property, only whether it's worth what you're hoping to borrow. The valuation ensures that the lender is assigning its money wisely.

If you rely solely on the valuation and serious structural problems are discovered after you purchase the property, you only have yourself to blame. Yet despite the obvious risks, around 75 per cent of buyers rely on the valuation and don't bother commissioning a survey.

Better: Homebuyer's report

It is well worth commissioning a homebuyer's report – the next step up from a valuation (see the preceding section) but not so detailed or expensive as a structural survey (see the next section). A surveyor tells you whether the purchase price is reasonable and whether there's anything you should know about the condition of the property. He also suggests what decisions and actions should be taken before exchange of contracts.

If you have a specific concern, mention this to the surveyor before he undertakes the survey. Most surveyors will look at a particular aspect of the property if asked, although you may have to pay extra for this. Confirm the cost beforehand.

Choose a homebuyer's report if the property:

- Is in good condition – that is, doesn't require significant renovation
- Is conventional in type or of traditional construction

A homebuyer's report costs from £650 plus VAT for a three-bedroomed house costing around £330,000. This includes the cost of the lender's valuation.

Best: Full structural survey

A structural or building survey is the most comprehensive type you can get and is vital if the property:

- Is very old – that is, built before 1914
- Is in poor condition and needs a lot of renovation
- Is not of traditional construction – for example, is a thatched or listed building
- Has been extensively altered
- Is going to be significantly altered by you
- Is very expensive

Expect to pay between £750 and £1,500 plus VAT for a building survey, depending on what you want to know and the size of the property. It's money well spent if a problem is unearthed. Sometimes the surveyor suggests that you get a specialist survey done if he thinks a particular issue needs more investigation, such as whether trees on the property will affect the foundations and need removing by a tree surgeon.

If you opt for a homebuyer's report or structural survey, you can often get this done at the same time as the mortgage valuation. Doing so saves time and hassle because only one surveyor needs to get access to the property. But remember that not all surveyors can carry out both types of survey, so be sure that the surveyor you hire can perform a survey as well as a valuation.

Dealing with problems uncovered in the survey

If your survey reveals that the property is fine, that's great news and it's all systems go. Quite often, however, the survey reveals that a problem may exist, and the surveyor may recommend that further investigations are required. Before you panic, remember that this happens quite a lot and is often just the surveyor covering her back. But the specialist survey may well reveal a significant problem, which could affect your decision to purchase the property.

If the surveyor calls for further reports, the lender will insist upon them.

When the property is valued at less than the asking price

Sometimes the lender's valuation assesses that the property is worth less than the asking price, which is bad news if you need to borrow the full amount in order to purchase it. Lenders aren't in the habit of letting buyers have more cash than a property is worth. But if you can find the extra cash from your savings to make up the difference, there's nothing to stop you from going ahead with the purchase, even if you're paying more than the surveyor thinks the property is worth.

Even if you haven't got enough cash to cover the shortfall and don't fancy taking on any more credit, all is not lost if the property is valued at less than the asking price. The surveyor has handed you a useful bargaining tool: Go back to the seller and inform him that your lender doesn't believe the property is worth what he's asking for it. And if your lender thinks that, the likelihood is that other lenders will take a similar view so the seller will have trouble flogging the property to another buyer. If the seller won't budge, you may have to accept that the property isn't going to be yours. You may even have had a lucky escape.

Coping with structural problems

If the survey reveals problems with the property, such as subsidence, all is not necessarily lost. Your lender may still be prepared to let you have a mortgage but will insist on holding back some of the funds until you have rectified the problem to the surveyor's satisfaction.

The downside in this scenario is that you need to have enough cash saved to fund the repairs out of your own pocket because you won't get the funds from the lender until after the work has been done. If you don't have enough saved, you will have to extend your overdraft, take out a personal loan, or pay for the work by credit card. Make sure you shop around for the cheapest rate before using one of these methods.

If you opted for a building survey, the surveyor will give you an idea of the cost of the work needed: It's up to you to decide whether you can afford to get it done. In this situation, try haggling with the seller. He might be persuaded to knock a couple of grand off the purchase price. But if the seller won't shift and you can't afford the repairs, you may have to give this property a wide berth and find one that doesn't require extensive building work or renovations.

Exchanging Contracts

As soon as both solicitors have completed their work, the survey's findings are satisfactory, the searches haven't unearthed any problems, and your mortgage application has been approved, a date is set for completion. You also have to sign the contract. Once this is done, your solicitor exchanges contracts with the seller's solicitor.

At the point of exchange, you must electronically transfer the deposit to your solicitor's bank account.

This is the point of no return: You can't back out after exchange of contracts unless you're willing to incur significant financial penalties.

Don't forget the stamp duty

Stamp duty is a tax imposed by the Government on all property purchases above £125,000, so you can't avoid paying it if your property is more expensive than this. It is banded according to property price at these rates:

- ✔ 1 per cent on properties worth between £125,000 and £250,000

- ✔ 3 per cent on properties worth more than £250,000 and less than £500,000

- ✔ 4 per cent on properties costing £500,000 and above

Stamp duty is due soon after completion, so make sure that you have the funds available to cover it.

Buildings insurance

Once you've exchanged contracts, the property is your responsibility from an insurance perspective. In some cases, the seller cancels his buildings insurance from this date. Your solicitor will insist that you take out buildings insurance for the new property before you exchange contracts in case anything happens to the property before completion.

Even if you haven't completed on the purchase, if the house burns down after you've exchanged contracts, you still have to complete on it. Buildings insurance covers you if any such problems occur. And make sure you arrange buildings insurance well in advance so there are no hold-ups at this stage.

Completion

This is it: The day the property legally becomes yours – the keys are handed over and you can move in. Completion can happen the same day as exchange of contracts, or it can happen several months later, depending on what you and the seller agree. Usually though, completion takes place one to four weeks after exchange of contracts.

In the run-up to completion, arrange for the meters in the property to be read and ensure that all the utilities – gas, electricity, water, and telephone – are transferred over to your name from the date of completion. You don't want to spend your first night in your new home sitting in the dark, now do you?

Chapter 10

Going, Going, Gone: Buying Property at Auction

In This Chapter

▶ Working out whether buying at auction is for you

▶ Preparing yourself before the sale

▶ Ensuring that your bid is successful

*T*he auction scene in *Only Fools and Horses* in which Del Boy and Rodney Trotter are set up for life after flogging an antique watch for millions of pounds is one of hundreds of auction scenes that have appeared on television. As a result, even if you've never set foot in an auction-room, you probably think you have a fair idea what an auction is like – you can get caught out if you so much as scratch your ear and end up with a hideous vase costing thousands of pounds; there's always a bidding war (usually between people who know each other); and the sale price is nearly always a complete surprise to all involved. Oh and when it comes to art, there is always a forgery or two.

Fortunately, auctions in real life are quite a bit different, and few people actually spend serious amounts of money as a consequence of mistakenly scratching their nose! If you're buying a property, checking out the auction-room for real may be worth it. An increasing number of buyers – first-time and experienced alike – find property bargains at auction.

You need to be careful, however. Although auctions are a quick way of buying a property – cutting out weeks of heel dragging and the chance of being gazumped – some sellers use this speed as an opportunity to get rid of a property quickly, hoping the buyer won't ask too many questions. If you don't know what you're doing, you could easily make a big mistake.

In this chapter I guide you through the process of buying a property at auction and identify the pitfalls you need to watch out for.

Pros and Cons of Buying at Auction

Some 5 per cent of all property sales are now done at auction, according to the Royal Institution of Chartered Surveyors (RICS) – and increasingly property developers aren't the only ones who go down this route. In the following sections, I look at the advantages and disadvantages of buying a property at auction.

Why you'd want to: The pros

An increasing number of first-time buyers are purchasing property via auction for several reasons:

- **A quick sale is guaranteed:** Once the hammer comes down, the sale is binding and you have up to 28 days to complete (when the property is legally yours and you get the keys). There's no chance of being gazumped – when the seller accepts a second, higher offer from another buyer after already accepting your offer.

- **Bargains galore:** When people think of auctions, they think of bargains and there are certainly plenty to be had. Quite often, properties going under the hammer are in need of extensive refurbishment, and the price reflects this. So if you're prepared to put in a bit of hard work, you may well stumble across a bargain.

- **Free and fair competition:** If you're not the only bidder interested in a property, at least you have a fair chance of successfully bidding because the playing field is open. You know exactly how much someone else is prepared to pay – not always the case when you're buying through an estate agent who plays one buyer off against another in order to push up the price.

Why you wouldn't: The cons

You also need to be careful. Buying at auction is fraught with potential pitfalls:

- **Getting the wool pulled over your eyes:** Many sellers use auction because they want a quick sale. Their motivation may well have something to do with the fact that the property has major structural problems. These sellers hope that you won't bother with all the necessary surveys, perhaps because time is short or you don't want to 'waste' money on a survey for a property if you then lose out during the bidding and someone else ends up buying it. To avoid such problems, be wary of cutting corners and *always* get a survey done.

Getting your feet wet without buying

Attend several auctions to see what happens. You shouldn't intend to bid this time around; instead you just want to get a feel of what's required. Most big auction houses run several property auctions a year around the country. Check in local and national newspapers and the property press, such as *Estates Gazette* and *Property Week*, for details.

The Internet is also a useful source. The Essential Information Group works with 150 auction houses, providing a list of coming auctions on its website (www.eigroup.co.uk).

Register with the big auction houses so that you get advance notice of any auctions.

✔ **Changing your mind is not an option:** Once the hammer has come down, the sale is binding and neither buyer nor seller can pull out without paying a financial penalty. As the successful bidder, you will exchange contracts on the day of the sale so you must be 100 per cent certain that's what you want. Properties are sold unconditionally, not subject to contract, survey, or finance.

If you change your mind and back out of the deal, you lose your deposit and may face legal action from the seller if he can't sell his property or has to sell it to someone else for less money than you had agreed to pay.

Although buying at auction does have potential pitfalls, if you put in enough preparation *before* the sale, you can get a bargain and reduce the chances of it turning into an expensive mistake. In the following sections, I show you what steps to take to protect yourself.

Getting Started – Action to Take before the Auction

Unlike buying almost anything else at auction, when you buy property, you have to do some legwork first – and quite a bit of it in some cases. If you turn up on the day without having seen the property you're planning to bid for or without having organised your finances, you're likely to run into trouble. Several steps are essential if you're going to successfully bid for a property at auction.

The guide price isn't always a good guide to the sale price!

Convinced that this was the best way to get a bargain, a friend of mine was keen to buy at auction. She sent off for a catalogue and spotted a derelict property, with a guide price of £110,000. Much work was required but this wasn't likely to be a problem as her husband is in the building trade and could do most of it himself.

My friend arranged a mortgage in principle and sat back and waited for the auction. But on the day, everything went horribly wrong: A bidding war broker out between her and two other buyers who were just as keen to buy the property. Although she knew she might be able to get a bigger mortgage and had some savings (originally for refurbishment and new furniture), she couldn't keep up and decided, regretfully, to pull out when the bidding reached £180,000.

It's just as well she did. The hammer finally came down at £276,000. It was later revealed that the reserve price was just £100,000, a third of the bid price – resulting in one very happy seller. My friend believes that the location of the property, near Teddington High Street, and the fact that the house was part of a pretty row of well-maintained cottages, with lots of potential, had a lot to do with such a high sale price.

She was wise to pull out when she did because she'd never have been able to cover the purchase price and pay for refurbishment, even with her husband doing the work. This is a classic example of how the guide price can wildly differ from the asking price. Remember, you need to know when to bow out gracefully.

Registering interest with an auction house or estate agent

If you don't know when an auction is taking place, you haven't a chance of even getting there to put in your bid. So you need to get yourself registered with as many auction houses and estate agents specialising in auctions as possible.

Look in your local paper and the property press, such as *Estates Gazette* and *Property Week*, for details of property auctions; contact those auction houses running these and get yourself on their mailing lists. This ensures that you're notified of an auction weeks before it occurs and can apply for an auction catalogue detailing all the different lots for sale. And if you have Internet access, check for details of auction houses in the area where you're hoping to buy.

If the reserve price isn't met, the property isn't sold on the day of the auction. However, there might be a way of buying the property afterwards. See the section 'Buying a Property after the Auction' at the end of this chapter.

Reading the catalogue

Getting hold of the auction catalogue that lists all the properties for sale is vital. The auction house usually publishes its catalogue several weeks before the sale. Most auction houses charge an annual fee if you want the catalogue sent automatically to you. Each catalogue contains a number of houses, flats, and plots of land. It also contains all the details of the property, including any Special Conditions of Sale and any planning restrictions. Make sure that you understand how the property is described:

- ✔ **Vacant possession:** Empty properties. Ideal if you're are buying somewhere to live. Also suitable are those with tenancies due to expire shortly because the tenants are moving out.

- ✔ **Tenanted properties:** Properties with existing tenants living in them. Ideal for investment purposes. If you're looking for a property to rent out and you buy one of these, you may not have to bother looking for another tenant (depending on the length of the current tenant's tenancy agreement).

Each lot should also have a guide price, which is different from the *reserve price*. The *guide price* is not the asking price, but it is indicative of the minimum price the seller expects to get for his property. Only a guide, this price can be exceeded at auction (see sidebar) – which is exactly what the seller hopes will happen. The guide price can also increase during the marketing period. The guide price is always higher than the reserve price, which is the minimum the seller will accept for the property. The reserve price isn't published; only the seller and auctioneer know what it is, and it's usually set just before the auction.

Viewing the property

Viewing a prospective property is essential. Just as you wouldn't buy a house through an estate agent without seeing it first, you shouldn't rely on the description in the catalogue, or the picture, when making your decision. Even if you think you're getting a bargain, you're still spending a lot of money, so view before you bid.

If you don't make the effort to view the property, you may end up paying far more than it's worth or having to pay for structural repairs you haven't budgeted for because you didn't realise they were needed.

The auctioneer often arranges group viewings on popular lots; contact him and find out what the arrangements are, then go and take a look at the property. Handle this viewing in the same way you would if you were buying a property through the estate agent. Make sure you check the property carefully – both inside and out – and find out why the owner is selling. For more details on viewings, see Chapter 5.

Time is likely to be short – you may have only a couple of weeks between receiving the catalogue and the auction, so arrange to view the property as soon as possible.

Arranging a survey

As well as asking a builder to give you a quote, get a survey done before the auction. Many buyers don't bother because they see it potentially as money down the drain; after all, there's no guarantee that their bid at auction will be successful. But if you don't have a survey and subsequently discover major structural problems that potentially cost a fortune to correct, it's too late. Once the hammer has come down, you can't pull out.

The cost of the survey depends on how detailed it is, which in turn depends on the condition of the property and how large it is. The bigger the property, the more expensive the survey. You can find a chartered surveyor to carry out the survey by contacting the Royal Institution of Chartered Surveyors (www.rics.org.uk). See Chapter 9 for more details on the different type the surveys available and how much you should expect to pay. Try to get a survey done at least a week before the sale so that you have time to think about the findings and investigate further, if necessary.

If you don't arrange a survey, you risk bidding far more than the property is worth. But if you do commission a survey, and major problems are unearthed, you can make an informed decision as to whether to give the property a miss or put a limit on your bid. You can then use the remainder of your budget to pay for the extra repairs.

Setting a budget for renovation and other stuff

When you buy a property at auction, don't forget to factor into your budget the other costs you'll incur. You'll have to pay fees for any professional advice you obtain from builders, surveyors, solicitors, and a mortgage broker (see 'Arranging your financing in principle' later in this chapter). You also have to pay stamp duty on properties costing more than £125,000 (see Chapter 11 for more details).

In addition, most properties sold at auction need some work, which varies from property to property. Some lots are complete wrecks that need total gutting and rebuilding; others need complete internal refurbishment. Factor the cost of renovations into your budget.

The best way to get an accurate estimate of the work needed is to take a builder or surveyor along when you view the property before auction. He can give you an accurate assessment of the work needed to get the property up to scratch and the likely cost. While you won't get a definitive quote, you will have a good idea of how much it will cost.

Unless you're a property developer or builder, working out how much a new roof is likely to cost is near impossible. And if you drastically underestimate the costs, you could run well over budget, which could hold the project up for weeks or months while you raise extra cash.

Be realistic. If refurbishment is likely to cost more than you can afford or more work is involved than you feel comfortable taking on, you might need to find a less challenging project.

Getting your solicitor on the case

Another task *before* the auction is to inform your solicitor that you're plan-ning to bid for a property. Send her the auction catalogue so that she can inspect the details of the lot you're interested in. She will then be able to contact the seller's solicitor (their details are usually at the back of the auction catalogue) to get hold of the various legal papers that you need to make an informed decision about whether you should bid for a lot. These papers include:

- ✔ Special conditions of sale
- ✔ Title deeds
- ✔ Searches
- ✔ Details of the lease (if it's a leasehold property)
- ✔ Planning permissions

Legal documents are available to view at the auction-room just prior to the sale. But as your solicitor is unlikely to attend, she won't be able to go through them. Make sure that you sort out the legalities before the auction; otherwise, you could end up buying a property that never had planning permission or has a lease with oppressive conditions.

Arranging your financing in principle

If you need a mortgage it's important that you have the necessary finances in place *before* auction. If you wait until you've successfully bid for a property before applying for a mortgage, there's a chance that the funds won't be approved before completion, which is non-negotiable. Finding out that you've got adverse credit problems once you apply for a loan, for example, could hold the process up by several months. And this isn't ideal if you have to complete within 28 days!

The solution is to get an agreement in principle from a lender, stating that it has approved you for a mortgage, provided that it can verify your earnings. Most lenders instruct a surveyor to complete a valuation before the auction, so you need to give them as much notice as possible.

Arranging insurance

If you successfully bid for a freehold property at auction (see Chapter 19 for the difference between these and leasehold properties), you're responsible for buildings insurance from exchange of contracts (which happens on the day of the sale). So make sure that you arrange this in advance of the auction. See Chapter 12 for more details on insurance.

Getting the deposit together

If you successfully bid for a property, you're expected to put down 10 per cent of the sale price there and then. How you pay depends on the auction house's policy. Some require that you pay by banker's draft, while others accept cash, building society cheque, or personal cheque. Check with the auction house as to what it prefers before the sale.

Because you pay the deposit *before* you get a mortgage, you must have the funds available. The best way to pay the deposit is out of your savings; alternatively, ask the bank to let you have an overdraft (or extend your existing one), take out a personal loan, or get a cash advance on your credit card. Whichever route you take, shop around for the lowest rate of interest and pay it back as soon as you can to avoid paying a fortune in unnecessary charges.

The Day of the Auction Dawns

By the time the auction comes round you should have your finances in place, your survey completed, and your solicitor happy for you to bid for the property. Attend at least one auction to ensure that you know what you're letting yourself in for. Now you reach the nerve-wracking part – the bidding itself.

A lot can change between an auction catalogue being published and the day of the sale. The seller may have pulled out or the guide price may have increased, for example. Give the auction house a call on the morning of the sale to check that the property you're interested in is still going on sale. Otherwise, it could be a wasted trip. If your lot is still up for sale, find out whether there are any last minute amendments or alterations to the catalogue. These will be printed as an addendum and available at the saleroom on the day of the auction.

Getting there early

If you're attending the auction (you can also bid by proxy over the telephone or Internet if you can't make the sale; see the section 'Bidding by proxy', later) arrive half-an-hour early. This gives you time to register if necessary (some auctioneers don't ask you to), find a good seat where the auctioneer can see you, and calm your nerves. It also helps to watch the bidding for a while to get a feel for how it's going and whether properties are meeting their reserve price.

Bring your auction catalogue, cheque book, and some identification – such as a driver's licence or passport. Also bring your solicitor's contact details; the auctioneer will require these if your bid is successful.

Controlling your nervous tic

Mistaken bids at auction are the bread-and-butter of sitcom plots, but in real life, thankfully, they are rare as most auctioneers require that you raise a paddle with a number on it when making a bid. But waving your arm in the air if you don't intend to make a bid is foolish so sit on your hands if you're worried about catching the auctioneer's eye.

The wrong bid could mean you spend thousands of pounds on a property you didn't want. And as the sale is binding, claiming that it was a mistake is not an excuse. If a mistake is made, let the auctioneer know straight away: don't wait until the end of the sale.

Making sure you don't get carried away

Once you've experienced the frenetic atmosphere of the saleroom, you can see how people get carried away and spend far more than they intended. Auctions attract many wealthy property developers who bid literally millions of pounds on property, so your £120,000 upper price limit may seem piddling in comparison.

But you've got a budget you need to stick to just as they have, although admittedly theirs is much bigger than yours. You can bet your bottom dollar, though, that nothing would persuade them to pay more than they can afford – developers are too shrewd for that.

If you can't trust yourself to stop when you reach your limit, ask a friend, relative, solicitor, or surveyor to bid on your behalf. Explain what your upper limit is and ask them to stick to it. Someone who's bidding for you is less likely to get carried away; she won't be emotionally involved (her heart isn't set on the property), and she's using someone else's money – yours.

If you bid more than you can afford, you will struggle to finance the purchase. Your lender won't let you borrow more than the property is worth, so you'll have to find the shortfall somewhere else. And if you chip away at the budget you've set aside for refurbishment, you could set back your repairs and renovations by many months.

Going, going gone: Handling the bidding

Once your lot is called, it's your turn. The auctioneer reads out the lot number, full address, and a short description of the property. Then he invites bids at a certain level; bid by raising your hand or catalogue. The property is 'knocked down' to the highest bidder, and the lot is sold once the auctioneer has said 'Going, going gone'. Following are some tips to keep in mind:

- ✔ If you're bidding, don't leave it to the last minute. If you do, you may miss out.

- ✔ Make sure that the auctioneer can see you – in a crowded room, this may be difficult. Try not to sit in the front row, however, because you won't be able to see what's happening behind you to gauge how well the sale is going.

- ✔ Make sure that you're bidding for the property you *think* you're bidding for. It might sound obvious but it's worth double-checking. You don't want to end up with one you don't want.

- ✔ To bid, put your hand or auction catalogue purposefully in the air and make sure that the auctioneer sees it. Some auction houses have a paddle bidding system with a number on it, so check whether this is the case beforehand.

What to do when your bid is successful

If your bid is successful – congratulations! Now you have to do the following things:

- **Pay the deposit:** This is usually 10 per cent of the sale price. You will also be told when you have to complete – usually within 28 days.

    This deposit makes the sale binding. If you don't pay the remaining 90 per cent of the purchase price within 28 days, you forfeit your deposit and lose the property.

- **Sign a *Memorandum of Agreement:*** This document confirms the sale and acknowledges the receipt of a deposit.

- **Provide identification:** You'll be asked for some ID and your solicitor's details.

When these things are done, you're given a signed copy of your contract. Pass this onto your solicitor as soon as possible. Make sure that you don't leave the saleroom without it.

As soon as you exchange contracts at the sale, you're responsible for insuring the property. Set this up before the sale and then confirm with the insurer that you want to proceed with the policy. If you're buying leasehold rather than a freehold property, you don't need to take out cover as this is the freeholder's responsibility.

Bidding by proxy

If you can't make the sale, you can bid by proxy, if you arrange this in advance. To bid by proxy you can do any of the following:

- **Bid over the phone during the sale:** In this arrangement, someone in the auction-room bids on your behalf.

- **Bid in writing:** In this situation, you specify a maximum bid, and the auctioneer bids on your behalf.

- **Bid over the Internet:** Contact the auction house for more details.

However you bid, you need to provide a cheque to cover your deposit in full; this won't be cashed if you're bid isn't successful.

Chapter 11

Getting a Mortgage

. . . .

. . . .

*U*nless you're a Premiership footballer, a film star, or can call upon a sizeable trust fund or inheritance, it's unlikely that you'll be able to buy a property outright for cash. More likely, you'll have to borrow the money – and that means taking out a mortgage. Securing a mortgage can be daunting because of the vast sums of cash involved. Nevertheless, the proliferation of mortgage deals in recent years makes getting a home loan that suits your circumstances easier than ever. And with interest rates at historically low levels, you don't have to sell your soul to the devil to get one.

But this proliferation of choice has its downside. With so many lenders offering a range of different, and sometimes complex, deals, it can be hard to see the wood for the trees. For most homeowners, their mortgage is their biggest single outgoing every month, so finding the right one is crucial. In this chapter I will guide you through the different mortgages available and help you avoid paying more than you should.

Finding a mortgage doesn't have to be scary. With the right advice and by doing your own careful research, you can find a decent deal that you aren't going to regret 10 years down the line.

How Mortgages Work

A mortgage is a loan for the express purpose of buying a flat or house. The majority of homebuyers take out a mortgage for 25 years (the length of the mortgage is the *mortgage term*). The aim is to pay back the money you borrow, plus interest, by the end of the term – and the property will be yours.

Because homebuyers are so used to hearing about a 25-year timeframe, many assume that you have to take a mortgage out for this length of time. But that's not the case.

You can vary the mortgage term to suit your circumstances; most lenders will let you take your mortgage over as few or as many years as you want, although there are some restrictions. Most lenders require that you take out a mortgage for a minimum of five years and that you pay it back by the time you retire.

If you're 20 years old and want to take out a mortgage over 40 years, for example, most lenders will be happy to let you do this. Or if you're expecting to receive a lot of money over the next couple of years, you can take a mortgage out for two or three years if you wish, although the repayments would prove prohibitive for most people. Likewise, most people pay off their mortgage by the time they stop working but in some cases you can continue your mortgage into retirement as long as you can demonstrate to your lender that your retirement income will cover the mortgage repayments.

There is a growing trend towards longer mortgage terms, particularly for first-time buyers. The advantage of paying your mortgage over 30, 40 or even 45 years is that your monthly repayments are significantly reduced, which is ideal for those on relatively low incomes. But the downside is that there will be many more of these repayments so you will end up paying a lot more interest in the long run. This is why the 25-year mortgage term is so popular because the repayments tend to be the most manageable for the majority of borrowers.

Table 11-1 shows how much you'd end up paying back if you took out a £120,000 repayment mortgage over 15, 20, or 25 years at a rate of 5.85 per cent. Note that over the longer term (25 years), you may pay less every month but you end up paying more over the term of the loan than if you'd opted for a 15-year mortgage term.

Table 11-1	Cost of a Mortgage Over Different Time Scales	
Mortgage Term	*Monthly Repayment*	*Total Amount Payable*
15 years	£990.08	£178,214.40
20 years	£835.66	£200,558.40
25 years	£747.69	£224,307.00

Source: London & Country Mortgages

Mortgages come with age restrictions. You must be at least 18 and should finish paying back what you've borrowed before you retire, unless you can prove retirement income sufficient to cover the repayments.

How mortgage rates are set

Before taking out a mortgage it helps if you understand a bit about how they work. The mortgage rate – the amount of interest you pay the lender in return for borrowing money to buy your property – reflects the Bank of England base rate. The Bank of England's *Monetary Policy Committee* (MPC) sets the base rate on the first Thursday of each month. The decision to cut, raise, or leave the base rate alone depends on several factors, including inflation, consumer confidence, and the state of the housing market. If there are signs that inflation is rising, for example, the MPC raises rates in an effort to curb consumer spending. However, if the economy is showing signs of slowing down, the MPC cuts rates in order to boost consumer borrowing.

Often within minutes of the MPC meeting, lenders adjust their mortgage rates accordingly. So if the base rate is raised by 0.25 per cent, most lenders' standard variable rate (SVR) also increases by this amount. This affects those on every type of mortgage rate apart from fixed and sometimes capped rates (see 'To fix or not to fix'

later in this chapter). However, nothing prevents lenders raising rates more than the base rate increase, or not raising them as much. Market forces mean lenders tend to stick together and follow the same pattern. But if a lender wants to buck the trend and attract some extra business, there's nothing to stop it doing so – except perhaps its profit margin!

If you're on a variable, discounted, or tracker rate, you're exposed to movements in the base rate, with a strong chance that your mortgage repayments will change straightaway. This is great if the base rate is falling because it means that your mortgage repayments will fall as well, but it can make things very difficult for you if it's going the other way.

If you're on a fixed rate deal or, in some cases, a capped rate, you won't be affected by an increase in the base rate until you come to the end of that offer period. However, the downside is that you won't see the benefit of a base rate cut either.

Who offers them

Mortgages are offered by banks, building societies, and specialist lenders – which tend to be offshoots of major building societies and concentrate on niche markets, such as the self-employed or those with credit problems. As their name suggests, building societies were established with the original intention of providing the opportunity to purchase homes to those whose needs were not met elsewhere. And with more than 7,000 mortgages available from over 100 lenders, finding one that suits you shouldn't be impossible. It might just take a little time!

Don't assume that the bank you have your current account with should be your first port of call when applying for a mortgage. Banks have different strengths. Even if you chose yours because of its excellent current account, it doesn't follow that it will also have the best mortgages.

Shop around for the best mortgage by using an intermediary, such as an independent mortgage broker if necessary (see 'Using a mortgage broker' later in this chapter). Remember how much cash you're spending. Getting the best deal at this stage is vital if you don't want to pay over the odds in the long term.

How much should you borrow?

What the lender is prepared to lend you and what you should borrow are two different things. The Department for Business Enterprise and Regulatory Reform identifies the question 'How much can I afford to borrow?' as one of the most important a homebuyer should ask herself before applying for a mortgage.

Typically, lenders let customers borrow up to four times their salary or three times joint salary if they're buying a property with a partner or friend. So if you earn £20,000, you can borrow £80,000 on your own or £120,000 if your partner earns the same amount as you. But this isn't going to get you very far when you consider that the average national house price in the UK was £197,247, according to the Halifax House Price Index at the time of writing.

In an effort to bridge the gap between what you can afford and what you can borrow, some lenders have increased their *income multiple* – the number of times your salary you can borrow – to five or six times income, depending on your particular circumstances. This will enable you to buy a more expensive property.

In recent years, some lenders have moved away from strict income multiples in favour of affordability criteria when deciding how much you can borrow. This is designed to look at the bigger picture of your finances to see how much you can realistically afford to repay. Lenders look at your outgoings as well as your income when deciding how much you can borrow.

Five times income is becoming increasingly common. While you may think you can cope borrowing this much, if interest rates shoot up, your repayments could rocket. Rates may be relatively low, but in the early 1990s they were as high as 15 per cent and repossession was common. And if history repeats itself, it could spell disaster for your budgeting.

It's important not to overstretch yourself. Even if you find a lender who is willing to lend you more than four times your salary ask yourself whether you would be happy with that level of repayments every month. Remember: You still have to eat!

Choosing between Repayment or Interest Only

There are two ways to repay your mortgage – by paying a slice of the capital plus interest every month (*repayment*) or by just paying the interest each month (*interest-only*). With the latter, you should set up an investment vehicle to pay off the capital at the end of the mortgage term. Whether you choose a repayment or interest-only mortgage largely depends upon your attitude to risk.

Repayment loans

If you want a guarantee that all the capital you borrow is paid off by the end of the mortgage term, a repayment loan is the only option. Each month, you pay a proportion of the interest on the loan plus a slice of the capital. If you keep up with the repayments, at the end of the mortgage term, all the capital will be paid off and the property will be yours.

Although the monthly mortgage payments are higher than with an interest-only loan, most people opt for a repayment mortgage because they don't want to take a gamble on the roof over their head.

If you want peace of mind, the only way you get any guarantee that the mortgage will be paid off at the end of the loan period is by opting for a repayment loan.

Interest-only loans

An interest-only mortgage does exactly as it suggests: Each month you pay back just a chunk of the interest on the loan. You don't repay any of the capital until the end of the mortgage term when you must pay it back in full; otherwise, your lender can repossess your home.

Interest-only mortgages can appeal to those on tight budgets because the monthly mortgage payments are lower than with a repayment deal. For example, if you borrow £80,000 on an interest-only basis at 5.65 per cent over 25 years, your mortgage repayments would be £376.67 per month. But if you take out a repayment loan instead, you end up paying £498.46 per month.

While interest-only mortgage payments are obviously lower than with a repayment deal, you must also set up an investment vehicle to pay off the capital at the end of the mortgage term. Most people use endowments (although these are very unpopular now), individual savings accounts (ISAs), or pensions to do this. The following sections explain these options.

Endowment mis-selling and the bear market

In 1986, endowment-backed mortgages accounted for 80 per cent of all mortgages and were at the height of their popularity as a result of the booming stock market, according to the Council of Mortgage Lenders. By 2001, this share had fallen to 10 per cent of the market.

This decline in popularity was linked to a falling stock market. Many people thought shares would continue to rise forever, with likely returns of 4 to 8 per cent per annum. At these rates, endowment holders would be able to pay off their mortgage – and get a tidy surplus, which they could do what they liked with. But it was too good to be true. In April 2000, share prices plummeted and continued to struggle over the following years. Endowment policies were hit hard, with insurers forced to send out re-projection letters to endowment holders telling them whether their policies were on track to pay off their mortgage.

The letters were coded: red for policies where there was likely to be a serious shortfall; amber for those likely to slightly miss their target, and green for policies which were still on track to meet projections. Between July 2001 and December 2002, over 4.3 million letters were sent out, according to the Association of British Insurers. Of these, only a third (31 per cent) were green; the rest were either amber (27 per cent) or red (42 per cent). In other words, nearly two-thirds of the endowment mortgages faced a shortfall.

Many policyholders claim that the risks weren't spelt out when they took out their endowment; in other words, they were mis-sold. Many now say they wouldn't have chosen an endowment in the first place if they had realised it was linked to the stock market. Some have successfully proven their case and received compensation. But many people weren't mis-sold. They took out an endowment because they liked the fact that their monthly mortgage repayments were lower than they would have been with repayment loans, and they hoped to get a windfall once they'd paid it all off. And they would have done if the stock market had played ball.

Endowment mortgages

You've probably heard about endowment mortgages during the past few years. It would be impossible not to notice that they've come in for a lot of stick because many could potentially fail to provide enough cash for homeowners to pay back their mortgages. The question about whether endowment policies were mis-sold continues to rumble on (see the sidebar 'Endowment mis-selling and the bear market').

Two types of endowment policy exist – with-profits and unit-linked:

  ✔ **With-profits endowments:** Your monthly payments are pooled with those of other investors. At the end of the year – and depending on investment performance – bonuses are paid out by the insurer you invest your money with. At the end of the mortgage term, you get a one-off *terminal* bonus, which can be a large proportion of your final payout but isn't guaranteed.

✔ **Unit-linked endowments:** Your premiums buy units in stock-market linked investments. The value of these investments goes up and down on a daily basis. Unit-linked endowments can grow quicker than with-profits, but as is usually the case, an investment promising greater returns also involves higher risk.

Equities can go down as well as up. Don't gamble on the roof over your head unless you have enough cash in reserve to cover any potential shortfall.

ISA mortgages

ISAs are tax-free investment vehicles, which replaced personal equity plans (PEPs) and tax-exempt special savings certificates (TESSAs) in April 1999. Two types of ISA exist: Cash, and stocks and shares. For the purpose of mortgages, equity ISAs are used. You invest a monthly sum into an ISA, either through a personal portfolio of ISA investments or through a specialist ISA mortgage package. The money (hopefully) increases over time, tax-free. If your ISA does well, you may be able to repay your loan before the end of the term.

The advantage of an ISA is that you don't have to pay the high levels of commission that you do on endowments and pensions. They are also far more flexible because switching investments and stopping or re-starting payments is easy. You also have more say over where your money is invested and your returns are free of tax.

But before you sign on for an ISA mortgage, keep these things in mind:

✔ ISA mortgages are linked to the stock market. The bear market that has had such a crippling affect on endowments has also affected ISAs. In fact the volatility of the stock markets since March 2000 has been so bad that the popularity of ISA mortgages has dropped dramatically and many lenders no longer offer them.

✔ If you use an ISA as a repayment vehicle, you're limited to how much you can invest each tax year (between 6 April and 5 April the following year). This limit is £7,000 per person, so you may find it difficult to generate the capital you owe during the mortgage term.

Everyone aged 18 and over is allowed to invest up to £7,000 tax-free in an ISA each tax year. If you buy your property with another person, you can each utilise your allowance and invest up to a total of £14,000 each year in ISAs.

If you take out an ISA mortgage, don't forget to insure your investment contributions in case you lose your job or have an accident and can no longer work. Any of the usual protection products (see Chapter 10) should be suitable.

ISA mortgages are extremely high risk. Don't take one on unless you're sure you know what you're doing.

Pension mortgages

Backing your interest-only mortgage with a pension is another good way of maximising the tax breaks available. Instead of investing in an endowment or ISA, your extra monthly payments go into a personal pension fund, and you also pay premiums into a life assurance scheme.

The idea is that when you retire, you end up with a tax-free lump sum – up to 25 per cent of your pension pot – which you use to pay off the capital you owe. You use the rest to purchase an annuity, which is a guaranteed income for life and forms your pension. Because you can't get hold of your cash lump sum until you retire, pension mortgages tend to run for a lot longer than endowment mortgages – they can be as long as 35 or 40 years.

Pensions are a highly tax-efficient way of saving. For every 60p a higher rate taxpayer invests in his pension (78p for basic rate taxpayers), the Government tops up this contribution to £1. This tax relief should lead to higher investment returns than investing in an ISA or endowment simply because you have more money going into your pension fund.

Pension mortgages have their problems. There are no guarantees, and what you end up with is linked to market performance and the skills of the fund managers who handled your investment. For this reason, pension mortgages can be risky. Pension rules also tend to be very complicated, so you're likely to need professional advice if you opt for a pension mortgage. If you have a pension mortgage, keep a close eye on the performance of your fund to ensure that it's on track to pay off your mortgage. If it isn't, you have to think about alternative arrangements to cover any shortfall.

Pension mortgages are extremely tax-efficient, but they are linked to the stock market and highly complicated. For these reasons, they're ideal for sophisticated, self-employed higher-rate taxpayers. Everyone else should give them a wide berth. In addition, if you're a member of an occupational pension scheme at work, you can't have a pension mortgage anyway.

To Fix or Not to Fix?

Once you've decided on how you're going to repay your mortgage, you need to choose which type of home loan you're going to take out. The type you choose depends on your circumstances and attitude to risk. Your main options are:

- ✔ Variable
- ✔ Fixed
- ✔ Discount
- ✔ Base-rate tracker

- ✔ Capped
- ✔ Flexible
- ✔ Offset or current account
- ✔ Cash back

In the following sections, I explain in detail how each type works, along with the pros and cons.

Variable rate mortgages

Every lender has a standard variable rate (SVR), which is linked to the base rate and used as the basis for calculating many of its other deals – such as discounted rates. You can have a mortgage on the lender's SVR but it is expensive – it costs more than a fixed or discounted deal, and the rate moves up and down in line with the base rate. So if the MPC increases interest rates, the lender will usually raise its SVR accordingly. (See the sidebar 'How interest rates are set' earlier in this chapter to understand the impact that MPC decisions have on interest rates.)

Many homeowners end up on their lender's SVR when their fixed or discounted deal comes to an end. When this happens you should remortgage to another deal to cut costs. The advantage of being on the SVR is that, in most cases, you're not tied in and can switch to another deal at any time without penalty. This could be useful if you're thinking of moving in the near future. But you will have to pay a higher rate of interest for this flexibility. And some lenders may charge you a penalty for switching if you have recently come to the end of a fixed or discounted deal and there are overhanging redemption charges for a number of years. If this isn't the case, find a fixed or discounted rate deal pretty smartish.

Although SVRs vary from lender to lender, they tend to be fairly similar because the market is so keenly priced. But while a mortgage on the lender's SVR isn't the most competitive deal to have, the SVR is a useful indication as to whether the lender is competitive in its fixed and discounted rates. If a lender's SVR is very high compared to the base rate and other lenders' standard rates, you can probably assume that the lender's discounted rates are not competitive either. Give this lender a wide berth and find one with a lower SVR – and better deals.

Six out of ten UK homeowners are on their lender's SVR. This is alarming because it means many people aren't getting the cheapest mortgage they could be. Your lender's SVR, even if it is competitive, is almost certainly likely to be higher than a fixed or discounted deal. So once the special offer on your mortgage has come to an end, make a point of remortgaging to another deal, otherwise you end up paying over the odds.

Longer-term fixed rates and the euro

Alistair Darling, the Chancellor of the Exchequer, is keen for UK homebuyers to opt for long-term fixed rate mortgages over 25 years – rather than the short-term fixed and discounted deals most buyers favour. The Chancellor believes that long-term fixed rate loans will create more stability in the mortgage market and reduce vulnerability to sharp changes in interest rates. In April 2003, the Government commissioned Professor David Miles of Imperial College London to look at the feasibility of establishing a market for longer-term mortgages, which are prevalent in the US and on the Continent.

Long-term fixed rate deals are nothing new in the UK, with a handful available since the late 1980s. But few people take them out because the rates are rarely as competitive as those on shorter fixes and penalties are often quite stringent. Many 25-year fixed rate deals don't allow you to exit without paying a penalty until year 11, so why not get a better deal by opting for a five-year fixed rate, which is bound to be cheaper and more flexible?

Fixed rate mortgages

Fixed rate mortgages are exactly as they sound. For a set period of time, your mortgage payments are guaranteed, no matter what happens to the base rate. If you take out a five-year deal fixed at 5.70 per cent, you'll be charged interest at 5.70 per cent.

Because your mortgage payments are fixed, budgeting is a lot easier than it is if you're on a variable rate. For this reason, fixed rate deals are ideal for first time buyers and those who are on tight budgets.

Mortgages are usually fixed for two, three, or five years. but you can take out a 10-, 15-, 20-, 25- or even 30-year deal. Relatively few people are keen to fix their mortgage for this long, though, because circumstances can easily change over such a length of time. At the end of the fixed-rate deal, you automatically revert to your lender's SVR for the remainder of the mortgage term and it's time to shop around for another offer.

Generally, the longer the fixed rate you opt for, the higher the rate of interest you pay. Therefore, a two-year fixed mortgage usually has a lower rate than a five-year deal. If interest rates are very high, and there's a possibility that they'll come down within a couple of years, you may want to opt for a two-year fixed and then take out another fixed rate deal at the end of that period. If, on the other hand, rates are exceptionally low and, therefore, more likely to go up than down, a five-year fixed is a good bet. (And besides, if rates do actually fall slightly during this time, you still get a cheap deal.)

Before you sign on for a fixed rate deal, consider these things:

✔ Most fixed rate deals carry stiff penalties if you redeem them during the offer period, which could amount to as much as a few thousand pounds. To avoid paying a penalty, don't fix for five years, for example, if there's a possibility that you'll be moving in three. Some deals are portable though and you can take them with you if you do move during the fixed rate period.

✔ While a fixed rate cushions the volatility in the market and protects you if interest rates rise, the downside is that you don't benefit if interest rates fall. Over the course of five or more years, rates could drop significantly.

If you're worried about budgeting, opt for a fixed rate deal. Be prepared to move quickly, however, as some lenders offer competitive rates for a very limited period of time. Delay – and you're likely to miss out.

Discounted variable rate mortgages

Most lenders offer discounted deals, which tend to be a couple of percentage points below their SVRs. Discount rates are usually taken over two or three years. As with fixed rate deals, the shorter the term, the lower the rate.

The big advantage of discount deals is that they tend to be lower than fixed rate deals initially. You also benefit from any cut in the base rate because your rate is linked to your lender's SVR. But here also lies the problem: If the base rate goes up, your mortgage payments increase accordingly. If there's a lot of volatility in interest rates, your mortgage payments could fluctuate dramatically from month to month.

Only opt for a discount rate if you can afford to be wrong – in other words, if you can cope with an increase in your mortgage repayments. If you can, a discount rate will usually give you a better initial rate than a fixed rate deal, plus you'll benefit from any interest rate cuts during the discounted period.

Base-rate tracker mortgages

A tracker mortgage tracks a set margin below or above the base rate. For example, if the base rate is 5.75 per cent, you may pay 5 per cent (0.75 per cent under until the rate changes). The advantage of tracker mortgages is that the lender can't widen the margin and charge you more than 0.75 below the base rate.

As an incentive, many lenders offer substantial discounts on tracker deals for six months or more. These discounts can result in very attractive rates and, given that tracker deals don't carry penalties after the offer period, you can then switch to another deal when the discount comes to an end.

As with a mortgage on the lender's SVR, tracker mortgages go up and down – there's no certainty. But unlike a discount – which is connected to the lender's SVR which can be changed on a whim – you know where you stand with a tracker because it's linked to the base rate.

Capped rate mortgages

With a capped rate mortgage, you know the absolute maximum you'll be paying each month. Your mortgage rate can rise but only as high as the cap. If the base rate continues to rise after the cap has been met, your mortgage repayments aren't affected. Capped rate deals are usually offered over 3, 5, or 10 years.

Because the rate is capped rather than fixed, it can fall, allowing you to take advantage of any cuts in the base rate. This makes a capped rate deal attractive because you can benefit from the best of both worlds.

Capped rate deals come at a price. They tend to be more expensive than fixed rate deals, and fewer are available so you have less choice.

Flexible mortgages

A number of lenders offer flexible mortgages, although terms and conditions and benefits vary considerably. All flexible mortgages have a facility for varying repayments, so you can pay more or less than your mortgage payment each month, or nothing at all. This ability to overpay, underpay or to take a payment holiday depends on how much money you have built up in your mortgage 'account'; if you have overpaid by several hundred pounds, you can take payment holidays, but you can't miss a payment completely if you haven't built up anything in reserve.

Flexible mortgages are ideal for the self-employed or anyone whose income fluctuates. When you're flush, you can pay more than required so that when finances are tight, you can miss a payment or two – and not be penalised for doing so. The other advantage of overpaying is that you reduce your interest payments, enabling you to pay your mortgage off more quickly.

Interest is calculated daily on flexible deals, which makes a big difference in how much interest you pay over the term of your loan; essentially, you end up paying less. See the sidebar 'A year to the day: A comparison' to find out why.

Flexible mortgages tend to be more expensive than fixed or discounted deals. If you don't use all of the flexible options, you may be better off steering clear of a flexible mortgage.

If you're drawn to a flexible mortgage simply because you want the ability to overpay when you can afford to, remember that many standard mortgages with offer periods, such as fixed and discounted deals, enable you to overpay a limited amount – usually around 10 per cent of the outstanding mortgage – without penalty each year. This is more than enough for most of us.

Offset and current account mortgages

Another option is the offset or current account mortgage (CAM). These mortgages are similar although they differ slightly on a number of points:

- **Offset mortgages:** Offset mortgages enable you to use your savings to reduce the amount of interest you pay on your mortgage. It works like this: You open a savings account and/or current account with your mortgage lender. You make your monthly mortgage payment each month, as usual, but your savings and current account are counted against your mortgage balance in order to reduce the interest you're charged, while remaining separate. If you owe £60,000 on your mortgage, for example, but have £12,000 in your savings account and say, £500 in your current account, you'll be charged interest at your mortgage rate on £47,500. By leaving money in your current or savings account for as long as possible each month, you reduce the interest you owe on your mortgage further still, because the rate is calculated on a daily basis.

- **Current account mortgages (CAMs):** CAMs work in a similar way to offset mortgages although your home loan, current account, savings, and even credit cards and personal loans are all lumped together in one account rather than everything kept in separate pots. On your monthly statement you get one overall figure – usually a minus – telling you how much cash you have after all your savings are offset against your debts. You pay a set monthly amount from your account to cover the mortgage and your savings are used to reduce the amount of interest you owe.

  Even a small amount of money can make a big difference to the amount of interest you owe. Consider this example: If you take out a £100,000 mortgage over 25 years at 7.5 per cent interest and spend all your salary every month except £100, which you leave in the account, you will pay off your mortgage six years and nine months early, saving £40,263 in interest. The residue of money left in the account every month may not seem much, but the key thing is that it eats away at the capital you owe.

Because the interest on offset mortgages and CAMs is calculated daily, you pay what you owe on that day. If you have just been paid, it doesn't matter that you'll soon spend all that cash; for several days, a large chunk of money has been offset against your mortgage. In the long run, this enables you to repay your loan a lot quicker.

A year to the day: A comparison

Old-fashioned loans – quite a few of which are still in existence – charge interest on an annual basis, which works out much more expensive than loans for which interest is calculated on a daily basis. The main difference between daily and annual calculation of interest is as follows:

✔ **Daily calculation of interest:** At the end of every day your mortgage lender calculates how much you owe on your loan. The great advantage of this is that when you make a mortgage repayment, your money gets to work straightaway, reducing your mortgage debt – and the amount of interest you pay over the term of the loan. As mentioned earlier in this chapter, the interest is the killer in terms of mortgage costs.

✔ **Annual calculation of interest:** If your lender calculates the interest you owe on an *annual* basis, your mortgage payments are knocked off the total you owe once a year, rather than when you make them. So if your interest is calculated on 1 January, nothing you pay during the rest of the year is used to reduce your mortgage. You end up paying more interest (because you owe more capital for longer) even though you have actually paid the cash to the lender.

Some lenders calculate interest on a *monthly* basis; this works in the same way as annual calculation but a repayment doesn't make a difference to the amount you owe until the following month. So for around 30 days, your lender benefits more from you paying off a chunk of capital than you do.

Here's the thing to remember: Calculating interest on an annual basis is an arcane, outdated method. Avoid lenders who still adhere to this practice, where possible.

Critics of offset mortgages and CAMs argue that they are so flexible that borrowers who aren't disciplined won't pay their mortgages off on time. For example, some CAM providers let you borrow the difference between your mortgage (say, for example, £62,000) and the value of your house (say, £150,000), so in this example, you could get your hands on an additional £88,000 to do with what you like. If you're not disciplined and tend to see these options as too much temptation, or if you're a first-time buyer poking her toe in the water for the first time, you'd be better off steering clear of a CAM and opting for a fixed or discounted deal.

Another problem with CAMs is that everything is lumped together into one statement each month. While seeing all your debts and savings on one piece of paper is handy, it means your grand total will be in the red by a serious amount. Many people can't cope seeing that they are £120,000 overdrawn, for example. Others prefer not to switch their current account to their mortgage lender, preferring to stick with their existing bank.

Although offset mortgages and CAMS are a great way of reducing your interest payments, they tend to be more expensive than fixed or discounted deals. However, rates have become more competitive.

Why APRs aren't key to picking a mortgage

With so many different types of mortgage to choose from, working out the best value deal can seem impossible. Sometimes it feels like even mathematicians would struggle to compare deals with different rates of interest once offers and charges have been taken into account.

To make this job easier, annual percentage rates (APRs) were introduced. Under the Consumer Credit Act, lenders must provide the APR next to the headline mortgage rate in order to enable borrowers to compare the cost of different loans. The APR takes into account the total cost of the mortgage, including setting up costs, arrangement fees, when interest is calculated, and any discounts or special offers in the early stages.

However, APRs can be unreliable so don't rely on them. You're far better off getting an individually prepared quote listing all upfront and ongoing costs.

Unless you have several thousand pounds in savings, which can be offset against your mortgage repayments, it may not be worth opting for an offset mortgage or a CAM. Offset mortgages and CAMs tend to be more popular with mature borrowers as they are more likely to have various savings lying around, or first-time buyers who regularly receive substantial bonuses which they can put towards paying off their mortgage.

Cash back mortgages

Money is usually tight for first-time buyers because they have so many costs to think about. Cash back mortgages are designed to solve this problem: When you take out your mortgage, you get a cash lump sum from your lender. The amount varies between lenders from a flat fee of a couple of hundred pounds to a percentage of the amount you borrow (it can be as high as 8 per cent of the mortgage). You can do what you want with this cash: put it towards new furniture, pay off a credit card debt, or even go on holiday if you need a break from all the stress of moving.

You don't get something for nothing – and that is very true when you opt for cash back mortgages. Most cash back deals work out as being quite expensive in the long run because the cash back is really a sort of advance, which is added onto the term of your mortgage. If you get £6,000 cash back when you borrow £100,000, for example, you're essentially borrowing £106,000 because the interest has to be paid back over the term of the mortgage. And interest rates tend to be higher on cash back mortgages than on straightforward fixed or discounted deals.

Asking granny for a loan

If you really can't raise a deposit from your own funds, check out other ways of getting your hands on the cash you need. If you're not too proud you could go, cap in hand, to rich relatives or friends who may take pity on your plight and stump up the readies. If they aren't willing to simply hand the cash over, you may be able to come to some arrangement where you pay them back over a few years (try not to over-stretch yourself and make promises you can't keep; remember, if they're willing to help you with a deposit, you're going to have mortgage

repayments as well and those take priority). If your family and friends can't help, your bank may be sympathetic and agree to extend your over-draft or let you take out a personal loan.

Resist the temptation to take on expensive debt. A cash advance on your credit card or a loan from a dodgy lender may be the only way you can raise a deposit, but at what cost? Make sure you work out how much borrowing the cash is costing you and whether it's really worth it. You'll have enough outgoings as it is without worrying about loan sharks banging on your door.

Early redemption penalties are also common with cash back mortgages; if a substantial sum is paid you could end up locked into the mortgage for five to seven years.

Rather than opting for a cash back mortgage, you may be better off picking a competitive fixed or discounted deal and then taking out a personal loan, extending your overdraft, or applying for a credit card with 0 per cent inter-est for a six-month introductory period to raise some extra cash. This way, you can get your hands on a few hundred pounds and don't end up paying interest on the extra money over 25 years or so (the key point of this strategy is that you would pay back the extra money very quickly). This also means you can then choose from a wider range of mortgages, rather than limiting yourself to just those offering cash back.

How Your Deposit (or Lack Thereof) Affects Your Mortgage

The deposit is the cash down payment you make on your mortgage, and the general rule is the bigger the better. Not only will your mortgage repayments be lower, you'll also qualify for a cheaper rate and won't have to pay a higher lending charge (HLC) – insurance taken out by lenders (but paid for by you) if you have a limited, or no, deposit. (See the section 'Higher lending charge' later in this chapter.)

Long gone are the days when first-time buyers saved up until they had a 10 per cent deposit, however. Nowadays, you can get away without any deposit at all because 100 per cent and even 125 per cent mortgages are available, so you no longer have to wait before taking the plunge.

Ideally every buyer would have a sizeable deposit to put down. Most people, in fact, use their savings (or their parents' savings) to raise a deposit of between 5 and 10 per cent of the purchase price (although your deposit can certainly be higher if you have a lot of spare cash or have sold a property to buy a new one). But not everyone has several thousand pounds lying around to use as a deposit. And if you don't want to waste valuable time saving up for a deposit when you'd rather buy here and now, you'll have to get a mortgage without one.

Getting a mortgage for the whole purchase price – or more

A growing number of lenders are offering 100 per cent or even up to 125 per cent loan-to-value (LTV) mortgages – this is the size of your mortgage in relation to the property value, so you don't need any deposit at all. These mortgages are particularly popular among first-time buyers because they enable them to get a foot on the property ladder before prices rise even further instead of 'wasting' several years trying to save up for a mortgage.

With a 100 per cent mortgage (or larger), you won't qualify for the most competitive deals that are open to those with a sizeable deposit. The higher rates are the lender's way of covering the risk in taking you on. If house prices fall, you also risk going into *negative equity*, which means you owe more than the property is worth. And if you had to sell the property quickly, for whatever reason, being in negative equity could be a big problem.

Higher lending charge

A higher lending charge (HLC) is a one-off insurance premium that some lenders charge borrowers who don't have much of a deposit. This can amount to several thousand pounds worth of HLC, which is added on to your loan. The HLC protects the lender in case you default on your mortgage payments, and the lender has to repossess your home and sell it at a loss. The HLC doesn't benefit you at all, yet you have to pay for it.

The HLC is expensive and outdated. Avoid lenders still charging the HLC where possible and opt for an HLC-free deal. If this isn't achievable, it may be worth saving up for a bigger deposit and putting your house purchase off until you can avoid an HLC.

Using a Guarantor

If you're a first-time buyer, having a low income is likely to be one of your biggest hindrances to getting the mortgage you need. As a result, an increasing number of people are relying on a guarantor to help them with their property purchase. Most lenders require the guarantor to be a relative – usually a parent – although some lenders also allow a friend to act as guarantor, as long as he is willing to guarantee that in the event of you defaulting on your mortgage payments, he will meet the shortfall.

When you apply for your mortgage, your guarantor goes through a similar application process, supplying details of his income and outgoings. The guarantor also has to sign a declaration saying that he understands exactly what being a guarantor involves. Your guarantor should also consult a solicitor for advice before signing anything so that he knows exactly what he is committing himself to.

If you use a guarantor, your lender often lets you borrow more than it would have if you weren't using a guarantor. But while you may be tempted to borrow as much as you can, keep in mind what you can reasonably afford to pay back. If you're going to struggle from the word go, this isn't a good start.

Negotiating the Maze: Where to Find the Right Mortgage

Some people apply to the lender directly when taking out a mortgage. But with so much choice, it is hard to know which lender to choose. In my opinion, if you really don't know what you're doing, you should use an independent mortgage broker to help you find the best product for your needs. Whatever you do, don't rely solely on your bank to come up with the best deal.

Why your bank might not be your best bet

Many people are governed by inertia when it comes to their financial affairs, which is why so many stick with the same bank year in, year out even though they would almost certainly get a better deal elsewhere. And if this is true of current accounts, it is almost certainly true of mortgages.

In the past, if you approached your bank for mortgage advice, you would likely end up with a mortgage from your bank. This is because, under Financial Services Authority rules, your bank was only licensed to sell its own products.

Why is this a problem? Well, you're unlikely to get the best mortgage rate, may incur a penalty for switching your mortgage even after the offer period, and will generally have limited your choice from the start. In other words, you're not giving yourself the best chance to find the best deal. Seeing that you're spending so much money, limiting yourself from the start is a rather foolish approach.

Using a middleman

Do yourself a favour and shop around using an independent mortgage broker. Why should you do all the legwork yourself? A broker spends all her time following the mortgage market, knows the best deals at that particular time (they are ever-changing), and can talk you through the whole process. If you need your hand held by an expert, a broker is the expert to do it.

If you decide to use a broker, make sure that you use a truly independent one. The best broker is one with access to the whole mortgage market, not just a handful of lenders. That way, he can do a full search and find the best available deal at that time.

Some estate agents provide their own mortgage service, which is likely to be far more limited than the broad market view offered by an independent broker. Give your estate agent a wide berth when it comes to financing your house purchase.

Using the Internet

The Internet is the most comprehensive source of information on mortgages, providing you with a wealth of information. Even if you aren't planning on actually applying for your mortgage online, you can still research the various loans and deals out there.

Researching online

The Web is great for researching the mortgage market. Several websites offer free calculators that enable you to quickly work out how much lenders will let you borrow and what your monthly repayments will be. For those who already have a mortgage, some sites also have calculators that let you work out whether remortgaging is worth your while.

Although these calculators are general guides and no guarantee of whether a lender will actually let you have the cash, they're a great place to start. Many of the big independent mortgage brokers also have tables of mortgage 'best buys' on their websites, which enable you to see the best available deals at a glance. When you're ready to sign on the dotted line of your mortgage application form, it's worth double-checking these tables to ensure that you have the best deal.

Here are some of the best sites, all of which are offered by big independent brokers:

✔ **Charcol:** www.charcolonline.co.uk

✔ **London & Country:** www.lcplc.co.uk

✔ **Savills Private Finance:** www.spf.co.uk

 Another excellent website worth looking out is www.moneysupermarket.com. At this site, you can compare over 7,000 mortgages, as well as home insurance policies and mortgage protection plans. Finding the right mortgage is very straightforward. You'll be asked several questions, such as the purpose of the mortgage – first-time purchase, self-build, or raising capital – as well as the location, price, size of your deposit, details about the property, and your earnings and outgoings. As long as you have this information to hand, completing all the details shouldn't take longer than 10 minutes or so. Moneysupermarket then provides details of all the suitable deals for you, along with links so that you can click through to the lender's home page to apply.

Moneysupermarket also offers a guide explaining mortgage terms. And even though the site is very clear and easy to use, if you get stuck, you can contact moneysupermarket's financial team over the phone. You can also arrange a face-to-face consultation if you prefer.

Applying for a mortgage online

The Internet is certainly changing the way the home buying process works. It is possible to save time and jump the queue by applying for a mortgage online.

Many homebuyers don't realise that applying for a mortgage online is possible. If you're confident that you have found the right deal and don't want mortgage advice, you can fill in an on-screen application form and submit it to the lender. You'll receive an email back informing you that the lender is processing your application.

Filling in a mortgage application form online is not for everyone, particularly first-time buyers. Mortgage application forms can be complicated, and many people like being guided through them by a broker. If you don't feel ready to fill out a form online, stick to pen and paper and asking for advice!

One Size Doesn't Fit All: Mortgages for Special Circumstances

As well as the standard mortgage deals available, there are a number of loans aimed specifically at certain groups of people. In this section, I look at mortgages tailored specifically for:

- Self-employed (self-certification mortgages)
- First-time buyers
- Those with poor credit histories (sub-prime)

Self-certification mortgages for the self-employed

When you apply for a mortgage, most lenders require three months' worth of wage slips to prove that you earn as much as you say you do. But not everyone can provide three months' worth of wage slips from an employer. If you're self-employed, you won't have this evidence of income. Yet with around 3.2 million self-employed people in the UK, the industry has found ways around this problem. As long as you have two years of audited accounts to prove your income, a mainstream lender (as opposed to a specialist lender) will usually let you have a standard mortgage.

But if your business hasn't been running for at least two years, you won't have enough accounts to satisfy a mainstream lender. And even if you have been going longer than two years, the problem for many self-employed people is that their accounts don't adequately reflect their income. If you employ an accountant, part of his job is to ensure that you don't pay more tax than is absolutely necessary, which is perfectly legal but means you may have a problem convincing a mortgage lender that you can actually afford to repay more than your accounts indicate.

If you fall into this category, you may have to opt for a *self-certification mortgage*. This enables you to certify your own income, by signing a document stating how much you earn. You don't need to prove audited accounts.

Most specialist lenders judge each case on its own merits rather than use strict income multiples, but as a general guide, many let you borrow up to four times your stated income. If you state that your earnings for last year were £40,000, for example, the lender will let you borrow up to £160,000.

It might be tempting to lie about how much you earn in order to get a bigger mortgage. But resist this temptation because it is fraud. You may have problems meeting your repayments if you overstretch yourself.

While rates on self-certification loans used to be much higher than on conventional mortgages (because of the perceived extra risk of lending to the self-employed), they have come down in recent years. However, they still tend to be higher than the rates for standard loans. You can choose between the same types of deal, although flexible loans may be most useful to the self-employed whose income might fluctuate.

You also have to stump up a bigger deposit in most cases – some lenders even want as much as 25 per cent of the purchase price. However, some specialist lenders are happy with a 15 per cent deposit, so all is not lost if you can't afford such a substantial down payment. You'll just have to shop around for a deal you can afford.

First-time buyer mortgages

A number of lenders offer specific first-time buyer mortgages with a variety of incentives, including free valuations, cash back on completion, no deposit required, and discounted rates. A mortgage broker will be able to point you in the direction of a lender offering such a deal.

While you may be a first-time buyer, it doesn't follow that you should take out a first-time buyer mortgage. Many of these deals are just marketing ploys. You can get all these offers on standard mortgages. Avoid restricting yourself to a limited selection of deals.

Sub-prime mortgages

If you've had credit issues in the past – missing loan or credit card payments, for example – you may have a patchy credit record. Lenders look at your credit rating to check your ability – and likelihood – to pay your mortgage. People with good credit histories usually qualify for most mainstream mortgage deals.

In recent years, a number of lenders have started offering loans to borrowers with a less-than-perfect credit history. These are called *sub-prime mortgages*. Rates are at a premium to mainstream deals, and depend on how bad your credit rating is.

Since the problems emerged in the sub-prime market in the US in 2007, with borrowers defaulting on loans, many lenders in the UK have priced their products much higher and reduced maximum loan-to-values, so you need a bigger deposit than in the past.

Buyer Beware: Things to Watch Out For

Mortgages can be a minefield because many products come with a sting in the tail, usually hidden somewhere in the terms and conditions. And if you don't spot this before you sign on the dotted line, you could end up with a deal that is not as competitive as it first appears.

Read the terms and conditions carefully. If you're using a broker, he should point out any potential nasties. But you can help yourself by watching out for the main things to avoid.

Penalties for early redemption

Most mortgage deals (other than standard variable rate loans) have some sort of redemption penalty if you cash your mortgage in within a certain period of time. If you take out a five-year fixed rate deal, for example, the only way the lender can offer you such a deal is if you stick with it for the five years, at least. If you cashed in your mortgage before then and paid no penalty for doing so, the lender would lose money. This is why lenders charge a penalty – a percentage of the interest owed on the loan – if you decide to switch mortgages before the stated time period is up. This practice is fair enough really and one most lenders follow when offering fixed or discounted rate deals, although not all lenders charge such penalties.

What aren't acceptable, in any situation, are *extended redemption penalties*. These are also known as *overhangs* because they run longer than the offer period. For example, some lenders offer two-year discounts at startlingly good rates. But the payback is that you're then tied into the deal for not two, but five years or even longer; if you try to redeem the mortgage at any time during that period, you face a substantial penalty, which can be in the region of thousands of pounds.

Accepting such a deal is clearly not in your best interests because it ties you to an uncompetitive rate – often the lender's SVR. To make matters worse, this sort of deal tends to be offered by a lender with a high SVR. So any of the earlier savings are lost by paying higher interest for years after the offer period has come to an end. So never take out a mortgage with an extended redemption penalty. The rate will undoubtedly look more attractive than loans without overhangs but there is a good reason for this – afterwards you're stuck on a higher rate for what can seem forever.

Compulsory insurance

Compulsory insurance, where a lender forces you to take out its insurance as a condition of taking out one of its mortgages, is a big rip-off; avoid it at all costs. Certain forms of insurance are essential when taking out a mortgage, such as buildings insurance; others, such as home contents insurance, are optional (both of these are explained in Chapter 12). The only way to get the best deal on this is to shop around. Taking what the lender offers is unlikely to produce the best deal.

Some lenders don't impose compulsory insurance, but they do try to make it as easy as possible for borrowers to take out their insurance because it's such a money-spinner for them. Often, on the mortgage application form they include a reminder that you must take out some form of cover and provide a box that you simply tick if you want to take out the lender's buildings insurance. Lenders are counting on the fact that you'll be so stressed by the whole mortgage application that one less thing to worry about is welcome. But even though some lenders offer competitive rates, you can't assume that this is the case.

Don't cross your fingers and hope that your lender offers competitive insurance. Shop around for the best deal. Go to Chapter 12 for information and guidance on shopping for insurance cover.

Not Forgetting the Not-So-Little-Extras

If the mortgage rate were the only thing you had to worry about, the finance side of buying a property would be fairly straightforward. Unfortunately, this isn't the case. You need to think about lots of not-so-little extras, explained in the following sections.

Some lenders refund the cost of certain fees as an inducement to taking out a mortgage with them; others offer free buildings and contents insurance or mortgage payment protection (see Chapter 12) for a limited period of time. Such offers can add up to a saving of several hundred pounds. As you shop around for a lender, be sure to ask about these incentives.

Lender's arrangement fee

Lenders charge borrowers an upfront fee, known as an *application, arrangement,* or *booking fee,* to reserve the mortgage. This fee is non-refundable. You may also have to pay a completion fee once you receive the money. These fees have risen in recent years – the average fee is around £1,000 although it can be higher. Some lenders charge a percentage of the mortgage amount instead of a flat fee, which can work out much higher.

The cheapest rates of interest often come with the highest fees. As a general rule, the bigger your mortgage the more important the rate is and the less important the fee. Work out the total cost of the mortgage – rate plus fee – before making a decision.

Some deals don't have arrangement fees. But the lender will charge a higher interest rate in order to make the money back, so you can end up paying a lot more in the long run than you would if you'd just paid an arrangement fee in the first place. Many lenders let you add the arrangement fee onto the mortgage, so you don't have to pay a lump sum up front. This can make cash flow a little easier, but you will pay interest on it.

Mortgage valuation fee

The lender charges you a fee for having the property valued – which seems a bit cheeky if you consider that the valuation is done to satisfy the lender, who wants to make sure that the property is worth what it's being asked to lend you to buy it. You don't benefit at all from this arrangement, apart from the fact that it brings you closer to getting your mortgage. The amount you're charged depends on the size of the property (see Chapter 9 for more details), but expect to pay upwards of £300.

The valuation fee is unavoidable although, if you're remortgaging, some lenders refund it. The lender sends a surveyor to value the property. You don't have to do anything at all; the valuation fee is added onto the money you borrow from the lender.

Mortgage broker fee

If you use a mortgage broker to help you find your home loan, you may have to pay a fee, depending on how the broker works. Some brokers are paid by commission, which means that the lender who supplies your mortgage pays the broker a sum for passing on your business. The amount varies depending on the size of your mortgage. The broker must tell you how much she receives from the lender.

However, if you use a broker who doesn't take commission, you have to pay him a fee for his time and expertise. The broker's fee varies from broker to broker but she will want to recover up to 1 per cent of the value of the mortgage, including fees and commission from the lender.

Make sure that you know from the outset whether your broker is paid by commission or is expecting a cheque from you after she has arranged your mortgage. Whether you choose fees or commission depends on the service you require. The more complicated your case, the more you need a fee-charging broker. Broker's fees are payable on completion.

Survey costs

Getting a survey is always wise. So expect to pay for a survey on top of the valuation (which doesn't really tell you anything about the condition of the property). As explained in more detail in Chapter 9, two different types of survey are available: a basic homebuyer's report or a full structural survey. Which one you go for depends on the condition and age of your property and how much money you want to spend. A homebuyer's report starts at around £600; a building survey can cost anything between £750 and £1,500, depending on the size of the property and exactly what you want investigated.

Skimping on a survey may seem like an easy way to cut costs. But think about how much money you're spending on the property – and how expensive it would be if you made a mistake.

Legal fees

Unless you do your own conveyancing or legal work, you have to pay a solicitor to do it for you (see Chapter 19 for more details on using a solicitor and legal costs). Again, costs vary, but expect to pay around £550 in legal fees for the purchase of a £200,000 property. Legal fees are usually payable on completion.

Land registry and local searches

As well as paying the solicitor a conveyancing fee, you may also have to pay him for the land registry fees and charges for local searches, which he undertakes on your behalf if the property you're buying doesn't have a HIP. (See Chapter 16 for more on HIPs.) These uncover whether the property had planning permission or not in the first place and whether any major works such as a supermarket are being planned for the empty plot next to your property.

The solicitor may bill you for these searches as he commissions them or he'll add the cost onto his final bill. Expect to pay in the region of £400 for these.

Stamp duty

You pay stamp duty to the solicitor at the same time as exchange of contracts (which means you can't pay the stamp duty out of the mortgage advance). The amount you pay depends on the value of your property, but it starts at 1 per cent on properties over £125,000, rising to 4 per cent for properties over £500,000. Stamp duty can, therefore, be quite a sizeable chunk of your budget, so don't forget about it or you could be in for a nasty shock when the solicitor sends you his bill.

Completing the Mortgage Application Form

Once you've decided on the mortgage you want, you have to complete a mortgage application form and supply several items to prove that you are who you say you are. If you're using a broker, she'll help you to complete your form. Identification proving who you are and information stating where you got the deposit from, for example, is necessary to crack down on fraud. Lenders take this very seriously.

As soon as you start looking at properties, start gathering together the information that your lender is going to want to see. Keep hold of wage slips, your most recent P60, bank statements, your passport, and some recent utility bills. These are all examples of the sort of things the lender wants to see. Getting them ready now can save you time – and stress – later.

Every lender has its own version of the mortgage application form, so it isn't possible to tell you exactly what information you'll be required to provide. But most lenders follow the same pattern. Most forms run to several pages, and you're required to give the following information:

- **The name, current address and date of birth of each applicant.** If you have not lived at your current address for at least three years, you have to provide the address(es) of where else you have lived.

- **The address of the property you intend to buy and how much you want to borrow.** You're also asked for a contact name and number for someone who can give the lender access to the property to arrange the valuation. This person is usually the estate agent handling the sale, but where the owner is selling privately, you have to give the owner's name and contact details.

- **Your solicitor's name, address, and contact number.** The lender wants evidence that you have instructed a solicitor because it will be dealing with him during the application process.

- **The size of your deposit and where you got the money from.** Again, the source of your deposit is important in order to reduce the risk of money laundering. Beyond that, the lender doesn't really care whether you saved up your deposit, got it as a present from a relative, or took out a loan. All are considered to be acceptable sources.

- **Each applicant's job title, employer's name and address, salary, and length of employment.** This information is necessary in order to convince the lender that you earn enough to meet the mortgage repayments each month and aren't over stretching yourself.

✔ **Each applicant's bank account details, including name and address of branch, sort code and account number, and number of years you have banked with them.** This information enables the lender to check your basic creditworthiness.

✔ **Whether either applicant has any county court judgments (CCJs) against them or has ever been declared bankrupt.** This information allows the lender to find out whether you have defaulted on any loans or mortgages in the past – in other words, whether you're likely to meet your repayments each month.

✔ **Details of any personal loans, outstanding credit card debts, or other monthly outgoings.** By finding out about your current commitments, the lender can work out whether you can afford to finance your mortgage.

✔ **Whether you want to take out the lender's buildings insurance or not.** If you do, tick the box. But I recommend that you don't take out the lender's insurance until you've shopped around and made sure that it's the best deal available at the time. If you get your insurance else-where, make sure that you have it arranged by the time you exchange contracts, or your solicitor won't let you go ahead.

✔ **Each applicant's signature and the date.** The signature is an important declaration that all the information you have provided is correct, so don't forget to autograph the application form!

Problems Getting a Mortgage

Once you've completed your mortgage application form and returned it to the lender, you can't do much apart from sit back, cross your fingers, and wait for it to be approved. And if everything is in order, it should be.

But sometimes the lender rejects your mortgage application because the information you gave doesn't stack up. One in four applicants is rejected, so you're not alone. The main reasons for a mortgage being rejected are the following:

✔ Unstable job or income history

✔ Missed repayments on some form of credit

✔ County Court Judgments (CCJs)

✔ Bankruptcy

✔ Not being on the electoral roll

✔ Not having a bank account

- Mortgage arrears
- Repossession
- Unemployment

Even with a bad credit record, you should be able to get a mortgage although you will have to pay more for it. Non-standard borrowers (also known as *sub-prime* – see 'Sub-prime mortgages' earlier in this chapter) are often charged a higher rate of interest than on a mainstream loan. Instead of automated credit scoring, specialist lenders look at each case on an individual basis. However, they are likely to lend you less and require a bigger deposit than on standard loans. There can also be very severe early redemption penalties.

Given that rates are higher with non-standard mortgages, your aim should be to try and get back on track with a cheaper mainstream product within three years or so. Of course, the way to do this is to keep up with your mortgage repayments.

Credit scoring

Financial problems in your past could well come back to haunt you when you apply for a mortgage. But many people who think they have a clean slate aren't prepared for it when their mortgage application is rejected – although this is quite common.

The reason for this rejection is probably to be found on your credit file. These are records of all your financial affairs and are held by the main credit reference agencies: Equifax (www.checkmyfile.com) and Experian (www.experian.co.uk). If you have missed a payment on a credit card or loan, for example, this is recorded on your credit file.

Before applying for a mortgage, get a copy of your credit file so that you can have any mistakes corrected. (You're charged £2 for accessing your file.) It may be that you haven't done anything wrong at all; your records could have been confused with a family member of the same name. By checking your file, you can have simple mistakes like these corrected.

Every time you apply for any form of credit, it leaves a 'footprint' on your file. So even if you're rejected for a credit card, for example, a record of this application appears on your file. The more footprints you have, the more credit hungry you appear, and the louder the warning bells sounding for the mortgage lender. Footprints remain on your credit file for six months only. So if there are lots of them, it might be worth waiting a few months before trying again to get a mortgage.

County Court Judgments (CCJs)

Every mortgage lender wants to know whether you have any county court judgments (CCJs) against you and most will reject your application if this is the case. A CCJ is an adverse ruling against someone who has not satisfied their debt payments with their creditors. Once recorded against you, it stays on your credit file for seven years. Usually, you have to satisfy any CCJs against you before you can get a mortgage.

All is not necessarily lost, however: some specialist companies accept applicants with CCJs. The bigger the problem and the greater the number of CCJs against you, the higher the mortgage rate you can expect to pay. But if you have a sizeable deposit, many lenders won't load the interest rate significantly.

No track record of borrowing

If you live at home with your parents and have never had a credit card or personal loan, you may think you'd make a great mortgage customer because you haven't got any debts. But lenders are looking for people who can repay debts, such as credit card payments, loan repayments, or rent to their landlord. If you can't demonstrate this, you'll struggle to get a mortgage.

If you've got a regular income, a sizeable deposit, and want to borrow a standard multiple – say four times income – you may be able to convince a lender that you're a good risk.

Chapter 12

Insurance: Ignore at Your Peril

In This Chapter

▶ Avoiding relying on the State for help with your mortgage if you lose your job

▶ Protecting your mortgage payments

▶ Covering your home and its contents

*T*he range of insurance policies available to cover your property, its contents, your mortgage repayments, and even your life, is so vast that finding the right one can be as complicated as finding a mortgage. With so many companies offering insurance – from mortgage lenders and traditional insurers to insurance brokers and even supermarkets these days – unearthing the cover you need can be daunting. But with a little research, you can sort your way through the insurance maze, and in this chapter, I show you how to find the right cover.

With plenty of other demands on your wallet, you may be tempted to scrimp on insurance if money is especially tight. Perhaps you intend to put off buying insurance for a few months until you have surplus cash available and time to research the market properly to find the most competitive policy. But putting it off can be false economy. Think what could happen if you don't get around to arranging cover before disaster strikes: You lose your job or get burgled. Ask yourself whether you could meet the mortgage payments while on the dole or fork out for a new television, stereo, and laptop that's been stolen. In this chapter, I look at how you can ensure that you have enough cover.

While being under-insured is foolish, it's possible to be over-insured as well. Having more cover than you need serves no purpose. Check whether you have any existing cover through your employer or whether you have life assurance already – through an endowment policy, for example (see Chapter 11 for more information on endowments). Making wise decisions about insurance is vital.

Avoiding the Temptation to Scrimp on Cover

While cutting costs by scrimping on insurance is tempting, it's false economy. 'Your home is at risk if you don't keep up the repayments on a mortgage or other loan secured on it' is an oft-quoted saying to remember. Many home-owners don't realise just how true these words are: The State does little to help if you can't afford your mortgage payments because you lose your job, for example. So taking out insurance to make sure that your mortgage is paid off is a very good idea; without it, you could end up losing your home.

On your own, son: Why you can't rely on the Government for help

According to research from the Association of British Insurers (ABI), one in five consumers believes they can rely on the Government to provide them with financial assistance to pay their mortgage each month if they are unable to work. However, this is not the case.

While the Government is keen to encourage us to become responsible homeowners, little help is available if you're sacked or can't work through illness and you can't afford your mortgage repayments. The Government scaled down its help with mortgage repayments in the mid-1990s and is now encouraging homeowners to take out mortgage payment protection insurance (MPPI) to protect themselves.

Although Jobseeker's Allowance is payable if you lose your job, under Department of Social Security rules, those people who buy a property after 1 October 1995 have to wait *nine* months before they receive help with their mortgage repayments. Even then, State support is capped and means-tested so you must be receiving Income Support or Jobseeker's Allowance to qualify, which means your savings mustn't exceed £8,000. And benefits only cover the first £100,000 of the loan anyway, so if you meet all the above conditions but have a bigger mortgage, you still have to meet the shortfall yourself.

Those who bought their property before 1 October 1995 get no help for the first two months of being out of work. They then receive 50 per cent of their mortgage repayments for the next 18 weeks and 100 per cent after that.

The only way to ensure your mortgage payments are met if you lose your job is to take out insurance. Mortgage payment protection insurance (MPPI) allows you to set the deferral period yourself so that you know after 30, 60, or 90 days, your mortgage repayments will be covered for a fixed period of time (usually up to a year) by which time you'll hopefully have found another job. See the section 'Protecting Your Mortgage Repayments' for details.

Knowing what to look for in an insurance policy

Given that the whole area of payment protection is an unregulated market and can be complicated and expensive, finding the right cover can be rather hit-and-miss if you don't know what you're doing. However, the ABI and Council of Mortgage Lenders (CML) have come up with some minimum standards, which the industry aims to adhere to. These include improved transparency and simplicity of policies so that you can understand the protection being offered and how insurance can benefit you.

These trade bodies also recommend that consumers help themselves by making sure that they know what they are getting into. Ask your insurer questions, such as what happens if you're self-employed or how long you have to wait before making a claim, before committing to a policy.

The CML and ABI have produced a free leaflet in consultation with the Government: *Take Cover for a Rainy Day*. This leaflet explains in detail how mortgage protection works, how to buy it, and how to make a claim. Log on to www.cml.org.uk or call the CML consumer line (020 7440 2255) for more details.

Protecting Your Mortgage Repayments: Your Insurance Options

There are several types of cover available, enabling you to pay your mortgage each month, receive a monthly sum to cover all your expenses, or get a lump sum to pay off your mortgage in the event of your dying before you've had a chance to pay it back.

If you buy any form of life cover, you have to reveal your full medical history and may even have to undergo a medical in some cases. While you may be tempted to conceal a history of diabetes or heart disease in the family in order to get lower premiums, such a move isn't wise. If you omit some information or blatantly lie, the policy will be invalid once you're found out. If your medical history or family problems are an issue, find another insurer.

Although it's tempting to be guided by price, particularly when money is tight, when it comes to protecting your mortgage payments you must ensure that you're guided by cover. Policies vary widely, so make sure that you're covered for what you think you are.

If money really is tight, some forms of insurance may be more essential for your particular circumstances than others. Below I detail the main features of each type of insurance available and assess how important it is that you take it out. In this section, I look at the following:

- ✔ Life insurance (also known as life assurance)
- ✔ Mortgage payment protection insurance (also known as accident, sickness, and unemployment cover)
- ✔ Critical illness cover
- ✔ Permanent health insurance (also known as income protection)

Life assurance

If you have a partner or children who won't be able to pay the mortgage if something happens to you, your first step is to take out life insurance (also known as assurance). If you die before the end of the mortgage term, your mortgage is paid off.

If you're single with no dependants, you can cross life assurance off your list of insurance to buy without a second thought. But if you plan to leave your property to someone in your will, you may want her to receive it mortgage-free: If so, take out life assurance.

There are two main forms of life insurance available; which one you take out depends on what sort of mortgage you have and how much cover you need. The two main types are:

- ✔ **Level term assurance:** The most basic and straightforward form of life cover available. You get an agreed amount of life cover, which is usually equal to the amount you borrowed, over a fixed period of time – usually the mortgage term. So if you die before paying off your mortgage, your dependants receive a lump sum to enable them to do this. This type of insurance is particularly attractive to those with interest-only mortgages (see Chapter 11 for more details) because the amount of capital you owe remains constant until the end of the mortgage term. The added attraction of level term cover is that monthly premiums are relatively low.

    Interest-only mortgages backed by an endowment policy already have life cover so you don't have to take out a separate policy. There is no point duplicating cover.

- ✔ **Decreasing term assurance:** With this type if insurance, the amount of cover decreases over the life of the policy roughly in line with how much capital you owe on the mortgage, rather than remaining the same as with level term assurance. For this reason, decreasing term assurance is ideal for those with repayment mortgages. If you die before the end of the mortgage term, a proportion of the sum originally assured is paid out, which should cover what's remaining on the mortgage.

Mortgage payment protection insurance (MPPI)

Also known as accident, sickness, and unemployment insurance (ASU), MPPI covers your mortgage payments for up to a year (in most cases) if you can't work due to an accident, sickness, or losing your job. If you're sacked for misconduct or resign, however, the policy doesn't pay out.

You don't have to take out all three elements. If your employer already covers you for accident or sickness, you need only take out the unemployment element. Check with your employer to find out what you're covered for. Doing so can reduce your premiums considerably.

Anything that reduces the premiums on MPPI is welcome because this cover isn't cheap – and the more dangerous or stressful your job, the higher the premiums are. MPPI tends to cost, on average, £6 per £100 of monthly benefit. So if your monthly payment is £600 and you pay the £6 per £100 charged on average, the monthly cost of MPPI will be £36. Premiums are assessed on a number of factors:

- ✔ Your occupation
- ✔ Your health
- ✔ Your deferment period (if you're entitled to sick pay or redundancy from your employer for three months, you may want to claim MPPI after that time)

To keep premiums down, you can usually opt for a deferment period of up to 90 days before you can claim. In this case, you need to have savings to cover at least three months' worth of mortgage repayments.

Shopping around and using a broker could result in much lower premiums. The comparison website, moneysupermarket.com for example has cover from as little as £10.08 a month to cover a £600 mortgage payment, from provider Helpupay.

The main disadvantage of MPPI is that most policies pay out only for a year, unlike income protection (see the section 'Permanent health insurance (PHI)' later), which pay out indefinitely until you're able to return to work. However, you may feel fairly confident that you will be able to find another job within a year, and if this is the case, the termination of benefits after a year shouldn't prove to be a problem.

A further restriction with MPPI is that it can only be written on an 'any occupation' basis, meaning that if you're unable to do your current job, it won't pay out if there is some other kind of work you can do, however menial. Income protection, on the other hand, offers the option of being written on an 'own occupation' basis, so if you can't do your job, the policy pays out.

Many mortgage lenders offer MPPI but the cover tends to be expensive and inflexible. If the insurance is tied to your mortgage, you lose it if you move and you'll also pay nearly twice as much as you'd pay if you got an insurance broker to search the market for you.

Look for a policy that is fully portable so you can take it with you if you change mortgage provider. And remember: It's cheaper to take out MPPI when you start your mortgage than delay it and take it out further down the line.

Critical illness cover (CIC)

CIC is designed to cover your mortgage payments if you can no longer afford them in the event that you become seriously ill and can no longer work; it doesn't pay out if you've been made redundant. A range of conditions is covered by CIC, including strokes, cancer, and heart attacks. Instead of a monthly payment direct to your mortgage lender (as with MPPI), you get a lump sum if you're diagnosed as having a condition covered by CIC.

Be careful to check the number of conditions covered, which varies widely between insurers: The Halifax covers 25, while Bupa covers 37. As a general rule, a policy covering at least 25 conditions should be adequate. Check what conditions are excluded. Many insurers don't offer cover in the event of your contracting AIDs, for example.

CIC also tends to be more expensive than life cover as you're more likely to develop a specified condition during your mortgage term than you are to die. But the good news is that it can be written on an 'any occupation' or 'own occupation' basis, so check the terms and conditions carefully before taking out cover to see what you're signing up for. This is particularly true if you're buying CIC from your mortgage lender, many of which only write this type of insurance on an 'any occupation' basis.

Permanent health insurance (PHI)

Also known as income protection, PHI provides an income for people unable to work due to ill health. Instead of specifically covering your mortgage repayments, PHI pays out a proportion of your gross income – usually 50 to 65 per cent – until retirement. This can, of course, be used to cover your mortgage repayments if necessary.

As the policyholder, you can decide how long to wait before the policy pays out; you can defer this income from one month to two years after you become ill and cannot work. The shorter the deferral period, the higher your monthly premium, so try to strike a balance between affordable premiums and a deferral period you can comfortably cope with.

You can also choose whether benefits are payable when you're unable to do your regular job or any job. There are exclusions to what is covered by income protection. Not being able to work through pregnancy or childbirth, alcohol-related illnesses, or AIDs don't trigger a payout.

Some insurers charge women up to 50 per cent higher premiums than men for PHI because statistically they are more likely to claim on their policy. However, not all insurers do this, so if you're female, shop around to find an insurer who doesn't.

Flood, Fire, and Theft: Covering All Eventualities

Nobody knows for sure what is around the corner, but insurance protects us from what could happen. As well as covering your mortgage repayments, it's wise to cover the property itself. Buildings insurance is unavoidable and lenders insist upon it before lending you the money to buy a property. Although home contents insurance is optional, it's also vital.

Buildings insurance

When it comes to your home, the only type of insurance that is compulsory is buildings insurance. Mortgage lenders won't let you have a mortgage in the first place if you don't have buildings cover. Buildings insurance covers your property (and anything you'd leave behind if you moved, such as a fitted kitchen or bathroom) if it is badly damaged by fire, suffers bad subsidence, or a tree falls on it. The insurer pays out the money for you to have the property rebuilt to its original state.

With buildings insurance, the property is covered for the cost of rebuilding – not the market value – in the event of it being completely destroyed. So, if the market value of your property is £300,000 but it would only cost £150,000 to rebuild it to the same standard, ensure that you have buildings cover for £150,000. While there's little point in being over-insured, you need to make sure that you've got enough cover. The cost of rebuilding a property will rise over the years, so review your policy on an annual basis and increase your cover as necessary. If you're under-insured and have to make a claim, your insurer will not pay the full amount of the claim, which could mean you have to find the shortfall out of your own savings. And because rebuilding work can run into thousands of pounds, you may not have enough cash lying around to cover it.

The valuation commissioned by the mortgage lender (see Chapter 8 for more details) will include an amount for the cost of rebuilding the property, which you can use for building insurance purposes. However, if your lender is difficult and refuses to disclose this figure (it's under no obligation to do so), you can find ways round this. If you commissioned a homebuyer's report or full building survey (see Chapter 9 for more details), the surveyor should calculate the rebuild cost of the property. Even if you didn't opt for a fuller survey, most insurers supply quotes on the basis of information you provide as to the size and age of the property. You can even have a go at it yourself. Use the calculator available on the ABI's Web site. Go to www.abi.org.uk for more information.

If you buy the freehold of a property rather than the leasehold, you own the building and the land it stands on (and don't have a landlord). As the freeholder, you're responsible for arranging the buildings insurance. But if you're a leaseholder and pay annual rent and service charge to the freeholder, he is responsible for arranging the buildings insurance. The money you pay in service charge covers the insurance premiums.

If you own the freehold of your property, remember that many lenders try to persuade you to take out their own buildings cover, partly to reassure themselves that you have actually bought insurance but also because it's a lucrative sideline for them. But before you accept your lender's buildings cover, shop around. You can almost certainly get a better deal if you buy cover from a broker.

Some mortgage lenders charge borrowers a fee, usually around £25, if they don't take their buildings cover. Lenders claim that this fee enables them to check that you've taken out the insurance you say you have. Even if you do have to pay this, you will usually still come out ahead because you're likely to find more competitively priced cover elsewhere.

Home contents insurance

While buildings insurance is compulsory, home contents insurance – which covers any belongings within the property, such as furniture and clothing – isn't. But while many people cut corners and don't take out home contents insurance, if you're burgled or find your belongings damaged or destroyed by flood or fire, replacing them can be an expensive business. Better to be safe than sorry – take out home contents insurance.

Why does it always rain on me?

Heavy rainfall and flooding is a big problem for many homeowners. The floods of the summer of 2007 cost the insurance industry in excess of £3 billion pounds. Many of these homeowners may have trouble getting buildings and home contents insurance in future.

The ABI has agreed that its members will continue to cover homes on flood plains – low-lying areas at risk of flooding – as long as the Government commits sufficient money to new and improved flood defences. But while your insurer is obliged to carry on covering you, shopping around for another policy when it comes to renewing your insurance isn't likely to be easy. And because of the increased risk, you'll face considerably higher premiums than homeowners living in properties not at risk of flooding.

The insurance industry has every right to be concerned. More than two million homes are at risk from coastal or inland flooding (10 per cent of total homes in the UK). Around 400,000 homes are at very high risk of flooding (greater than 1-in-75 chance).

You can save yourself a lot of heartache and money by not buying a property on a flood plain in the first place. A detailed survey should unearth such a problem, but you can also do some research yourself and can check your prospective property's proximity to a flood plain by looking it up on the Environment Agency's Web site (`www.environment-agency.gov.uk`).

You can find two types of contents cover:

- ✔ **New-for-old policy:** Most homeowners opt for this type of cover because the insurer replaces the item you're claiming for. If your TV is stolen, for example, the insurer will provide you with a brand new replacement.

- ✔ **Cash policy:** With this type of policy, your insurer simply pays you the amount of money it costs to replace the item and you have to shop for the replacement yourself.

Whether you go with a new-for-old policy or cash, make sure that the amount insured is the cost of replacing all the items in your property – you don't want to be over- or under-insured.

Instead of guessing how much replacing all your possessions would cost, take a pen and paper and do an inventory. Walk from room to room, jotting down the items and likely replacement costs. Don't forget the clothes and shoes in your wardrobe, your CDs and DVDs, your jewellery, and so on. It is also worth keeping receipts for your purchases, as you can use these as evidence to back your claim in case of burglary. And if you have a video camera, I suggest filming your belongings and storing the tape – along with the written inventory – away from your property, in a safety deposit bank at the bank, for example, in case of fire.

Many mortgage lenders also sell home contents insurance and some even offer six months free buildings and home contents cover as a sweetener when you take out your mortgage. But as with buildings insurance, shop around to ensure that you have a competitive deal and are getting enough cover. When you shop for insurance, keep these points in mind:

✔ **If you have expensive pieces of jewellery or art, you may have to get these items insured separately.** Similarly, your insurer is likely to attach an extra premium for insuring any valuables you take away from the property on a regular basis, such as a laptop. Check with your insurer to be sure.

✔ **You may be able to lower your premiums if you beef up the security on your property.** Usually this requires installing a British Standard BS 3261 five-lever mortice lock on all external doors and window locks. Insurers also look upon a burglar alarm favourably as long as it's BS 6799 approved. Other ways to lower premiums include

- **Joining your local Neighbourhood Watch scheme.** A Neighbourhood Watch is a group of concerned neighbours who work together with the police to reduce crime in the immediate area.

- **Working from home.** When you work at home, you cut down on the chance of burglary during the day. If you tell your insurer, you may get reduced premiums.

✔ **If you live in an area your insurer considers to be high risk, finding cover may be more difficult.** Some insurers may refuse point blank to insure you; others may charge you a higher premium. If this is the case, shopping around is more important than ever.

While a freeholder is responsible for arranging buildings cover for the leaseholders at his property, she isn't responsible for providing home contents insurance. If you're a leaseholder, you have to arrange your own home contents cover.

Determining the right excess

The *excess* is a sum of money you must pay to the insurer when you make a claim on your policy. For example, if your policy has a £100 excess and you make a claim for £500, you will have to pay the first £100 yourself. The excess varies and you can usually increase it if you want to reduce the cost of your insurance premiums: The higher the excess, the lower your premiums.

While you may be tempted to opt for an excess of a couple of hundred of pounds in order to bring down your premiums, think carefully before you do. First, if something were to happen to your property, could you afford the excess amount? Make sure that the amount of the excess on your policy is a sum you're personally comfortable with. Shop around for another insurer if the one you have chosen has a very high excess.

Say that you have to replace your lounge carpet after a flood. Before you make a claim, evaluate whether doing so is wise, based on the amount of your excess and the value of the lost item. If the cost of the carpet is only £280, and your excess is £250, it's probably not worth your while to make a claim on your insurance policy. In this situation, you'll get the £30 to replace your carpet and probably higher insurance premiums as a result of making a claim on your policy.

Knowing Where to Buy Insurance

When you purchase insurance, whether it's life cover, mortgage payment protection, or buildings and home contents cover, you can go to several places. Mortgage lenders, insurance brokers, insurance companies, and supermarkets all offer different forms of insurance. Of course, some sources are better than others.

Mortgage lenders

Buying insurance from your mortgage lender may be the most convenient and hassle free way to buy cover, but it isn't the cheapest way of going about it. And if your employment situation or property is anything other than standard, you may be refused cover from your mortgage lender anyway.

Some lenders charge you a penalty (usually a £25 fee) for buying your insurance elsewhere. In most cases, it is worth swallowing the charge and shopping around, using an insurance broker, rather than accepting the lender's cover. Very rarely is the lender's cover the most competitive. Some insurers, such as Direct Line, pay this charge for you if you take out one of their policies.

Insurance brokers

A broker is the best source of insurance because he has access to a wide range of policies offered by many insurance companies. All you need to make is one call or do one Internet search to come up with the most competitive deal. And because you don't pay a fee for this (the broker earns commission from the insurer for passing on your business), drawing on their expertise won't cost you anything. Instead, you'll get the cheapest price because you simply pick the most competitive deal from the list you're provided with.

The Internet is also a good source of insurance brokers:

- For life cover, try broker Lifesearch (`www.lifesearch.co.uk`), which also has a calculator so you can work out exactly how much cover you need.

- Mortgage brokers Charcol and Savills Private Finance also offers life cover and buildings and contents insurance (`www.charcolonline.co.uk` or `www.spf.co.uk`).

- For MPPI (also called ASU for accident, sickness, and unemployment insurance) and CIC (critical illness cover), try independent financial adviser Chase de Vere's site (`www.moneyextra.co.uk`).

Mortgage brokers can also recommend an insurance broker if you don't know where to find one.

Make life easier for yourself and use an insurance broker. You've got enough to occupy your time without taking on unnecessary tasks.

Insurance companies

Buying your cover direct from an insurer is a better move than purchasing your lender's cover, but you still need to compare prices from several companies. Such a search can be time-consuming, particularly if you're buying several forms of insurance. A company that is strong in, say, MPPI may not have the best deal on home contents cover if it offers it at all.

Supermarkets

As the insurance market opens up, you can now pick up cheap home contents insurance from your local supermarket, along with a pint of milk. But while policies such as contents insurance are fairly straightforward, you won't find CIC for sale among the fruit and veg. And even if you're tempted by the cheap price of the home contents package, if your situation is not standard and doesn't fit the supermarket's risk profile, you may not be able to get cover.

Off-the-shelf policies tend to be one-size-fits-all. While this is fine if you don't have any valuables that need insuring separately, most people won't have such straightforward insurance requirements. You're probably better off with an experienced insurer who assesses customers on a case-by-case basis.

Chapter 13

When Money's Too Tight to Mention: Low Cost Routes to Homeownership

. . . .

In This Chapter

▶ Buying property with the help of a housing association

▶ Finding out whether you qualify for any of the schemes available

▶ Taking in a lodger – and using her rent to get a bigger mortgage

. . . .

*I*f you really can't afford to buy a property, no matter how many times you crunch the numbers, you may think you'll be stuck renting scruffy bedsits forever. But there are ways and means through which even those on low incomes hoping to buy in an area where property prices have escalated as a result of high demand can purchase their own home.

Housing associations offer a range of schemes designed to help those living or working in the local community get on the property ladder. These schemes are increasing in number and popularity because of the booming property market of the late 1990s/2000s that has priced many first-time buyers, particularly teachers, nurses, and policemen, out of the market.

In this chapter, I look at the various ways you can buy a property if money is tight. From buying with a housing association to arranging for a Rent-a-Room mortgage, in which the lender takes the potential income from a lodger into account when calculating how much you can borrow, there are ways of making your dream of owning a flat or house a reality.

Buying a Property with the Help of a Housing Association

Housing associations offer a variety of assistance for first-time buyers who want to get onto the property ladder. The main scheme is HomeBuy (its availability depends on where you live), of which there are three main types:

- ✔ **New Build HomeBuy** (formerly shared ownership)
- ✔ **Open Market HomeBuy** (where you part buy a property and get a Government loan for the rest)
- ✔ **Social HomeBuy** (where housing association and local authority tenants are helped to buy their existing home)

The Government has also launched the **First-Time Buyers Initiative.**

The following sections explain these schemes in more detail.

Introducing New Build HomeBuy

The New Build HomeBuy scheme enables social tenants, key workers and other priority first-time buyers to buy a share of a home. Here's how it works:

1. **You buy a share in a property – usually 50 per cent – from a housing association.**

   You don't have to buy a 50 per cent stake in the property: You can buy anything from 25 to 75 per cent, depending on what you can afford.

   Before you decide how big a share of the property to buy, calculate what your mortgage repayments will be and how much rent you'll have to pay to the housing association. Don't forget to budget for service charges, and remember that you have to pay the usual survey and valuation costs and legal fees as you would if you were buying without the help of a housing association.

2. **You have the option to *staircase* up to full ownership – by buying the remaining shares in the property – as, and when, you can afford to.**

   When you buy a further share in the property, you must have the property revalued by an independent valuer, recommended by the housing association.

3. **Each month, in addition to paying your mortgage, you also pay rent to the housing association on the portion of the property it owns and a service charge to cover the building's maintenance.**

   This rent is kept artificially low – around the same amount as the mortgage repayments on that amount would have been.

When you buy through the HomeBuy scheme, the housing association grants you a lease. Even though you don't buy the property outright initially you have the usual rights and responsibilities of an owner-occupier and are responsible for repairs and bills. There are restrictions, however, to the changes you can make. If you want to make alterations, you must ask the housing association for permission. Certain restrictions also apply if you sell the property; see 'Selling up' later in this chapter.

Here are a couple of other things to keep in mind about buying through New Build HomeBuy:

✔ If you're a key worker and then change your job, you have five years to buy the property outright or to sell it to someone of the housing association's choice or back to the housing association.

✔ You may be able to avoid stamp duty – completely legitimately, of course – by buying a shared ownership property. Stamp duty is payable on properties over £125,000 (see Chapter 9 for details). If your property costs less than £250,000, and you buy a 50 per cent share initially, it falls below the stamp duty threshold. If you staircase by 10 or 25 per cent each time, you will again fall below the threshold – unless the property shoots up in value. So you can eventually purchase the full 100 per cent without paying any stamp duty. On a £250,000 property, you can save £2,500 – the Chancellor of the Exchequer may not be pleased, but I imagine you'd be thrilled!

For more information on HomeBuy, contact your local housing association. To find a housing association registered in your area, you can also try the Housing Corporation, which funds English housing associations (www. housingcorp.gov.uk) or Scottish Homes (www.communitiesscotland. gov.uk).

Qualifying for New Build HomeBuy

If you're interested in New Build HomeBuy, contact your local housing association to find out whether it runs such a scheme. Generally speaking, you need to be a key worker, existing social housing tenant, or in priority housing need. You will have to complete an application form and the housing association will assess your application.

Many housing associations have long waiting lists, so if you're interested, put your name down straightaway. Waiting lists in popular areas are likely to be longer than in less popular ones, and the housing association should be able to give you an idea of how long you're likely to have to wait.

Housing associations can help you clamber onto the first rung of the property ladder

Housing associations are the main type of Registered Social Landlords (RSLs) – non-profit making bodies providing social housing for people who can't afford their own homes. These associations are run as businesses, but profits are ploughed back into the organisation to maintain existing homes and to buy new ones.

The role of the housing association is becoming increasingly important as people live longer and the number of people living on their own rises, creating a greater need for housing. And with house price inflation continuing to escalate, particularly in crowded urban areas, homeownership is becoming beyond the reach of an increasing number of people.

Finding a property

After the housing association decides that you qualify for New Build HomeBuy, you can start looking for a property to buy – the property has to be one owned by a housing association.

Housing associations own many properties, including flats and houses, so you should be able to find one you'd be happy to buy. Prices vary according to location, but expect to pay less than the 'going' rate – this is supposed to be affordable housing after all!

View properties as you would if you weren't buying through a housing association, taking care to ask similar questions. See Chapter 5 for more details on what to look out for when viewing a property.

Getting a New Build HomeBuy mortgage

Once you find a property you want to buy, you need to find a New Build HomeBuy mortgage. Not all lenders offer these because they are considered more risky than conventional borrowing because a third party – the housing association – is involved. And people who apply for these would otherwise struggle to buy a property.

Lenders are looking more favourably upon such schemes than in the past, however. As house prices have risen, the type of person using this scheme isn't necessarily a credit risk but someone who simply doesn't earn enough to buy in the area they live or work in.

Here are a couple of things to remember about shared ownership mortgages:

> ✔ If your housing association doesn't allow 100 per cent staircasing, it can be difficult to get a mortgage. Check before you commit yourself to anything.
>
> ✔ Before you settle on a mortgage, be sure to shop around for the best deal. Interest rates vary dramatically.

If you have a poor credit history, you may still be able to get a mortgage, although your options are more limited. Check with your housing association first. If it is happy for you to go ahead, shop around for a lender who feels the same way. A broker can point you in the right direction.

Selling up

Because housing associations exist to service the community and provide affordable housing, you can't simply stick your property on the market and sell to the highest bidder when it's time to move on. The maximum you can sell your property for is determined by an independent valuer appointed by the housing association. And in many cases the housing association also nominates prospective buyers. Before you buy, check whether this is the case.

You don't have to own 100 per cent of the property in order to sell up. If you own 50 per cent, say, you get 50 per cent of the sale price, with the housing association keeping the rest.

Understanding Open Market HomeBuy

Open Market HomeBuy helps eligible applicants buy a home on the open market with the help of a government equity loan.

The three types of equity loan are:

> ✔ You receive a government equity loan equal to 17.5 per cent of the purchase price. You're free to raise a mortgage for the remaining portion with any high-street bank or building society.
>
> ✔ You receive a 12.5 per cent equity loan from the housing association and a further 12.5 per cent equity loan from your mortgage lender. There is no interest to pay on the equity loan from the housing association – ever – or on the loan from the lender during the first five years. This loan is only offered by four lenders: Advantage, Halifax, and Nationwide and Yorkshire building societies.
>
> ✔ You receive a 32.5 per cent equity loan: 15 per cent from Yorkshire Building Society, plus 17.5 per cent from the Government. You take out the mortgage to go alongside the loan with the Yorkshire Building Society.

Open Market HomeBuy is primarily targeted at key workers and public sector tenants. But housing associations may also consider applications from other first-time buyers as long as their household income is no more than £60,000 per annum.

When you sell the property, the amount you pay back depends on how much your property has increased (or decreased!) in value during the time you've owned it and what percentage you borrowed in the first instance. If you opted for the 17.5 per cent equity loan from the Government, you pay 17.5 per cent of the market value of the property back to the Government. If, for example, you buy a £200,000 property with £35,000 from the Open Market HomeBuy scheme and sell in seven years' time, you must repay 17.5 per cent of the open market value at that time. If your property is then worth £250,000, you would repay £43,750. If you opted for the 12.5 per cent loan from the housing association and 12.5 per cent from the lender, you have to pay back a total of 25 per cent of any increase in property value.

If you're a key worker – such as a nurse, teacher, or in the police – and you're no longer employed in a key worker profession, or you move to an area not covered by the scheme, you will have to repay the government's equity loan. This is known as 'clawback' and you have two years in which to pay it back.

For more information on Homebuy in England, contact the Housing Corporation (www.housingcorp.gov.uk) or your local housing association. In Wales, take a look at the information on the Welsh Assembly Web site at http://wales.gov.uk/topics/housingandcommunity/housing/publications/homebuy?lang=en.

The application process

The first step is to fill out an application form to find out whether you qualify for the scheme. You can obtain a form from a registered social landlord operating the scheme in your area. However, money available is limited so even if your local council operates such a scheme, the waiting list is likely to be very long.

The housing association checks the information you give and may ask for more evidence of income and savings. If it is satisfied with your answers, you receive a letter confirming that you qualify. You also receive approval to look for a home up to a certain price limit, depending on the area you live in.

Finding a property

Unlike New Build HomeBuy, with Open Market HomeBuy you can buy any property in England (or Wales, if you're buying via the Welsh scheme) that is for sale on the open market and fit to live in – that is, it doesn't need extensive work. But there are restrictions:

✔ **The property should be close to your place of work.** Open Market Homebuy insists that the journey from the property to your usual place of work by car or public transport shouldn't take longer than 90 minutes.

✔ **If you want to add an extension to your property or carry out other improvements, you must get permission from the housing association first.**

Finding a mortgage

Once you've found a property and agreed on a price with the seller, you need to apply for a mortgage and commission a survey (if you decide to have one). You also need to appoint a solicitor to act on your behalf.

Don't enter any legal agreement to buy a property until the housing association gives its stamp of approval. After you receive mortgage approval, notify the housing association of the property's details; as long as it approves the property, the sale goes through in the same way as any other sale, apart from the fact that a proportion of the funds are coming from a source other than you.

Getting to Grips with the First Time Buyers' Initiative

The First-Time Buyers' Initiative (FTBI) is aimed at first-time buyers who can't afford to buy a home outright. Half of the homes available under the scheme are for key workers. Priority is also given to those in private rented or temporary accommodation. The scheme is available through English Partnerships, the national regeneration agency.

Under the scheme, buyers must purchase at least half of the property on a designated FTBI development with English Partnerships retaining the rest. There is no interest to pay on the percentage of the equity you don't own for the first three years. After this, you pay 1 per cent per annum. This will increase each year by a fixed percentage until it is a maximum of 3 per cent after five years in the property.

When you sell your home, you pay back the Government a share of the sale proceeds equal to the initial percentage contribution you received.

For more information, contact your local HomeBuy agent. Details of agents can be found on the Housing Corporation's Web site (www.housingcorp. gov.uk).

The Rent-a-Room Scheme

If you don't qualify for any financial help from a housing association, here's another way of getting help to pay your mortgage – rent out a room in your home. Under the Rent-a-Room scheme, you can earn £4,250 a year tax-free from letting a single room in your home to a lodger. Unfortunately, lenders won't take this income into account when calculating the mortgage you can have.

For more information on the tax implications of renting a room, go to www. direct.gov.uk.

If you buy a house under the Rent-a-Room scheme, keep these points in mind:

- ✔ If you can't let your spare room once you've bought your property, you will have to find the extra cash from somewhere to meet the mortgage repayments. Think about how you would manage without this extra income before committing yourself to such a mortgage.

- ✔ If you're renting out a room in your property, don't forget to notify your insurer or it could affect the validity of your policy in the event of a claim.

Part IV
Selling Your Home

'It can be rather interesting having
more than one estate agent.'

In this part . . .

Obtaining the best price you can for your home in the shortest possible time involves a lot of hard work on your part in getting your property ready for viewings and choosing the right estate agent. Or you may decide to take on the advertising, showing prospective buyers round, and negotiating the price yourself, without an agent.

In this part, I cover all these issues, so that you have the information you need to set you on the way to successfully sell your home.

Chapter 14

Deciding When It's the Right Time to Sell Your Home

*B*ecause property prices move up and down, timing is extremely important when you come to sell your home. If you put it up for sale when the market is quiet and prices are weak, you'll be lucky to find a buyer reasonably quickly who is also prepared to pay what you want. In a quiet market, it's more likely that finding a buyer will take ages and that you'll get less cash than you would have if you'd sold at a time when house prices were buoyant.

If you aren't desperate to move by a certain date and have the luxury of being able to time your sale to coincide with a booming housing market, chances are you'll get a better price for your home. In this chapter I show you how to pick the optimum time to sell.

Of course, not everyone can choose when to sell. The timing of your move may be out of your hands. Maybe you fall pregnant and need to move from your one-bed flat to a roomier home before the baby is born. Or maybe you have to relocate for work, want to move to the catchment area of a good school, or need to raise cash to get out of financial difficulties. In this chapter, I also look at how to get the best price for your property when you have no choice about when you sell.

Knowing When to Sell

Particularly if you've never sold a property before, you may not realise that there's a right time to sell your home. But there is. It's when you can get the best price for your home, in the shortest possible time. The problem is that often the optimum market conditions for selling property don't tie in with your personal circumstances. In other words, you aren't ready to sell at a time when the market is hot. When you think about selling your home, your aim is to ensure these coincide as much as possible so that you can move when you want and – crucially – get the price you want.

If you're not desperate to sell, you have a much greater chance of getting the price you want for your home. Not only can you reject the first offer you get, which may be lower than the asking price, but you also have plenty of time to get your home in tip-top condition for viewings – which is particularly important if your home requires lots of work.

When you sell your home, you have to pay off your outstanding mortgage, if you have one, and some deals demand you pay thousands of pounds in redemption penalties if you do this before a certain date. So before you sell, be sure to check with your mortgage lender to see whether your home loan includes a penalty for paying it off early. If so, and you can't postpone moving, it may be worth your while to rent out your property until you no longer incur a penalty for selling. See 'When It's Wise to Rent Out Rather Than Sell Up' at the end of this chapter for details.

Expanding rather than relocating

If you're selling because you need more space, keep in mind that you don't actually have to move to get the room you want. Why not expand the home you've got? Build an extension on the back or side of the house, convert the loft, or create a basement by digging underneath it. Extending your existing property can be cheaper than moving to a bigger house because you don't have to pay thousands of pounds in stamp duty. It's also usually a lot less hassle than packing everything up and moving – if you can stand builders coming and going while the work is completed and the inevitable dust.

If the idea sounds tempting, work out the cost of the expansion carefully beforehand; a surveyor or builder can help you do this. If the whole point of expanding is to save money,

make sure that the project won't end up costing more than the move would have.

Keep in mind, however, that not all property lends itself to an extension. If you own a one-bedroom flat in a purpose-built block, for example, you won't be able to build onto it. You may also need planning permission to extend your home if it's a listed property or the extension is particularly ambitious. Check with your local planning authority beforehand (see Chapter 8 for more details).

Before deciding what work you want to do, seek professional advice. Most people employ a builder to carry out renovations and extensions; you're also likely to need a surveyor or architect to draw up the plans. See Chapter 8 for details on how to find a surveyor, architect, or builder.

Many people move through necessity not choice, usually because they need something bigger. If you're getting married, expecting another baby, or making room for an elderly relative, you're probably facing a date by which you absolutely *must* move somewhere bigger. The problem is that you may be facing a depressed market and low prices. If more space is a must, you have some options: You may be able to expand your current property and not move at all (see the sidebar 'Expanding rather than relocating'), or you may be able to rent out your current home now and sell it when the market is more robust. See the later section 'When Renting Out is Wiser Than Selling Up' for information on this.

Recognising a seller's market

The best time to sell your home is in a *seller's market*, where the number of buyers outstrips the number of properties for sale. In a seller's market, buyers compete with each other over the available properties, which usually means your home sells quickly and you get more than the asking price. A seller's market is every seller's dream.

The problem with a seller's market is that you're probably also buying another property, so you end up competing with several buyers and may pay over the odds for it. The only way round this scenario is to sell your home when the market is buoyant and rent until prices fall a little.

Discovering whether the housing market is buoyant or not is easy because most homeowners are obsessed with discussing house prices. Just listen to the conversations around you. You can also look out for the monthly announcements from the Halifax, Nationwide, and quarterly ones from the Land Registry as to whether prices have risen or fallen. (This information tends to be widely reported in the press and on TV and radio.) Although the findings vary from index to index, they provide a broad idea of what direction property prices are moving in.

If property prices are rising, you may be tempted to delay putting your home on the market in case prices edge higher still. But doing so isn't always a good idea. Trying to time the market can backfire badly if it crashes before you have a chance to sell. Property prices can't – and don't – go up indefinitely. If property prices have already risen considerably, you probably have made a decent profit. Don't be greedy and hang on longer – particularly if putting the sale off is inconvenient.

Avoiding a buyer's market

What you really need to avoid is putting your home up for sale during a *buyer's market*. The opposite of a seller's market, a buyer's market is when more properties are for sale than there are buyers to buy them. If you try to sell at this time, you're likely to have difficulties finding a buyer. And chances are pretty slim that several potential buyers are going to compete to purchase your home – unless it's highly desirable or unusual. In addition, in a buyer's market, the buyer has more scope for haggling, so prices tend to fall; your bargaining power, as the seller, is severely diminished.

The advantage of moving house in a buyer's market is that you're probably buying as well, which means that you may get a better deal on your new home—offsetting the fact that you're also selling in a buyer's market.

To check whether the housing market favours buyers or not, take a look at the property 'for sale' adverts in your local paper and estate agent's window. If a large number of properties are taking weeks or months to sell, or – worse still – are reduced in price, it's not such a good time to think about selling.

If other homeowners are struggling to sell, there's a good chance you'll struggle too unless you have an unusual or desirable home or are prepared to accept a lot less than the property is worth – never a good idea. Even if you're really desperate and must move, alternatives to selling your home in a buyer's market are available. You could, for example, rent out your home until the market picks up.

Other times to sell – or not

There really is a best time of year to sell your home – and that's springtime. Estate agents are usually rushed off their feet as buyers opt for a fresh start in another home. February to May is the busiest time of year for property purchases. And if your property is on the market at this time, you're more likely to find a buyer relatively quickly who is also prepared to pay what you want than if you put it on the market in the height of summer when everyone is on holiday.

If you have a say over when you sell your home, choose the spring. Start getting your home ready the previous autumn, attending to all those little jobs you never got round to before. If you're really organised, you could take some photos of your home in the summer – before putting it up for sale the following spring. A garden in full bloom looks far more attractive than lots of bare wintry branches.

Autumn is also a good time to sell your home – although not as good as the spring. But with people returning from their holidays and wanting to move before Christmas, the market usually picks up a bit at this time.

Other times, however, aren't good for selling your home. As the preceding section explains, if you do have a say in when you sell, steer clear of a buyer's market. Following are other times to avoid selling your home:

- **Falling prices:** If prices are moving downwards, you may be tempted to sell before they fall any further. But buyers are probably holding off until they feel the bottom has been reached (that is, prices have no further to fall), so you may struggle to sell your home anyway. Avoid the market completely until prices have stabilised.

- **The height of summer or depths of winter:** As a rule, buyers aren't interested in moving during these times, so fewer of them are out there. And this means fewer prospective buyers for your property.

  Summer can be very quiet for the property market because most people disappear on holiday. And once they return, they're too busy paying off their credit card bills and won't have any money to spare. Christmas and New Year is also a bad time to try and sell your home: Again, owing to the combination of holiday and lack of cash. If you absolutely have to sell at Christmas, remember to tone down the decorations. An inflatable 10-foot snowman on the front lawn might be your idea of heaven but potential buyers will see it as a huge distraction – and it might prevent them from seriously considering your home.

- **Being unprepared.** If your home isn't ready to sell – sparkling clean, free of clutter, and in good repair – you won't get the best price for it. See to this work before putting your home on the market.

Figuring Out the Cost of Selling

Buying a home is an expensive business. What many people forget is that selling is also expensive. You must budget for several fees and charges when you decide whether selling is worth your while:

- Repairs, cleaning, and painting and decorating your home before putting it on the market
- A Home Information Pack (HIP) if you have three or more bedrooms
- Solicitor's fees
- Estate agent's commission
- Removal costs

You can find more information on these expenses in the sections that follow. Table 14-1 shows how these expenses work out pound-wise if you sell your home for £200,000. Note that this list doesn't take into account the cost of painting, decorating, or repairs so you may have to do to get your home ready.

Table 14-1	Typical Cost of Selling a £200,000 Property
Item	*Cost*
Home Information Pack (HIP)	£400
Solicitor's fees:	£500
VAT on solicitor's fees:	£87.50
Estate agent's commission (2 per cent):	£4,000
VAT on agent's commission:	£700
Removal costs:	£400
TOTAL COST OF SELLING	£6,087.50

Adding the cost of buying into the equation

As well as the legal and estate agent's fees you must pay when you sell a home, you're likely to be buying another home, which means you have to cover all the costs involved in buying too (things like stamp duty, fees for local authority searches and the Land Registry fee, valuation and survey expenses, the solicitor's conveyancing fee, and more).

Say you've sold your house for £200,000. Your expenses probably don't stop there. Presumably, you're buying another house to move into. If the other house costs £280,000, you assume other expenses as well, this time as the buyer. To buy a £280,000 home, for example, you would add the following expenses to what you've already paid to sell your home (refer to Table 14-1):

Item	*Cost*
Stamp duty (3 per cent of £280,000)	£8,400
Solicitor's fees	£800
VAT on solicitor's fees	£140
Total cost of buying:	**£9,340**

If you add the cost of selling (£6,087.50 in the example; refer to Table 14-1) to the cost of buying (£9,340 in the example), you could pay over £15,000 just to move to a slightly bigger property. This amount doesn't include the difference in purchase price – £80,000. In other words, you end up spending just under £100,000 to move. Before you take this leap, weigh up whether it's worth the cost, the time, and the hassle.

Preparing your home for sale

The amount you spend on decorating your home, undertaking repairs, and cleaning depends on its current state. If you're a sensible homeowner, you probably deal with repairs as and when required. Likewise, if you decorate your home every five years or so, your home's décor should be in a fairly reasonable state of repair. But if this isn't the case, you're going to have to get out the paintbrushes. Here are some of the repair and maintenance chores you may have to undertake:

- **Clean your house thoroughly:** Cleaning is cheap and makes a real difference. Ensure your home is spotless and then critically assess whether you need to replace anything before splashing out on new wallpaper and a bathroom suite.

- **Paint to spruce things up:** Usually you can get away with a fresh lick of paint to tired-looking cupboards, walls, and the front door (see Chapter 15).

- **Make necessary repairs:** Deal with repairs that are essential to selling your home. If you have a bad case of damp and aren't prepared to fix it, expect to knock a few thousand pounds off the asking price, because the buyer will have to rectify the problem when she moves in.

 Before undertaking any work, assess what really needs to be done. There's no point replacing the bathroom suite or kitchen cabinets if you don't have to because such changes are expensive and time-consuming – a real consideration if you don't have the time to do it anyway.

Solicitor's fees

Although the seller doesn't pay as much in legal fees as the buyer, your solicitor still has quite a bit of work to do on your behalf (see Chapter 19 if you're selling a property in England, Wales, and Northern Ireland; see Chapter 21 if you're selling in Scotland). Sellers are usually charged a fee according to the value of their property and the work involved: The more expensive your home, the more you pay. If you sell a property for around £200,000, for example, you can expect to pay £500 or so in legal fees. And don't forget that you have to pay VAT at 17.5 per cent on this amount (in this example, the VAT works out to be £87.50).

The buyer pays for disbursements or searches and the Land Registry fee only if the property has less than three bedrooms (see Chapter 19 if you're selling in England, Wales, and Northern Ireland; see Chapter 20 if you're selling in Scotland). Otherwise, the seller has to provide a Home Information Pack (HIP). (See Chapter 16 for more information on HIPs, otherwise known as sellers' packs.)

If you can, use the same solicitor to handle your sale and purchase – it usually works out cheaper. It's also far easier to chase one person over hold-ups than two.

Estate agent's commission

Using an agent to sell your home costs from 2 to 3 per cent of the sale price, depending on what sort of contract you have. If you opt for sole agency, expect to pay around 2 per cent of the purchase price in commission, payable on completion. If you sell your home for £200,000, for example, you have to pay £4,000 to the agent. Don't forget that you will have to pay VAT (17.5 per cent) on top of the agent's commission. In this example, then, you could end up paying an extra £700.

Whatever the fee, get it in writing beforehand and make sure it includes advertising costs. (See Chapter 16 for more details on agents and costs). Alternatively, if you want to save a few thousand pounds you can sell your home privately; Chapter 17 has the details.

HIPs

The cost of the Home Information Pack (HIP) is a relatively new one for sellers to factor in. You can obtain a HIP from your estate agent or a specialist HIP provider – some charge a flat fee of £295 plus VAT so shop around to keep costs down. (Go to Chapter 16 for more on what's included in a HIP.)

Removal costs

One of the worst bits of buying a new home is the actual move itself. You can do the work yourself, but it's exhausting, time-consuming, and a hassle. At the very best, you may smash a favourite vase; at worst, you could put your back out and have to take weeks off work. And because you'll probably have to hire a van anyway, why not just get the professionals to do it all?

The best way to pick a removals firm is if a friend or relative recommends one. Otherwise, contact these moving associations:

- ✔ **The British Association of Removers (BAR),** the trade association of the removals industry. BAR can provide details of three members in your area. Call 01923 699480 or go to the BAR Web site at www.bar.co.uk.

- ✔ **The National Guild of Removers and Storers.** This association has details of members in your area. Call 01494 792279 or go to www.ngrs.org.uk.

If you hire a removal firm, keep these points in mind:

✓ **Prices vary across the country, so get a couple of estimates before hiring a firm;** expect someone to come round to see what needs moving before you get an estimate.

According to the Woolwich House Moving Survey, the average cost of removals from a three-bedroom semi-detached house in England and Wales is £379. Local moves are cheaper than cross-country moves. Expect to pay an extra £200 to move from London to Manchester, for example.

✓ **Check the terms and conditions of the contract carefully.** If you're quoted an hourly charge rather than a set fee, check what hours the movers work and how long they expect the move to take. The cost of packing your stuff is usually included; if not, expect to pay around £10 an hour for this service.

✓ **You can reduce costs by packing yourself.** Keep in mind, however, that the removal firm's insurance won't cover any breakages that occur during transport.

If you do the moving yourself, check your insurance. Most home contents policies will cover your belongings while they're in transit but verify this before you move.

When Renting Out Is Wiser Than Selling Up

If you're relocating for work, you may need to sell your property in order to buy another one near your new place of employment. But if market conditions aren't great, you may be reluctant to sell at that particular time (refer to the earlier section 'Avoiding a buyer's market' for information on selling during a slow market). In such instances, you may want to consider renting out your home until the market picks up. And until it does, you rent somewhere handy for work. Then when prices do improve, you can sell your home and think about buying another one (perhaps continuing to rent until prices fall again so you get more for your money).

Of course, if you can afford it, you could buy another property near your place of work (taking advantage of the fact that it is a buyer's market) and rent out your existing property. The rent should cover the mortgage. Then, when house prices rise again, you could finally sell up.

If you're thinking of renting out your property, you must notify your mortgage lender because you're changing the conditions of the original deal you agreed with the lender. Also be sure to inform your insurer; otherwise, your cover may be invalid.

Check out my book *Renting Out Your Property For Dummies* (Wiley) for more information on becoming a landlord.

Chapter 15

Creating the Right First Impression

· ·

In This Chapter

▶ Cleaning and de-cluttering your property

▶ Deciding what needs repairing or replacing

▶ Financing your improvements

· ·

*F*irst impressions count, particularly when you're selling your home. You want prospective buyers to be in no doubt that your home is the one for them – and you can't do that with a bad first impression.

Creating a good impression can take time, effort, and money. And knowing what you need to do to make your property attractive can be difficult. You're so used to living there that you may not notice your home's defects. But although you may be oblivious to a crack in the hall ceiling, chipped skirting boards, or the lingering smell of the dog, you can bet your bottom dollar that prospective buyers won't be. And such factors usually register as a black mark against a property.

The better your house looks and the more care you take presenting it, the more likely you're to get the price you want – and quickly. Take time and effort to clean thoroughly, remove clutter and questionable furnishings, and give your home a fresh lick of paint.

In this chapter, I discuss how you can make it easy for prospective buyers to see the potential of your property – and envisage themselves living there.

Ensuring that Your Property Is Irresistible

As soon as you decide to sell your home, you need to get it up to scratch. An estate agent will probably handle viewings and negotiate the price but you have to give him something to work with – a property in tip-top condition –

clean, tidy, and welcoming. How much work is required depends on the condition you normally keep your home in. Tackle the necessary tasks in the following order:

1. General cleaning

2. Ditching the clutter

3. Making repairs and improvements

4. Painting and wallpapering

5. Cleaning carpets and floors

6. Final cleaning

General cleaning

A good spring clean not only makes your property look better, it also gives you the opportunity to assess whether further work is needed. Only by scrubbing the dirt off the skirting boards, for example, can you assess whether they need re-painting or simply cleaning.

Clean thoroughly so that everything is left gleaming. Anything still dull, worn, or tarnished needs replacing. Pay special attention to the following:

- **The windows and glass panels in doors:** Hire a window cleaner to do the outside of the property and tackle the inside yourself. Clean windows let in more natural light and create a good impression. Remember that on a sunny day, dirty windows are even more obvious. While you're washing windows, note any cracked panes that need replacing. Check wooden frames too. Do they need repainting or replacing?

- **Windowsills, especially those at the front of the house:** Because they are visible from the street, they are one of the first things the prospective buyer sees. A cluttered windowsill gives an untidy impression, so make sure that yours are clear. The one thing you can get away with on a windowsill is a nice big bunch of freshly-cut flowers.

- **Curtains and blinds:** Clean, iron, and re-hang curtains and nets. Use a mild detergent diluted with water to wipe blinds clean.

- **Floors:** Scrub and clean all floors. See the section 'Cleaning the carpets and floors' later for details on what to look for.

- **Light fittings and lampshades:** These can be easy to forget, so give them a good wipe down.

- **The bathroom:** Make sure that baths, toilets, sinks, or showers are sparkling clean. Thoroughly disinfect the toilet with bleach, and make sure all drains are unblocked and not omitting foul odours. Make sure tiles are clean (re-grout them where necessary).

✔ **The kitchen:** The cooker and oven should be spotless – a task that's likely to require a lot of elbow grease. Don't forget to scrub the floor, and clean out the fridge and defrost the freezer just in case prospective buyers take a look in there.

Ditching the clutter

A successful seller is someone who sees her home through the eye of a buyer. One person's idea of vital furnishings and ornaments is another's idea of clutter.

If prospective buyers can't imagine their belongings – and themselves – in your highly individualistic house, they won't buy it. Tone down personal effects – one photo of the kids is enough. Too much clutter makes your home feel small so tidy away as many of your personal belongings as you can. Keep surfaces clear. If you have a lot of furniture, store some of it until you sell your home.

Making repairs and improvements

Fix anything that's broken. If you're lucky, most of the repairs will be minor – fixing broken cupboard doors, replacing broken tiles in the bathroom, or re-grouting. Some properties may require fairly major work, such as dealing with a damp patch on the bedroom ceiling. If you have any unfinished do-it-yourself projects, complete these – nothing's worse than a property that looks like a building site.

If carpets are worn or threadbare, think about replacing them as this will create a much better impression. But don't get too carried away: Recarpeting the house from top to bottom is unnecessary and expensive. Likewise, don't buy the priciest carpet available because you're unlikely to recoup the cost. Opt for medium quality instead.

If you're unsure about replacing the bathroom or kitchen, ask the agent for advice before spending a lot of money. She will have a good idea what improvements appeal to buyers and which don't. This will prevent you from spending money unnecessarily.

Painting

After you've completed the necessary repairs, the property is ready for a lick of paint. Depending on when you last painted and your preference when it comes to colour, you'll either be facing a lot of work or a little.

You need to think about two things when you paint – your choice of colours and the quality of the work. Both can have an impact on how quickly you sell your property. Paint walls in light, neutral colours. If you have garish wallpaper or dark-coloured walls, consider painting over them.

Do the job right. You don't want a botched paint job, with splashes of paint on floorboards or on skirting boards. If you can't afford to get in the professionals, ensure that you prepare the walls carefully first. Remove nails and screws and fill any holes with plaster filler. Clean the walls so they are free of dirt before you begin. And don't forget dust sheets to cover floors and furniture.

Don't forget to paint doors, doorframes, skirting boards, window frames, and ceilings (in white!) or they will look dirty next to your bright, newly painted walls. And don't forget to remove splattered paint from the floor, windows, woodwork, and cabinets, using white spirit as necessary.

Final cleaning

Once you've done the general cleaning, made any necessary repairs and painted where required, you're ready to re-clean everything. Although another spring clean may be the last thing you feel like doing, cleanliness is next to godliness, and you can't beat a sparkling clean, fresh-smelling house.

As you do your final clean, keep these points in mind:

- ✔ **If your kitchen and bathrooms are dirty or grimy, buyers wonder about the state of the rest of the property.** Nobody wants to spend the first day in their new home scrubbing the previous owner's grime off the bath. See 'General cleaning' for suggestions on cleaning bathrooms.

    Clear the crumbs and clutter from work surfaces in your kitchen, but don't leave them so bare that they look clinical. A couple of strategically placed, expensive-looking appliances (like a stainless steel kettle or a blender) and a pretty fruit bowl kept topped up create interest and give a bit of a lived-in feel.

- ✔ **Buyers really do open the kitchen cupboards and the fridge door.** Give your appliances a thorough clean.

- ✔ **Smell is important.** Prospective buyers will be put off if your house smells bad, even if it is spotless. So while you're cleaning the property, pay special attention to whiffs. Open windows to get rid of cigarette smoke and use natural-smelling air fresheners: Not ones with a nasty artificial smell.

Once you've done the final cleaning, your job is not finished because you still have to keep your house this clean all the while it's for sale. This can be a hassle if it's on the market for ages, or you're not fastidiously tidy. But you must ensure that your property is ready for viewings at short notice. Although estate agents try to give you a call to warn you that they're bringing a buyer round, this call may come only a half-an-hour before they arrive.

Heavenly scents

Do you need to go as far as baking your own bread to encourage buyers to put in an offer? It certainly smells delicious, but if scores of prospective buyers are traipsing round at all hours of the day, evening, and weekends, you probably don't have time to crank up the oven and get up to your elbows in dough. And in summer, an oven going at full blast is simply going to make prospective buyers think you're mad.

So what about freshly brewed coffee? It smells great and is easier to make than fresh bread. But the smell can be overpowering and isn't to everyone's tastes. Also be wary of using air-fresheners, because these usually smell very artificial and can be a bit overpowering.

Instead, I suggest you dot as many freshly cut flowers as you can afford around the house. Very fragrant flowers such as freesias smell wonderful and have the added benefit of brightening up a room and giving it a fresh appearance. If you prefer, choose flowers in a single colour that ties in with the colour scheme of the room. You can't go wrong with flowers because they add a touch of class to your decor.

Just make sure they're fresh – you don't want dead flowers dropping all over the carpet. Dead flowers are far worse than no flowers at all and create a poor impression because it looks like you simply don't care.

Salesman's Tour Part 1: Assessing the Impression Created by Each Room

As well as general cleaning and repairs, carefully assess each room to ensure that it has a clearly defined purpose. Buyers can be easily confused by a bedroom that doubles as a gym, or a dining room that's used as a bedroom. Make sure that each room serves its original purpose. If you've converted the dining-room into a fourth bedroom, remove the bed, wardrobe, and other clutter and bring in a table and chairs to turn it back into a dining-room, which is a much bigger selling point than a downstairs bedroom.

As you tour your property, jot down work that you need to do to ensure that everything is as it should be in that type of room. As you assess each room, bear in mind your target audience and think about how you can appeal to them. If your property is a modern apartment likely to appeal to young professionals, for example, is your furniture and décor in keeping with that? If your furniture looks out of place, think about putting it into storage and hiring items more in keeping with the surroundings and the demands of your target market.

Here's a quick list to help you make your property appear at its best:

✔ **The hallway:** The hallway is the first room that the prospective buyer sees, so it's vital that the hallway creates the right impression. Remove bikes and junk which could trip prospective buyers up and simply look untidy. Hide the coats you don't use on a day-to-day basis and put your shoes away, particularly if you're an Imelda Marcos wannabe. If you paint one room, make it the hallway as it's the first room the buyer sees.

✔ **Kitchen:** Paint tired-looking cupboards in light, neutral colours and replace door handles with modern, expensive-looking ones. Ensure that cupboards and doors fit well and aren't hanging off their hinges. Replace grubby work surfaces and broken or missing tiles. Worn-out flooring can also be replaced relatively inexpensively with some bright lino.

✔ **Sitting-room:** Check that your furniture looks right. If you've got chintz sofas in an open-plan warehouse space, they will appear out of place. If your furniture is old or tatty, hire more appropriate sofas, tables, and so on while you're selling your home. And remember that soft lighting can make a big difference. Opt for lamps rather than a harsh bulb without a lampshade in the middle of the room.

✔ **Dining-room:** A real selling point, show it off to its best advantage if you have one. Lay the table with your best dinner service and cutlery and use fresh flowers as an inviting centrepiece.

✔ **Bathroom:** Get rid of carpet unless it is brand new. Lino looks better, is more hygienic and is cheaper than tiling the floor. Think about installing a shower attachment if there isn't one as most buyers expect one. Expect to pay around £100 for a basic power shower from a DIY store. Invest in fluffy white towels, which look great – and you can take them with you when you move. Buy a new shower curtain and hide the laundry.

Most buyers want a white bathroom suite and won't accept a coloured one. If you have a coloured suite, consider replacing it with a new white, modern suite. A standard white suite, including basin, bath and toilet starts at around £300, which won't break the bank and could result in a quicker sale.

✔ **Bedrooms:** Masculine bedrooms are a big turn-off for women buyers so try to make them more inviting. Make the beds. Ensure bedding is clean, ironed, matching, and of good quality. Hide your mess away but ensure that it doesn't fall out of the wardrobe if a prospective buyer opens a door. And opt for soft lighting.

Salesman's Tour Part II: Getting the Outside Ready

The exterior of the property creates the first impression in the mind of the prospective buyer. And a messy exterior doesn't do justice to a beautiful interior. Here, I explain what you need to pay attention to when preparing the *outside* of your home for viewings.

Kerb appeal

Don't underestimate the importance of *kerb appeal* – the appearance of the property from the street. To enhance this, do the following:

- ✔ Make sure that the gate opens easily and closes properly (if you have one). If it's hanging off its hinges the buyer will wonder whether the rest of the house is in a similar state. Give it a fresh lick of paint as well and replace any broken panels.

- ✔ If you have a fence or wall, ensure that it is in good repair and isn't leaning to one side. Give it a fresh lick of paint if necessary.

- ✔ Trim hedges and prune trees. Get rid of weeds, clear the lawn of rubbish, and cut the grass. You might favour the wild look with waist-high grass, but prospective buyers probably won't share your taste.

- ✔ If you have a driveway, check that no weeds are poking up through the gravel or tarmac.

- ✔ Give the garage door a lick of paint, if necessary.

- ✔ Spruce up the front door and the area around it. Paint it, if necessary, and polish the knocker, letterbox, and number. If you have a doorbell, test that it's working. You don't want to leave prospective buyers standing on the doorstep pressing a broken buzzer in vain.

A new door mat is a nice touch: It encourages people to wipe their feet and gives the impression that you care about your home. Steer clear of tacky slogans – you can't beat a *plain* mat.

Window boxes full of colourful flowers are also welcoming, as are well-maintained hanging baskets. Create some balance by putting matching boxes or baskets either side of the front door. (And don't forget to take them with you when you move!)

✔ If there's a caravan on your drive or a clapped out old banger, remove them. Some people have an aversion to caravans, and most people have a dislike of junk. They also detract attention from the property and in the case of the caravan, may make it difficult for the buyer to actually see the house properly. Store these in the garage or away from the property until you've sold it.

✔ Take a good look at the roof and make arrangements for any needed repairs as soon as possible. Also check that the guttering isn't broken or detached from the exterior. Prospective buyers are put off by these problems because they'll have to get them fixed as soon as they move in.

Back garden

Overgrown, unkempt gardens full of weeds are no selling point. So if you're lucky enough to have a back garden, make the most of it. Your garden doesn't need to look like it's had a *Ground Force* makeover; just make sure that it's neat and well-kept. Simply by cutting the grass, weeding the flowerbeds, pruning the trees, and trimming the hedges, you give the impression that you care – and make it easy for buyers to imagine themselves relaxing and entertaining friends.

You don't have to spend a fortune on expensive shrubs and flowers – and if I were you I wouldn't bother unless they're portable, that is, in pots so you can take them with you.

Other things you can do to make your garden inviting include hiding all your junk out of the way in the garden shed, keeping the rubbish bins out of sight, and scrubbing the patio clean.

Hiding the Dog – and the Kids!

While Fido is no doubt your pride and joy, not everyone might feel so passionately towards him. Lots of people love dogs but not dog smells or hair on sofas and beds. Some people are allergic or simply don't like pets. If you have pets, you don't necessarily have to hide Tiddles away in the cupboard but conceal as much evidence of her as possible. Get all the hair off the sofa, or cover with a throw if necessary. The same goes for the beds. Hide away litter trays so they don't give off any nasty odours.

If you have a cat that sprays in the house you have more of a problem, as the smell can be very off-putting. While you may have grown used to it and hardly notice it, a non-pet owning prospective buyer will pick up on it immediately. It also damages the walls and furniture so it is very obvious. You can purchase various sprays, such as Febreeze, which minimise the smell as much as possible. Spray this around the property before a viewing if it is a real problem and light some scented candles to mask the pong. Re-paint the walls and replace any wallpaper that's affected.

 If your dog is particularly friendly or otherwise, it might be worth asking a neighbour or friend to look after him while prospective buyers are being shown around. This will remove the chance of him jumping up at them and knocking them over, or doing the opposite, growling at them and actually going for them. If the dog is out of the way until the viewing is over it removes a distraction you can do without, allowing you and your prospective buyers to concentrate on the property.

Chapter 16

Using a Pro to Sell Your Home: Getting the Most from Estate Agents

. . . .

In This Chapter

▶ Understanding what an estate agent does

▶ Finding a good agent (or several)

▶ Understanding the contract before you sign

▶ Checking up on your agent and deciding when to take your business elsewhere

. . . .

Despite the obvious attractions of selling your home privately – you don't have to deal with estate agents or pay their commission – most people end up using an agent. Leaving the advertising, viewings, and price negotiations to someone else is simply much easier.

But things can – and do – go wrong. Anyone can set up in business as an estate agent because you don't need any formal qualifications. And even though professional bodies exist, such as the National Association of Estate Agents (NAEA) and the Ombudsman for Estate Agents (OEA) scheme, these are entirely voluntary, and only a third of agents are members. If you have a complaint about an agent who doesn't belong to one of these bodies, little redress is available. Therefore, it is important that you protect yourself against rogue agents – in this chapter I show you how.

The Role of the Estate Agent

The estate agent may be the middleman, but when you sell your home, if you're like most people, you probably couldn't do without him. Yes, selling your home yourself may be cheaper because you avoid paying the agent's commission – a percentage of the sale price, usually between 1.5 and 3 per cent. But the question is whether you can get the right buyers through the door and negotiate the price you want, all within a reasonable amount of time. If the answer is 'no', you've no choice but to hire an agent.

Most sellers use agents because agents are experts at selling property. Every week, thousands of prospective buyers call into their local estate agents, read the ads they place in local and national newspapers, and browse their Internet sites. Most buyers make an agent their first port of call. For this reason, an estate agent is one of the first people you want to call when you sell your home.

The agent works for you rather than the buyer because you pay him commission. He guides you through the selling process and is responsible for several vital steps in ensuring a successful sale:

- ✔ **Giving an estimate.** The estate agent's first job is to give you an idea of how much you can sell your home for. See 'Accepting the agent's estimate and setting the price' later in this chapter.

- ✔ **Suggesting improvements/repairs.** The agent's job is to sell your property, but he needs good tools to work with. If your home is untidy, cluttered, or full of unfinished do-it-yourself work, he may suggest you address the problem in order to achieve a successful sale.

   Let the agent guide you: If you're thinking about replacing a tired old bathroom suite with a gleaming new white one, ask the agent first whether he thinks this is necessary or worth the cost.

- ✔ **Writing the property particulars.** These are a description of your home. The agent uses this, along with a photo of the property (which he also arranges), in his advertising. Some agents charge extra for this, so check beforehand. To prepare the property particulars, the agent will inspect your home, measure the rooms, and note down special features that might interest prospective buyers. Although the agent tries to make your home sound as desirable as possible, he can't make false or misleading statements; doing so is a criminal offence.

- ✔ **Advertising the property.** Your success in selling your home rests on suitable buyers knowing it's for sale. Thus the advertising of your home is crucial. Ask the agent how he plans to do this – in the agent's window, in the local paper, via mailing lists, over the Internet, and so on. Most agents put a 'For Sale' sign up outside your property. The key is using direct advertising toward the right type of buyer.

- ✔ **Handling viewings.** Some agents rely on sellers to show their properties to prospective buyers, but you may prefer not to. Don't feel bad if you would prefer to leave this to the experts.

   If you are at home while the agent is showing people round, stay in the background. Be as discreet as possible. Don't stalk the agent and prospective buyers round your home, pointing out things they may have missed.

✔ **Negotiating a deal.** If you receive lots of offers, having an emotionally uninvolved third party who can negotiate the best deal is helpful. Even if only one offer is on the table, the agent is obliged to inform you promptly in writing. Be guided by your agent: If the offer is much less than the asking price. Ask him whether he thinks you should hold out for a higher offer or accept it. If you decide the offer is too low, the agent will try to negotiate a higher price with the prospective buyer. If the buyer refuses – and you're adamant that the offer is too low – you'll have to wait for another buyer to come along.

✔ **Arranging mortgages, surveys, and conveyancing.** Some agents offer these services, but you're under no obligation to take up all or any of these. Because you'll be taking out a new mortgage in order to buy your new home (unless you have enough cash to buy the property outright or are moving the mortgage from another property), I recommend that you refuse any home loan offered by your agent. You can find a much better deal by shopping around using an *independent* mortgage broker (see Chapter 11 for more on this). But when it comes to surveys or conveyancing, it may be cheaper to use the surveyor or solicitor your agent recommends because the agent should be able to get you a discount for putting work their way.

You should be put under no pressure to sign up for any of the services recommended by your agent. Some agents receive more commission on mortgage advice and insurance than on house sales. Be wary.

After you accept an offer on your home, instruct your solicitor to start conveyancing (see Chapter 19 for more details). At this point, the agent's work is done but you don't pay him until completion.

Wanted: An Honest and Competent Estate Agent

If you work with a good agent, you're likely to sell your home more quickly and for the price you want. Unfortunately, good agents are outnumbered by the bad. A bad agent will struggle to sell your property and may be unable to negotiate effectively on your behalf. If you've already found a property you want to buy, his incompetence could hold up the chain while you hang around waiting for a buyer.

Do your research carefully and pick a good agent. The work involved in finding a good agent is well worth the time and effort and could save you heartache further down the line. Check out the following:

✔ **Membership of professional organisations:** Charges are a big consideration when you choose an agent (see 'Working out the Cost' later in this chapter), but price should only be part of your decision. Far more important is membership of a recognised professional body which indicates that the agent meets certain standards and protects you against malpractice. Use agents who are members of the NAEA, the Royal Institution of Chartered Surveyors (RICS), or the OEA scheme.

Some agents claim to belong to a professional trade body and use its logo in its advertising when they aren't members at all. You can check the truthfulness of these claims on the following Web sites: www.naea.co.uk, www.rics.org.uk or www.oea.co.uk.

✔ **Personal recommendations:** As well as having a professional qualification, the best agent to use is one that a friend or relative has personally recommended to you. The likelihood is that, if your friend enjoyed success, you will too. But remember, not all agents are adept at selling all types of property. Opt for an agent who has a number of properties on his books similar to yours.

Interviewing your prospective agents

After you narrow your choice to two or three agents, invite all of them to (separately) value your property. The purpose of this is to ascertain whether you can envision working with them. To help you answer this question, ask each agent the following:

✔ What price should I ask for my home? Remember: The highest quote may not be the best one to go with. If you get three quotes, I recommend opting for the middle one.

✔ How will you market it – 'for sale' board, estate agent's window, local or national newspaper adverts, mailing lists and brochures, or on the Internet? The more outlets the better.

✔ How much do you charge? Check what is included in the price in order to compare costs between agents.

✔ Will you personally be handling the sale? If a more junior agent will be handling it, find out how closely they will be supervised.

✔ How experienced are you? If the agent seems a bit 'wet behind the ears' you may prefer someone more experienced.

✔ How do you want to conduct viewings? Do you want a key to show people around or do I have to be in? Go with what suits you best.

✔ What is the tie-in period on your contract? (See 'Making sense of the contract' later in this chapter).

Your final choice should be the agent who not only gives the most satisfactory answers to your questions but who knows a bit about the locality. It's also important that you like him. After all, he'll be your ambassador and you want to give the right impression to buyers.

Go with your gut feeling: If you don't get the right vibes from the agent, prospective buyers aren't likely to either.

Accepting the agent's estimate and setting the price

One of the agent's most important functions is helping you set the asking price. This shouldn't be too high (which dissuades buyers from arranging to view your home) or too low (you could miss out on thousands of pounds). The agent will bear in mind what similar properties in the area are fetching, the condition of your property compared with those, and the number of interested buyers. Here are a couple of things to keep in mind about the agent's estimate:

✔ The agent's estimate is just that – it's not a valuation and a lender won't accept it as proof of the value of the property. Only surveyors can make accurate valuations, but this can cost several hundred pounds and isn't necessary at this stage.

✔ Your property is only worth what someone is prepared to pay for it, so don't get too worked up over the asking price.

✔ You don't have to accept the agent's estimate, but I recommend that you be guided by it. Agents usually have a better idea than you of market conditions and, because they're not emotionally attached to your home, can be more dispassionate.

After you have the agents' estimates, you can set the asking price. Because estimates aren't an exact science and can vary a lot, I recommend that you get estimates from several estate agents (they're free) and put your home on the market at the average price.

Getting the asking price right first time is important. Although you may be tempted to pick the highest estimate, if your home is much pricier than similar properties, you'll only have to reduce the price when it doesn't sell. This doesn't send out the right signals to buyers, who may get the impression that you're desperate to sell or that something is wrong with the property. If your asking price is fair, stick to your guns until a buyer eventually comes along who is prepared to pay what your house is worth.

Set the price slightly too high rather than too low. Buyers usually offer below the asking price and if this is already low, they'll try to pay even less. If your home is on the market for slightly more than you hope to get, you are more likely to end up with the price you want.

Assessing the agent's market reach

It doesn't matter how hot an estate agent's negotiating skills are: If he can't find prospective buyers in the first place, he's of limited use to you. You must ensure that as many serious prospective buyers as possible get to see your property. Follow this advice:

✔ **Ask the agent how he plans to market your property.** Will your home be advertised in the local newspaper or nationally? National advertising is particularly effective if you own a large, expensive property.

Some agents charge extra for advertising on top of the standard commission. Check the charges before signing the contract and don't forget that you can negotiate these.

✔ **If your agent has an Internet site (as many do nowadays) log on and have a look.** Can prospective buyers take a virtual tour of the property? Can buyers register their details for e-mail alerts when a property goes on sale matching their criteria? An increasing number of buyers are using the Internet so it will help if your home is featured on it.

Making Sense of the Contract

Once you instruct an agent to act on your behalf, you enter a legally binding contract. Most contracts include the following:

✔ **Cost:** Agents work on a no-sale, no-fee basis, with commission ranging from 1.5 to 3 per cent of the sale price. Most of the complaints received by the Ombudsman are generated by dissatisfaction over commission. The Office of Fair Trading (OFT) advises that the contract should clearly state the exact amount you'll be charged. Failing this, the agent should state how the cost will be calculated and estimate what it will be.

Make sure that there are no hidden costs. Some agents charge a low commission plus additional charges to cover advertising and a 'For Sale' board. Others charge a higher percentage of the selling price but this includes all costs. Some agents charge a fixed fee rather than commission so insist on a full breakdown of the costs.

✔ **How long it will run:** Most contracts have *tie-in periods,* which stipulate how long the agent has to sell your home before you can cancel the contract. You'll probably be offered a fairly long tie-in period and should try negotiating this. I recommend that you sign up with an agent for no more than eight weeks. This gives him plenty of time to find a buyer. If your home remains unsold, take your business elsewhere. Don't be sentimental, you owe the agent literally nothing (as he doesn't get paid if he doesn't get a sale).

Find out how long the contract will run and whether you can cancel it at any time. If you don't read the small print, you may find you have signed up to an agent for several months. If the agent is useless, you're stuck until the tie-in period ends. If you instruct another agent who sells your property while you are still contracted to the first one, you have to pay commission to both.

✔ **The notice period:** This is the amount of time you have to continue working with an agent after you inform him that you want to cancel the contract. To figure out how long you could be saddled with the agent, add the notice period for cancelling the contract to the tie-in period. *Note:* The best contracts are those with a notice period and no tie-in period.

✔ **When payment is due:** Most agents are paid on completion. Check that the contract doesn't state that he gets paid on exchange of contracts otherwise you'll have to fork out thousands of pounds from your own pocket before the sale is completed – money you might struggle to come by.

Some contracts are complicated, misleading, and even unfair. If you don't understand something, ask. And if you don't like something, refuse to sign. The Citizens Advice Bureau (see Yellow Pages for your nearest branch) offers advice on contracts, or get your solicitor to take a look.

The contract will also include a number of terms, including:

✔ Sole agency

✔ Joint sole agency

✔ Multiple agency

✔ Sole-selling rights

✔ Ready, willing, and able purchaser

The following sections explain these terms in more detail.

Sole agency

With sole agency, one agent has exclusive rights to sell your property. Many sellers prefer sole agency for the following reasons:

✔ Because the agent earns all the commission if he is successful, he is likely to work hard to sell your property.

✔ It is the cheapest way to sell your home, with commission from as little as 1.5 per cent. And if you find a buyer yourself (see the next item in this list), you pay no commission at all.

✔ You don't pay commission if you find a buyer yourself unless the agent has 'sole-selling rights' (see the later section of the same name).

✔ Buyers often prefer dealing with sole agents because there is less chance of being gazumped – when the seller accepts an offer after already accepting an offer from another buyer. This is more likely when two or more agents are selling a property and competing for the same commission because, even after one agent has negotiated an offer that the seller has accepted, the other may continue to market the property.

Keep in mind, however, that if you instruct a second agent to sell your property after signing a sole-agency contract that is still in force, you're asking for trouble. If the second agent sells your home, you're obliged to pay commission to both him and the original agent.

Joint sole agency

One way of increasing the chances of selling your home is by instructing two agents to work together. Your local agent may recommend a link-up with a national partner to extend the reach of the advertising. To set up a joint sole agency, contact your local agent. The agents split the commission between them if they secure a sale – this is usually around 2 per cent. If you sell your own home you don't have to pay commission (as long as the contract doesn't give the agents sole-selling rights).

Multiple agency

If you instruct two or three competing agents to sell your home, this is known as multiple agency. The agent who finds a buyer gets commission, the others get nothing. Keep these points in mind:

✔ This arrangement can speed up your hunt for a buyer because several agents promote your home. But you also have to juggle a number of agents who want to arrange viewings at different times.

✔ Multiple agency increases the likelihood of your property being marketed by another agent after you've accepted an offer, and this puts off buyers because they are afraid of being gazumped. Some buyers also think that multiple agency means you are desperate to sell, which can affect the size of their offers.

✔ Competition doesn't always spur agents on. Because they get nothing if they don't find a buyer, some agents reserve their real effort for properties on which they have sole agency – and are guaranteed to earn commission if they secure a sale.

✔ Make sure that the contract is clearly worded so only one agent receives commission for finding a buyer. Expect to pay more than sole agency – usually around 3 per cent of the sale price.

If you use several agents, select them in the same way you would if you were using only one. See Chapter 4 for more details.

Sole-selling rights

The term 'sole-selling rights' should set alarm bells ringing. Never, ever agree to this. It means that when you sign a contract, that agent – and nobody else – can sell your property. Even if you sell your home yourself, you still have to pay the agent commission. Some sole-agency agreements include sole-selling rights clauses so check the small print of the contract.

Ready, willing, and able purchaser

Another term to watch out for is 'ready, willing, and able purchaser'. This means that if the agent finds a buyer who is prepared and able to buy your home and exchanges unconditional contracts, you have to pay the agent, even if the sale falls through.

Shooting from the HIP

If you're selling your property yourself, you are legally required to provide a Home Information Pack (HIP) before marketing your home. This is designed to give the buyer vital information about your property, which normally wouldn't be available until later and at their own cost. The pack must contain:

- ✔ Index
- ✔ Energy Performance Certificate (EPC) – telling the buyer how energy efficient your home is
- ✔ Sale statement – including the address of the property and whether it's freehold or leasehold
- ✔ Standard searches, including local authority and Drainage and Water
- ✔ Evidence of title (proving that you own the property and are in a position to sell it)

If the property is leasehold, you also require:

- ✔ Copy of the lease
- ✔ Details of rules and regulations in force at the time by managing agent or landlord
- ✔ Statements or summaries of service charge for previous three years
- ✔ Name and address of landlord and managing agent

Many estate agents offer HIPs and will do all the work for you. They may not charge a fee but will include it as part of the service. Alternatively, you can get a solicitor or specialist HIP provider to compile it. This will cost you a few hundred pounds, depending on the size of your home.

Checking Up on Progress

Keep an eye on your agent. He should provide feedback after a viewing, so you know how prospective buyers react to your property, but some are better than others at doing this. If you've had several viewings and no takers, you need to know why so that you can correct any problems with your home. Build a relationship with the agent so that he keeps you informed.

Agents are obliged to pass on to you all offers for your property, in writing. If you find out that he didn't, complain to the Ombudsman, if your agent is a member of the OEA (Ombudsman for Estate Agents) scheme.

Taking Your Business Elsewhere: When to Give Up on an Agent

If your home isn't selling, the problem may not be your property or the price but the agent. Following are warning signs that your estate agent isn't up to par:

- ✔ **You haven't heard from him in weeks:** Expect at least a call or two soon after your property goes on the market. If you don't hear anything at all for some time, that's not good enough.

- ✔ **You get no feedback after viewings:** Your estate agent should report back to you after every viewing to tell you how it went, what the prospective buyer thought, and whether he wants to make an offer. If you don't hear anything, contact the agent yourself.

Give your agent a couple of months to sell your home. If you aren't happy with his performance after this time, give him notice and switch agents (if your contract allows you to do so).

Take the same steps to find a new agent as you did to find the original one; you may just have been unlucky the first time. Discuss with the new agent whether the asking price is right and ask whether he has suggestions about the presentation of your property. Sometimes a fresh perspective is all you need.

Complaining about an Estate Agent

Dealing with an agent isn't always smooth sailing, as the 6,000 complaints the Ombudsman received last year testifies. But getting a result when you complain is far harder than you may think because agents aren't regulated. There's very little a trade body can do if an agent has messed up, so your challenge is to minimise the chances of this happening by following the tips in this chapter and choosing and monitoring your agent carefully. Sometimes though, you will be dissatisfied with your estate agent. See Chapter 4 for more details on pursuing a complaint against an agent.

Chapter 17

Going It Alone: Selling Your Property Privately

In This Chapter

▶ Setting the asking price

▶ Advertising your property

▶ Handling viewings with prospective buyers

▶ Accepting an offer

▶ Selling at auction

*O*ne in 20 properties is now sold without an estate agent, according to property portal HouseWeb. An increasing number of people are selling privately because it speeds the process up considerably because it cuts out the middleman. And you also save money because you knock out the estate agent's commission, which can be as much as 3 per cent of the sale price. If you're selling a property for £200,000, for example, the estate agent's commission works out to be £7,050, after VAT (value-added tax) is added on. No wonder an increasing number of people are looking at ways of avoiding this charge! Of course, going it alone isn't always easy. The reason so many people use estate agents to sell their home is because it makes life easier. Your agent handles the advertising, viewings, and price negotiations – tasks many people don't feel comfortable doing themselves. But if you're prepared to give it a go, selling your home yourself can be worth the extra effort. In this chapter I look at what's involved, as well as setting the asking price, marketing your home, and handling viewings. I also cover what you need to know about selling at auction.

Setting the Asking Price

Your property is worth what someone is willing to pay for it. The difference between receiving loads of offers – all at the asking price – and not hearing a dickey bird all comes down to the asking price and demand. While you can't influence demand, apart from making your property as attractive to buyers as possible, you need to get the price right. Although making as much profit as possible is tempting, setting the price too high doesn't always pay. You may find that you've priced yourself out of the market.

When you sell privately, you can determine a realistic asking price by following these strategies:

✔ **Get quotes from three different estate agents and then work out the average.** Simply call up agents and tell them that you're considering putting your house on the market via their agency and want an idea of the price the property would fetch. Agents are called upon to come up with asking prices all the time, so they won't think this request is unusual or out of order. You don't need to tell the agent that you have no intention of actually employing their services in selling your property.

An estate agent won't give you a valuation of you property – just an indication of what you could get for it. For a professional valuation, you have to employ a surveyor, which costs extra and there isn't much added value in doing this.

✔ **Compare your property with similar ones in your street.** If Number 43 down the road went for £180,000 three weeks ago, chances are that if your property is in a similar state of repair with the same sort of features, you can get the same sort of sum.

✔ **Be aware of things you can't see:** The owners of Number 43 may have installed a hot tub in their conservatory, put in double-glazing, or recently redecorated, and your place might not be as desirable. Or maybe when they put their property on the market, demand was greater, and that's why they got several prospective buyers so easily. Treat your neighbours' experience as a general guide – there is no guarantee you'll get the same price.

✔ **Scan your local papers and property Web sites.** The local paper will reveal the price similar properties in your area are being advertised for. And don't forget the property Web sites on the Internet as well: These provide a ballpark figure of the amount you can reasonably expect.

Before putting your property on the market, don't forget to prepare it for prospective buyers to view. Clean thoroughly, repair any broken tiles, fix cupboard doors that don't shut properly, replace worn carpets and faded curtains, and clear away the clutter. For more information on how to prepare your home for viewing, refer to Chapter 15.

Advertising Your Property

The easiest way to sell your home privately is if you personally know someone who wants to buy it. Maybe someone has approached you and asked whether you'd consider selling, or a friend of a friend has heard that you're thinking of putting your property on the market and wants to get in ahead of the rush. If this is the case, lucky you. You can save time, money, and the hassle of advertising.

But most people aren't in this position. Instead, you have to let prospective buyers know that your property is up for sale. This is where advertising comes in. Do it correctly, and money spent on advertising is money well spent. Do it badly, and you may as well throw your cash down the drain.

The key to success in selling your property is in reaching the small number of people who are interested in buying it. To do this, you must advertise in places where these people are likely to see your ad – the local newspaper or national papers, the Internet, specialist property publications, or on a board outside your home. In the following sections, I go into more detail as to how each of these works and show you how to write a property ad.

Putting up a property board

The first step to take if you're selling your house privately is to do as the estate agents do and erect a 'For Sale' sign outside your property. The idea is to catch the attention of prospective buyers who may pass by. The property board informs them that the property is for sale and provides a telephone number if they want more details.

You don't have to pay a fortune to erect a board. As long as the wording is legible and the sign is clean, even a homemade effort can be effective. Get a large piece of wood, paint it white, and write 'For Sale' and your telephone number for enquiries. Then nail this board firmly to a post and stick it at the front of your garden where it can clearly be seen from the road. If you're selling a flat or house that doesn't have a garden, nail your sign onto the outside wall.

Your aim is to attract people who are passing by, some of whom will be driving. So keep these tips in mind:

- ✔ Make sure that your writing is legible. That means neat and large enough to easily see from the road.

- ✔ Don't put too much information on the board. If you do, prospective buyers won't be able to take it in while they drive past. 'For Sale' and your phone number are enough. If they register that the property is for sale and are interested, chances are they'll pull up and take down your phone number.

You may be tempted to put 'Enquire inside' on the sign rather than a phone number, but I'd advise against this. Although it may seem like a good idea, you could end up with random people knocking on your door, disturbing your family's routine, and calling at the most inconvenient times. Inviting passers-by into your home is also a safety concern, unless a member of your family or a friend is present. A far better plan is to arrange a viewing over the telephone at a mutually convenient time (see 'Arranging a viewing' later in this chapter).

Advertising in newspapers

Nearly every national and local newspaper has an extensive property section. As well as pages full of big display ads paid for by estate agents to justify their commission to clients, you can also find scores of pages of classified ads, often placed by private sellers. Because the classifieds are probably going to be your main source of advertising for your property, you have to familiarise yourself with the paper's circulation schedule and the information included in the ads. Why? Because you have to write your own.

When writing a newspaper ad, remember what you're aiming for:

- To attract the reader's attention
- To keep the reader's interest
- To generate a desire to find out more information about your property
- To convince the reader to contact you for more details
- To arrange a viewing

You need to decide what sort of ad to opt for, where you're going to advertise, and what information you want to include. I cover each of these in the sections below.

Information to include in a newspaper ad

An effective newspaper ad is short and snappy yet conveys all the vital information the reader needs. The essential points to cover are:

- The property's location
- Period style
- Size, number, and type of rooms
- Any unusual features
- Whether it's leasehold or freehold
- Price
- A contact telephone number for interested buyers to use to get in touch with you

Make sure that the telephone number is one you can be contacted on during the day – a mobile phone number is best. There's not much point in giving your home number if you're at work all day.

Most papers use abbreviations of words that regularly appear so that you can fit in as much information as possible as inexpensively as possible. Familiarise yourself with these and use them, as appropriate. But remember that abbreviations can look untidy, so try not to use more than you need. Also avoid using your own abbreviations, which are likely to leave readers mystified. Table 17-1 shows common abbreviations used in newspaper ads.

Table 17-1	Common Newspaper Ad Abbreviations
Abbreviation	*Translation*
Apt	Apartment
bed	Bedroom
d/g	Double-glazing
det	Detached
dble	Double
exc	Excellent
ex l/a	Ex-local authority
ff	Fully fitted
FH	Freehold
flr	Floor
GCH	Gas central heating
gdn	Garden
immac	Immaculate
lge	Large
LH	Leasehold
ono	Or nearest offer
refurb	Refurbished
sq ft	Square feet
sep	Separate
ter	Terrace
WC	Water closet or toilet
yr	Year

Before you write your ad, look at other ads in the publication you're planning to advertise in. Doing so gives you a good idea of how you need to word your ad.

Including a photo of your property: Yes or no?

The saying 'A picture speaks a thousand words' is certainly true with something as emotive as property: Most people have a set idea of what sort of home they can live in – and what they can't.

The trouble with including a photo with your newspaper ad is that it costs a lot of money and could blow your advertising budget out of the water. But if you're advertising on the Internet, a picture or two of the property is vital.

If you decide to include a photo, make sure it is as clear as possible, shows the front of the property, and if you arrange it, is taken on a sunny day. If you aren't a budding David Bailey, consider paying a professional to take the pictures for you. Even if you do know your shutter from your flash, forking out a bit of cash to get a more professional finish is often worth the extra expense.

Many Web sites have their own photographers who can take photos of your property for a fee. Otherwise, you could look up photographers in the Yellow Pages.

What sort of ad should you go for?

Newspapers carry two sorts of ad: *Display* and *classified*. Display ads are more eye-catching, tend to be far bigger than classifieds, and usually include photos of the property. They are also much more expensive. Classified ads provide the buyer with the necessary info but are usually only a few lines long. For these reasons, they tend to be much smaller and, therefore, much less expensive.

Classified ads are likely to be your best bet because they're more reasonably priced than the huge display ads favoured by agents with big advertising budgets. Most newspapers offer bold print for an extra sum which you may be prepared to pay for because anything that makes your ad stand out from the crowd is money well spent.

A huge ad doesn't guarantee you more interest from prospective buyers. A classified ad that's worded correctly can be more effective than a badly worded display ad that takes up a lot more space.

Picking a newspaper to advertise in

All national and most local newspapers have substantial property sections. But because you probably have an advertising budget you want to stick to, you can't advertise in all of them. A local paper typically charges around £1 a word, with a minimum number of words, say 16, so an ad in a local paper would cost you a minimum of £16 plus VAT at 17.5 per cent. A national newspaper on the other hand, has much higher advertising charges. For a mono ad (black and white) stretching over a single column, you can expect to pay £53 for the ad itself, plus £10 per line. And don't forget to slap the VAT on top of that.

The trick is to be selective and choose those papers that are most likely to be read by your target market. If you're selling an end-of-terrace house in Manchester, for example, placing an ad in the London Evening Standard's property section is unlikely to result in many calls from interested buyers. Spend your money wisely.

To place an ad, buy a copy of the paper you're going to advertise in. The phone number you need to call will be prominently displayed inside. Alternatively, look on the paper's website. You may be able to complete an ad online, or find a number to call. To help you make your mind up about which type of paper you should advertise in, consider the following:

- ✔ **Local papers:** Whether your budget stretches to an ad in a national newspaper or not, your first port of call is your local paper. Most have reasonably sized property sections. Many local papers also have their own Web sites, which are updated more frequently than the paper – particularly because many local papers are published weekly. If your local paper has a Web site, find out whether your ad will appear online as well and if this service costs extra. Even with an extra charge, the online ad may be worth it because it means your ad will probably reach more potential buyers.

- ✔ **Regional papers:** You don't have to restrict yourself to one small-time local paper. There could well be some bigger regional newspapers covering your area with a bigger catchment of readers. Place an ad there too to broaden your chances of selling your property.

- ✔ **National papers:** If you have the spare cash, you may want to think about advertising in a national newspaper as well as your local one. The principles are the same as with a local rag. The ad needs to be carefully worded and include all the necessary information the prospective buyer needs. National newspaper advertising is best suited to those with expensive or unusual properties for sale.

You will have to pay a lot more to advertise in a national newspaper so consider whether it is worth it. I recommend trying the local paper first and if you have no joy after a few weeks, trying a national. Otherwise, you could be spending a lot of money unnecessarily.

Don't write off the free ads. *Loot* publishes a number of regional papers in the South East (including London, Croydon & Surrey and Essex) and the North West (including Manchester, Liverpool, and the Wirral & North Wales) and has an extensive Web site (www.loot.com) with details of thousands of properties for sale. If your area is covered by *Loot*, it's worth placing a free ad. You never know, you might get lucky!

Timing your ad

If you want it to appear in the next edition of the paper, make sure that you find out the submission deadline. If you miss it, you've lost out on as much as a full week of advertising.

Checking your published ad

After you place an ad, make sure that you buy a copy of the paper when it goes on sale. The reason? To check that the ad appears in the first place, to verify that it's worded correctly, and to make sure that your contact details are correct.

If you ad has been printed incorrectly because the salesperson who took your details down over the phone got it wrong, request that a free ad is run in the next edition.

Using specialist property publications

There are a number of specialist property publications available, many of which cover only the local area. Weekly property magazine *Hot Property*, for example, covers property for sale in London or the Home Counties. It also has a Web site (www.hotproperty.co.uk) you can use. Check out your local newsagent to see what specialist publications are available.

Advertising on the Internet

The Internet offers a number of Web sites you can use to sell your property. This is cheaper than advertising in your local paper, enabling you to include a lot more information in your ad. And some Web sites allow your property to appear until it is sold, unlike newspaper ads where you have to pay for the ad to be repeated over several weeks.

Selling over the Internet is by no means a foolproof process. Buyers can have a hard time locating properties for sale if the seller doesn't use one of the big Web sites, pages can be slow to download, and information can become out-dated. And nothing is more frustrating for a buyer than enquiring about a property that has already been sold. (And from the seller's perspective, the last thing you want are buyers ringing you up weeks after you have agreed a sale.) But if you're aware of the potential pitfalls and know how to minimise them, the Internet can be an effective way to show off your home to buyers.

Several good sites are available that you can advertise your property on. By far the best is HouseWeb's (www.houseweb.co.uk), which boasts 100,000 visitors a month. You pay a one-off price, and your property appears on the site until it's sold. HouseWeb prices start at £47 for a standard advert with one photo, but you can pay quite a bit more depending on the number of photos you include, whether you opt for normal, bold, or red type, and whether you have a link through to your own Web site). If you want to include a panoramic virtual tour, for example, where the buyer can examine the interior of your property online through a series of pictures, you'll pay £398, which includes VAT and the cost of the filming – a process that takes a photographer about an hour.

Writing the ad is straightforward. After you register on the site and write your ad (this is likely to include details similar to those that would appear in a newspaper, although you may also include the size and a description of the rooms), and uploaded any photos you want to include, the ad is automatically created and appears on the site. In addition to the ad:

✔ All HouseWeb ads also include a location map enabling the prospective buyer to see exactly where your property is.

✔ HouseWeb notifies buyers by email if a property meets their requirements. An interested buyer can contact you by email via HouseWeb or call you directly through a personal phone number that you can include in your ad.

✔ HouseWeb gives you, the seller, direct access to your ad so you can amend it at any time.

✔ To eliminate the problem of out-of-date information, HouseWeb insists you update your ad every 30 days in case you sell your property or it is under offer.

Here are a couple of tips to make your online ad more effective:

✔ When you advertise on the Internet, use photos. Most sellers do – if you don't, buyers will wonder why and may assume you're trying to flog a hideous-looking property. If you don't have a scanner and can't upload your own photos, many Web sites do this for you for an additional charge if you post them the hard copies. HouseWeb charges £10, for example, for this service.

✔ If you can afford it, include a visual tour. It may cost a bit extra, but it can cut back on timewasters. If you get a call from a prospective buyer following up your ad, she's already seen the interior of your property and is impressed enough to want to see it in person.

Handling Viewings

After your ad appears in whatever advertising media you select, prepare yourself for calls. With a bit of luck, they will come flooding in from serious prospective buyers, enabling you to arrange a number of viewings. Because you aren't using an agent, you have to organise a convenient time and date for yourself and the prospective buyer and guide him through the property, answering his questions. In the following sections, I look at how you can prepare for a viewing – and what to do to make sure it goes off without a hitch.

Taking the call

Your first contact with a prospective buyer is likely to be over the telephone. She may have spotted your ad in the local paper or driven past the property and seen the board you erected outside. As soon as you advertise your property, you need to be prepared to receive phone calls from interested parties and to deal with these in a professional manner.

Preparing for the call

To prepare for conversations with prospective buyers, have the following by the phone:

- ✔ **A copy of any ads you ran.** The prospective buyer may want confirmation of details, such as the size of the master bedroom. Even if you stated this information in the ad, you need to have it on hand just in case you need a reminder of what you said. The last thing you want to do is contradict yourself or sound flustered because you don't know the answer to a question.

- ✔ **A property knowledge sheet.** Compile a *property knowledge sheet* with details about your property. Make sure that it contains all the basic information about your property, such as its size and type. Also include important information about the local area, such as transport links, local schools, childcare facilities, leisure centres, and shopping facilities.

Although you probably know many of the details about the amenities in your area, be sure to research answers to questions you might be asked if you don't know them. For example, if you aren't religious or don't have school-age children, you may not know the places of worship or the area schools. Use the Internet or visit your local public library before you speak to prospective buyers.

Talking to prospective buyers

When you receive a call, answer the phone quickly and politely, taking care not to sound harassed. To sound professional and give the impression that you know what you're doing, say 'Hello' and state your name.

Keeping the caller waiting or being too casual in your approach when you do eventually pick up the phone doesn't impress, which is what you're trying to do. If you absolutely can't speak to the caller at that particular moment, politely ask him for his name, his telephone number and a convenient time when you can return his call. Then make sure you call exactly when you said you would.

During this phone conversation, you have three goals: To answer the buyer's questions, to sell her on your property so that she'll want to come around to see it, and to actually arrange the viewing.

Be friendly and chatty and try to build up a rapport with the prospective buyer. Some would-be purchasers are wary of buying privately because they aren't dealing with a recognisable firm of agents. They may be particularly concerned about the safety aspects of the viewing. So reassure them that you aren't a psychopath by being friendly and helpful and building up a rapport over the telephone.

Answering the buyer's questions

When you're speaking to the prospective buyer, she may want some more details from you before committing herself to a viewing. Her inquiries can save you time, as well as her time, if for some reason, the property isn't suitable. Maybe, for example, it isn't close enough to the local primary school or the mainline train station into London – factors which weren't clear in the ad.

Selling the prospective buyer on your property

While you don't want to waste your time arranging a viewing if the caller is only half interested, your goal is to get as many prospective buyers as possible, who have the means to purchase your property, round to look at it. The trick to turning a call into a viewing is to be as persuasive as possible, while listening to the caller's requirements at the same time. He may, for example, express concern at the fact that your home has only three bedrooms when he really wanted a fourth bedroom for guests. If you can convince him that the bedrooms are such a good size that he could easily put a sofa bed in at least one of them, you may be able to convince him to come and take a look.

Arranging a viewing

If the prospective buyer is still interested in viewing your property by the end of the telephone call, you can make the necessary arrangements:

✔ **Set a time and date convenient to both you and the prospective buyer.** Most buyers want to come around after work or at the weekend, particularly if they want to bring a partner and/or children. Although you may initially baulk at this, be as flexible as possible and put up with the disruption. Hopefully these disruptions will last for only a relatively short period of time.

Inviting complete strangers into your home while you're alone is inadvisable and can be downright dangerous. When you arrange a viewing, make sure you also arrange for a friend or relative to be there with you in case of trouble. If this isn't possible, I recommend arranging the viewing for a time when you can get somebody present. Don't take any unnecessary risks.

✔ **Provide the prospective buyer with the full address of your property, together with clear directions so that he knows how to get there.** This is particularly important if the buyer doesn't know the area very well or your property is hard to find. Make sure that directions are clear and easy to follow. If giving directions isn't your forte, ask a friend or relative who knows the area well and is good at directing people to provide them for you. Also try and avoid directing people past the council rubbish tip or sewerage works if possible. A local park or attractive village pub or two create a much better impression of the local area.

Don't be late for the viewing – or cancel it. Prospective buyers tend to see several properties. If you mess them about, there will be scores of other sellers more than happy to roll out the red carpet. If something unavoidable does crop up that that will make you late or necessitate your having to cancel the viewing altogether, give the prospective buyer as much notice as possible and, if you can, arrange another viewing.

Guiding prospective buyers round your property

When the buyer arrives, switch into professional mode. Answer the door with a smile and welcome her into your home (which, by the way, should be clean, tidy, and fresh smelling; see Chapter 15 for tips on how to present your home to prospective buyers). Offer to take her coat and ask whether she had a pleasant journey. If she came a long way, you may also want to offer her a cup of tea or a cold drink.

As you and the prospective buyer walk through your house, keep these suggestions in mind:

✔ **Allow yourself to be guided by the buyer if she seems happy to lead the way (not all buyers will feel comfortable leading).** If your buyer wanders into the lounge and starts commenting on the room before you've a chance to direct her into the kitchen, go along with it and point out any features that you think need highlighting. The key is to be flexible and see how each viewing pans out. The buyer may want to start in the garden instead: Let her guide you on this if she seems happy to do so.

✔ **If the buyer doesn't take the lead, start the viewing at the hallway and work round the ground floor of the property before moving upstairs.** Once upstairs, you may want to start with the Master bedroom and move on from there.

✔ **Avoid stating the blindingly obvious, such as 'Here is the bathroom'; it sounds patronising.** Far better to highlight certain features that the buyer (probably overwhelmed by everything she has to take in) could well miss. If you have French windows in the lounge, which open out onto a patio, for example, open the doors and demonstrate how convenient they are. This might be a better time to look at the exterior of the property as well, if you haven't already.

Answering prospective buyers' questions

It is highly unlikely that you and the prospective buyer will wander around your property in complete silence. Most prospective buyers have lots of questions to ask, such as whether you've had any trouble with the neighbours, what's the nearest bus route, and whether you have gas central heating or not. Answer questions as truthfully as you can. If you aren't sure of the answer, say so but promise to find out as soon as possible and get back to them.

Bluffing your way through the answers makes you look as if you're deliberately trying to mislead the prospective buyer – especially if something doesn't turn out to be what you said it was.

Predicting every question a prospective buyer will ask is impossible, but you can prepare yourself for the most obvious ones. Following are the kinds of questions you're likely to be asked and how you should reply:

✔ **Why are you moving?** This is either a straightforward question or an extremely complicated one, depending on the answer. If you're moving because you fancy living in the country after years of city life, say so. But if you're moving because you have outgrown your property, be truthful but try not say anything too negative. If you suggest that your property is too small, for example, your buyer is likely to focus on the fact that the house has only two bedrooms. Instead, you could say that you need an extra bedroom for the new baby, which is perfectly reasonable – unless, of course, you don't have (or aren't expecting) a baby!

✔ **Are you part of a chain?** A *chain* is the term that means several people are involved in a house sale. For example, you're buying a property from someone else, who is also buying another property. That's a chain, and they can get pretty long. The trouble with chains is that if one buyer drops out or one person misses out on the property they want, the chain is broken and the whole process is held up while that person finds another buyer or property. If your prospective buyer is purchasing her first property (and is therefore not part of a chain) she may, understandably, want to steer clear of a long and complicated chain. Make sure you're aware of the ins and outs of your chain and be prepared to supply this information to the prospective buyer.

✔ **What's included in the asking price?** Most properties are sold with the fixtures and fittings, such as the kitchen and bathroom suite, light fittings, and tiles, all as part of the asking price. If you plan to leave the carpets and/or curtains behind as well, mention this to the prospective buyer, particularly if you want some extra cash for them. If the prospective buyer has his eye on your best curtains, for example, you can offer them to him for, say, an extra £100.

✔ **What are the neighbours like?** If your neighbours play loud music at all hours, and the noise reverberates around your semi, saying that you never get a peep out of them is deliberately misleading and could get you in trouble later. As much as you may wish otherwise, you have to be honest. While you must tell the truth, don't spend ages slagging off the neighbours and going into great detail of the feud you've got running with the family across the road. If you do, you'll send your prospective buyer running a mile. Indicate that you've had a problem and stick to the facts. Then the buyer can decide whether she's still interested in your property or not.

You must tell the potential buyers about any disputes with a neighbour that you have formally reported to the local council or police. If you don't inform the buyer, you could be legally challenged or even sued at a later date if the buyer can persuade a court that, had she known the true situation, she wouldn't have bought your property.

Coming back for more

If your prospective buyer rings you after the viewing and asks to come back and take another look, rejoice – this is a very good sign. A second viewing indicates that the buyer is very interested in purchasing your property and either wants to clear up a couple of things in his mind or just wants to reassure himself that he has made the right decision to buy your property.

As with first viewings, arrange the second viewing at a mutually convenient time. You may feel that you don't need a chaperone this time because your prospective buyer seemed like such a nice person during your first meeting, but I still advise that you arrange for someone to be at the property with you. It's better to be safe than sorry.

With a second or third viewing, you can leave the prospective buyer to look around on his own; simply tell him that you'll be in the lounge if he has any questions. He'll be familiar with the layout from his first visit, and you'll have already highlighted the key features of the property. He is likely to have some specific aims: He may want to double check that the second bedroom is big enough for a double bed, for example. He may also have some questions he forgot to ask on his first viewing because they went out of his mind.

At the end of the second viewing, the prospective buyer may make an offer or say he'll be in touch. If it's the latter, you may want to chivvy him along a bit; perhaps mention you've had a lot of interest in the property and you wouldn't want him to miss out by taking too long to get back to you. Even if this isn't strictly true, it may instil a sense of urgency in the prospective buyer, resulting in a quicker sale, which is obviously good for you.

Dealing with Offers

Of course, in the best scenario, the prospective buyer makes an offer on your property. That doesn't mean you should immediately accept it. In fact, resist the temptation to accept the first offer you get, particularly if it's well below the asking price. If you have only just put your property on the market, wait a bit longer to see whether another buyer offers you the full asking price. For information on negotiating a deal, go to Chapter 18.

If someone offers you the full asking price, your property may be under-priced. You can either accept the offer if you're happy with the sum or hold out for a higher offer from another buyer, who may offer more if they know someone has already offered the full asking price.

Don't accept an offer from one buyer and then later accept an offer from another buyer – this is gazumping and is very distressing and expensive for buyers (you can find more details on gazumping in Chapter 8). Although you may tempted to go for the higher offer – and it isn't illegal to accept another offer after you already accepted someone else's – gazumping is a bad practice. It can be expensive for the first buyer, who may have forked out for a valuation and survey and instructed a solicitor. Treat others as you'd like to be treated: Imagine how you'd feel if you were gazumped – understandably furious. Stick with the buyer whose offer you accepted.

If you've shown several buyers around your property, and they are all keen to make an offer, consider opting for *sealed bids*. In this situation, you ask all interested parties to submit an offer to you in writing by a deadline. You then open all the offers and decide which one you're going to accept. You don't have to opt for the highest bid – you may prefer to go for the first-time buyer who isn't caught up in a chain – and you don't have to accept any of the offers you receive. Getting sealed bids is a good way to speed up the process *and* get a good price for your property – usually more than you put it on the market for in the first place. See Chapter 10 for more on sealed bids.

Chasing Prospective Buyers

Once you've accepted an offer, you need to instruct your solicitor, who will set the wheels in motion. The prospective buyer needs to arrange his financing, arrange a survey, and instruct his own solicitor. In addition, you may need to *chase the buyer,* that is, ensure that he's doing what he needs to do and when. (For those who use estate agents to sell their property, the agent assumes this role.)

Make yourself familiar with the various stages of the conveyancing process so that you know when something is taking longer than it should. Remember that purchasing a property in England, Wales and Northern Ireland can take 10 to 12 weeks. If the process is dragging on for several months, you have a right to know why. After all, you will have taken your property off the market and you may have missed out on other potential buyers who could have moved more quickly.

The hold-up may be on your side. Your solicitor may be dragging his heels for one reason or another. So while you're harrying the buyer, remember to put in a call to your solicitor, too.

Gentle reminders are a whole lot different from harassment. Don't turn into a stalker, bothering your buyer at all hours of the day and night. Try not to call more than once a week for an update, otherwise you'll put the buyer off and he may well pull out of the sale. Remember, in England, Northern Ireland, and Wales, a sale is not binding until exchange of contracts (in Scotland an offer is binding; see Chapter 20 for more details on the Scottish house buying process).

Under the Hammer: Selling at Auction

If you're privately selling a property that has complications such as subsidence or isn't in tip-top condition, or you need a quick sale for whatever reason, you may want to consider selling at auction. Selling at auction offers these possible advantages:

- ✔ **Auctions are good places to sell homes that have problems.** This is because the sale goes through much more quickly so buyers may be less likely to notice problems. And because they usually get a good price, they may be prepared to over look a bit of damp or subsidence.

- ✔ **If a bidding war breaks out among interested buyers, you could end up getting a better price for your property.** In such a situation, you could end up with more than you would have if you'd gone the 'normal' route and sold through an estate agent.

✔ **Selling at auction gives you a great deal of marketing exposure.** Most big auction houses advertise in national, trade, and local press, as well as on the Internet. Your property will also feature in the sale catalogue, usually with a photograph and detailed description.

Before you decide that an auction is the way to go, keep these things in mind:

✔ **Not all properties are suitable for sale at auction.** If yours is in pristine condition and you've spent a lot of time cultivating the garden and expect the sale price to reflect this, you may be better off trying to sell via an estate agent or on your own.

To find out whether your property is suitable for auction, consult an auctioneer who has an MRICS/FRICS qualification. The Royal Institution of Chartered Surveyors (RICS) has a detailed list of auctioneers in each area. Contact the RICS on 0870 333 1600 or the Web site (www.rics.org.uk). Or try The Essential Information Group, which works with 150 auction houses and provides lists of future auction (www.eigroup.co.uk).

✔ **Once the auctioneer has brought down her hammer, the sale is binding and neither you nor the bidder can withdraw.** You can change your mind about selling your property up until the auction and the property will be withdrawn from sale. But once someone has accepted your offer it's too late to change your mind about selling. The buyer pays a 10 per cent deposit on the day of the sale.

✔ **The sale must also be completed within a set date.** The buyer usually has 28 days to pay the balance of the purchase price to the auction house and the sale is complete.

✔ **If you sell your property at auction, you must ensure that it is vacant by a fixed date – usually four weeks after the auction.** Unless you have another property lined up to move into and are certain that you can do so by that date, you have to arrange to store your belongings and find somewhere to stay temporarily until you can move into your new property.

Going about it

If the auctioneer thinks your property is suitable for auction, discuss what you need to do before the sale. The auctioneer can tell you all about viewing arrangements and a possible sale date.

Most sales have a closing date for entries, which is six weeks before the date of auction. Make that sure you get you get all your searches done and your details submitted to the auction house in plenty of time.

Price

The auctioneer will discuss the *guide price* with you. This guide gives buyers an idea of how much you're expecting. You will also need to come up with a *reserve price* – the minimum price you're prepared to sell your property for – prospective bidders know that there is a reserve price, but they don't know what it is. Only you and the auctioneer are party to this information.

As the auction date approaches, you may have to adjust the reserve price if market conditions change dramatically. If a lot of people have shown interest in your property, you may decide to increase the reserve price.

Instructing your solicitor

Once the reserve is set, you have to instruct a solicitor to obtain the title deeds and the details of the lease (if there is one) and to prepare the special conditions of sale. Some auctioneers also request that you get local authority and Land Registry searches carried out on the property (see Chapter 19 for more details on the searches and costs involved). All this information is made available to prospective buyers through your solicitor.

Viewings

The auctioneer arranges viewings of your property with prospective bidders. Interested parties are also likely to commission a survey of the property – and their surveyor needs access to compile this report.

If the property is vacant – that is, you're living somewhere else – such viewings won't really affect you. But if you're living at the property, you have to be patient and flexible. Many auctioneers arrange group viewings for popular lots to cut back on the time and hassle. If this is the case with your property, I suggest you go out and leave them to it. The last thing you want is to be sitting there trying to watch *Coronation Street* while strangers are traipsing around your living room and poking their noses in your cupboards.

Sold!

If you manage to successfully sell your property at auction, the auctioneer signs a contract on your behalf in the saleroom. The purchaser has to pay a 10 per cent deposit on the day of the sale (see Chapter 10 for more information about buying a property at auction). The buyer loses this 10 per cent deposit if he doesn't pay the remainder of the sale price, usually within 28 days. But while you get to keep the buyer's forfeited deposit, you also have the hassle of trying to sell your property again.

If your reserve price isn't met at auction, you have a couple of options: You can try selling your property privately instead. Or you may have to face the fact that you have to accept less than your reserve price.

Cost of selling at auction

The auction house is paid by commission – usually around 2 per cent of the sale price, plus VAT. Many auctioneers also charge sellers an entry fee for including their property in the sale. This fee covers the original inspection of the property by someone from the auction house (to ensure that it is suitable for auction), as well as marketing and catalogue production costs. The price of this depends on the space you take up in the catalogue, which in itself depends on the value of your property; the bigger the property, the more space you should buy in the catalogue to give it prominence over fellow lots.

If you're tempted to go ahead with the auction, obtain an estimate from the auctioneer, in writing, stating how much you're expected to spend. Also remember that, even if you fail to sell your property, you may have to pay certain auction costs, such as the entry fee. Check with your auctioneer before the sale as to exactly what these fees are likely to be.

The auctioneer's bill for his commission and other expenses is usually sent to your solicitor who pays it on your behalf. After your mortgage and solicitor's fees have been paid, you receive the balance of the money.

Chapter 18

Negotiating a Successful Sale

*W*hen selling your home, one of the most important aspects of the process is negotiating the price. Rarely does a buyer offer the asking price without attempting to haggle first. Negotiation is part and parcel of the process, so both seller and buyer should be prepared for this. From the seller's point of view, a successful transaction is achieved when you find a buyer who is prepared to pay close to the asking price for your property – and the sale is completed within a reasonable timeframe.

Negotiating the price with a buyer and trying to get her to pay as much as possible for a property is a central part of the estate agent's role – the higher the price he achieves, the greater his commission. If you're selling through an estate agent, you don't have to get involved in negotiations if you don't want to. Your agent will simply ask whether you're prepared to accept an offer. But if you're selling privately, you have to negotiate directly with the buyer.

In this chapter, I look at how to negotiate the best price for your home if you're selling in England, Wales, or Northern Ireland. I also help you decide when to spot a timewaster, when to accept an offer, and when to hold out for a higher one. (For details on selling property in Scotland, see Chapter 21).

You Don't Always Get What You Ask For: Negotiating the Price

Sellers have to settle on an asking price when they put their home up for sale (unless the property is at the top end of the market and offers are invited instead). Yet few properties are sold for the asking price. Your property may fetch many thousands of pounds above the asking price in a buoyant market, or it may fetch thousands of pounds below the asking price in a slow market. Buyers expect to pay less than the advertised price for a property and sellers tend to set the price higher than the amount they would happily accept to allow for this.

The asking price is usually considered by both parties to be negotiable. Even so, you must set it carefully because it affects what you end up getting. If you fix it too low in the first place, you're likely to get much less than you had hoped for. Buyers nearly always offer less than the asking price unless they face a lot of competition from other buyers. If you price your home at the minimum you'd be happy to accept, you won't be happy going any lower, yet the buyer will expect to knock you down a little. So when setting the asking price (see Chapter 17 for more details on how to do this), always ask for several thousand pounds more than the minimum you would happily accept.

Typically, this is how offers are made:

1. **The buyer makes an offer through the estate agent, if you're using one, and directly to you if you're selling your home privately.**

   Buyers tend to make offers verbally, but the estate agent should put them in writing when conveying them to you.

2. **You must decide whether to accept or reject the offer.**

   The first offer is usually turned down as a matter of course because it's likely to be a fair way below the asking price. The buyer may be chancing his luck to see how you react. If it's a ridiculous offer, you should have no qualms about rejecting it. See the later section 'Contemplating Offers' for information on what to consider when you make your decision to accept or reject.

3. **The estate agent conveys your decision to the buyer.**

   If you reject the offer, the buyer can make another offer or give up and look for another property. If the buyer makes an improved offer, consider it carefully, even if it's still below the asking price.

   When deciding whether to accept an offer, take into account whether it's higher than the minimum you're prepared to accept (which, of course, you never reveal to the buyer) and how quickly you want to move.

Even if you don't like the buyer personally or she tells you she has great plans for filling in your prized pond as soon as she moves in, try not to let this influence your decision to accept her offer or not. You don't have to live with her and what she does with the property after she has moved in shouldn't affect you. It is only bricks and mortar – concentrate on getting the best price and dreaming about the changes you'll make to your new home.

4. **If you decide to accept an offer, tell your estate agent.** He will inform the buyer who will then contact his solicitor and pass on details of the property, the agreed price, your contact details and those of your solicitor. The conveyancing process then begins.

5. **Inform your solicitor that you've accepted an offer on your property.** Once he has received a written offer from the buyer's solicitor, he will draw up the draft contract.

   See Chapter 19 for details of how the conveyancing process works in England, Wales, and Northern Ireland, or Chapter 21 if you're selling a property in Scotland.

Here are some important points to remember as you negotiate:

- ✓ **Nothing is guaranteed until exchange of contracts (when both you and the buyer sign the contract).** Before then, both sides can pull out.

- ✓ **The price you agree with a buyer is not necessarily what you will end up getting.** Much can happen between agreeing to a price and exchange of contracts. Offers are made 'subject to contract and survey' and if the survey reveals any major structural problems, the buyer will want to pay less for the property. You don't have to agree to this, but you will have to be flexible if you're to achieve a successful sale.

- ✓ **If you're personally negotiating with the buyer, be firm but reasonable.** You, as the seller, have the upper hand; if you don't want to accept an offer, you don't have to – and the deal's off. But you need to weigh up whether the offer you've got is the best you're likely to get or whether you're prepared to hold out for another offer, which could take months.

- ✓ **Weed out the timewasters by checking that the buyer can afford your property, has already got a firm buyer for his own home – if he is selling one – and wants to move in around the time you were hoping to move out.** Only then should you accept his offer and take your home off the market.

- ✓ **There is no need to rush into a decision.** You can reasonably take a day or two to consider an offer before responding. You may even get a better offer from another buyer in the meantime!

Contemplating Offers

Whether you get one offer or several, you need to work out a strategy for dealing with them. Most sellers want to get the best price for their home in the shortest possible time. But this is not always the case. No two property transactions are the same, and your personal circumstances can go a long way towards dictating how you handle offers for your home. If you need a quick sale, you may have to accept a lower offer than you would if you weren't in a hurry. Circumstances that may affect how you vet offers include the following:

✔ **You have to sell quickly:** If you've already found the property of your dreams, are relocating for work, or expecting a baby and have outgrown your one-bed flat, you need a quick sale and may be more inclined to accept lower offers.

Try not to let prospective buyers know you haven't got all the time in the world, because they are likely to take advantage of your urgency and offer less than they would have otherwise, confident in the knowledge that you need to move fast.

✔ **You're in no rush to sell:** If you aren't bothered about when you move, you can afford to stand firm. If you receive offers below the minimum you're prepared to accept, you can wait for a better one to come along. In addition, you're likely to get more for your home eventually because you won't reduce the price in desperation if several weeks pass without a buyer making an offer.

✔ **The housing market is depressed:** Not everyone has the good fortune to sell at the top of the market (besides, unless you're prepared to rent until prices fall a little, you'll have to buy at the top as well). At certain times of the year – usually during the summer and around Christmas – property sales are just slow. Sometimes the market is quiet because buyers have lost confidence in it and are fearful that prices are about to fall. If you've had few viewings, your best bet is to sit the slow-down out and wait for the market to pick up, if you can. If you need to move quickly, you have to consider reducing your price (see 'Lowering the price' later in this chapter) to attract buyers.

✔ **Your home generates lots of interest:** Some people are fortunate to have homes that practically sell themselves even if the market is quiet. If you're in this position, you may well get several interested buyers, which means you're likely to get the asking price – and then some.

Considering the first offer that comes along

Getting an offer is thrilling because it means someone wants to buy your property and you move one step closer to your new home. But try not to get carried away. If the offer is close to the asking price, you may be very tempted to accept it. But beware of accepting the first offer that comes along, particularly if your property has only been on the market for a day or two. If you've managed to attract a serious buyer in that time, you either have an extremely desirable property, the market is buoyant, or the asking price is too low. If you can, wait a little longer to see whether you get any other – higher – offers.

Before accepting or rejecting an offer, ask your estate agent whether he thinks you're likely to get other – higher – offers. He should have a good understanding of current market conditions and be able to advise whether waiting a little longer for a better offer is worth your while.

If you're genuinely prepared to wait, you may find that the buyer raises her original offer if she's genuinely keen on your property. The new and improved offer may convince you to accept it. But don't reject an offer simply as a ploy to spur the buyer to offer more. She may not make an improved offer – maybe she decided the property isn't worth it – and you may have to wait many months for another buyer to come along.

Receiving offers from several buyers

Most sellers would love to receive several offers for their home so they can choose the most desirable buyer offering the highest price. Not only should this enable you to get a buyer who isn't in a chain (see the section 'Buyers in chains' later in this chapter), with his financing already arranged, but you may also get more than the asking price.

Part of the estate agent's job is to get the best – that means the highest – asking price for your home. If several buyers are interested in one property, your estate agent usually plays them off against one another. For example, if a property is on the market at £150,000 and one buyer is prepared to pay the asking price, the agent informs other buyers of this and asks if they're prepared to beat it. If a second buyer offers £155,000, this information is relayed back to the first buyer who has to decide whether to increase her offer. This continues until one buyer is left in the frame – and you end up with a purchase price that is higher than your original asking price.

Dealing with offers significantly below the asking price

You may find that prospective buyers are only happy to offer significantly less than the asking price on your home. There are several reasons why they may do this and you need to weigh up whether the reasons are good ones and whether you should accept a much lower offer:

✔ **Your home has been on the market for several months without a bite.** You may have despaired of ever receiving an offer and then when you do get one, it's much less than the amount you're hoping to receive. You have a choice: Either reject this offer and hang on, possibly for several more months, until a better one comes along, or accept it. If you can afford to wait, you may eventually achieve a better price. But if you need to move as soon as possible, you have to accept the lower price.

- ✔ **Your home is on the market at a much higher price than similar properties in the area.** Prices may have fallen since you first put your home on the market. If your asking price starts to look expensive, you may have to reduce it – or at least be prepared to accept a lower offer.

- ✔ **Your home needs major structural work.** Many people don't want to take on a property requiring major structural renovations. You must be realistic. If the next owner of your home will have to spend a lot of money putting things right, it's only reasonable that the purchase price should be lower to reflect this fact.

If you receive an offer significantly below the asking price, the action you take depends on your personal circumstances. If you desperately need to sell, you may have to accept a lower offer. But if this is the case, don't let the buyer know you're desperate or he will take advantage of this fact and offer even less.

Using sealed bids or 'best and final offers'

If several buyers are keen to purchase your property, one way of deciding between them and achieving the highest price is through *sealed bids* or *best and final offers*. These are very common in Scotland and some parts of the UK when the property market is booming. The big advantage of sealed bids is that there is a chance you'll get a few thousand pounds above the asking price.

Outfoxing the timewasters

A friend of mine rented out her two-bedroom flat in east London when she moved in with her boyfriend. She had no trouble finding good tenants, but when she became pregnant, she and her boyfriend decided to sell both flats and buy a house with more space.

Unfortunately, they made the decision at a time when the housing market was depressed. They received offers on the flats, but they were ridiculously low. Although my friend's flat was for sale at £270,000 – well in line with what she would easily have got several months before – prospective buyers were offering more than £40,000 below the asking price. Even in a quiet market, these offers were ludicrous. The buyers

weren't interested in upping their offers. It seemed that they weren't really serious about buying; just trying to see how low an offer they could get away with.

Luckily, my friend and her boyfriend were far from desperate. They decided to take both flats off the market and carry on renting out her flat. Once the market picks up a bit, the plan is to try selling both flats again. It's a bit of a squeeze living in a small flat with a new baby, but they'd rather do that than lose out on thousands of pounds.

If you've got the option of waiting, you're in a stronger position and are more likely to get the price you want – eventually.

With sealed bids, or best and final offers, buyers interested in purchasing your property must make an offer in writing to your estate agent or solicitor by a certain deadline. Once the deadline has passed, the agent or solicitor opens the bids and informs you of what the offers are. You get to decide which one you accept (if any).

The highest bid isn't necessarily always the successful one. A lower offer from a buyer who is in a position to move quickly could work out better for you. Look for offers from buyers who are chain-free, have found a buyer for their own home, or have a mortgage agreed in principle.

No gazumping!

Even if you have accepted an offer, nothing is guaranteed until exchange of contracts and both buyer and seller can pull out before this stage is reached. The price can change if the buyer's survey reveals problems with the property or the seller accepts a higher offer from another buyer after agreeing on a price with someone else. This latter situation is known as *gazumping*.

Although it's perfectly legal to accept an offer from another buyer before contracts are exchanged, even if you have already accepted an offer, it isn't fair – at least not without giving the original buyer a chance to match the new offer. Think how you'd feel if you were gazumped (which, since you're probably buying a property yourself, isn't so unlikely). In addition, gazumping can be expensive for the buyer who may have already instructed a solicitor or arranged a survey.

You may be tempted to accept a higher offer from another buyer, but resist doing so. Price isn't everything, and if someone made an offer that you were happy to accept at the time, be decent enough to stand by your agreement. Here's a good rule to follow – treat others as you would like to be treated yourself.

Not All Buyers are Equal

Price is important when it comes to selling your home, but it isn't the be all and end all. Whether the purchase is successfully completed or not depends on a variety of factors including the buyer's financial position, if she is in a chain, and whether the survey uncovers serious problems with the property.

Buyers to avoid

Some buyers spell trouble. They mess you about and hold up the sale, sometimes through no fault of their own but because they are in a complicated chain. Either way, they can make your life a misery and delay your sale. Below, I look at how you can spot them.

Those who've yet to sell their own homes

Avoid accepting an offer from a buyer who has yet to find someone to purchase his home. If a prospective buyer tells you that he has an interested buyer but she hasn't made a firm offer, wait until she has before taking your home off the market. If his 'buyer' falls through, you could hang around for months waiting for him to find another one when you could have found a serious buyer during that time. And in the interim, you may miss out on a property that you had your eye on.

Buyers who haven't arranged financing

If a buyer hasn't already got her finances arranged when she makes an offer on your home, there's a chance she may not be able to get that funding. If this is the case, you're wasting your time accepting her offer. Several wasted weeks could pass before you're finally able to pin the prospective buyer down about her lack of finances, during which time you could have sold your property to someone who'd sorted all this out in advance.

One of the best ways of ensuring that this doesn't happen is to ask the prospective buyer for evidence of her ability to raise the necessary funds. Most lenders will issue a certificate – known as *an agreement in principle* – stating that it will lend the buyer a certain amount of cash, subject to survey. While an agreement in principle isn't an absolute guarantee, it is useful as it demonstrates that the lender can't see anything glaringly wrong with the applicant. It also shows that the buyer is serious about purchasing a property because she's gone to the trouble of consulting a lender.

Make sure that you know a buyer's financial status before accepting an offer. This is a vital part of the estate agent's job.

Buyers in chains

Most people who sell a property buy another one at the same time. If your buyer is relying on someone else to buy his home so that he can purchase yours – he's part of a *chain*. If you accept his offer, you become part of the chain. If someone pulls out, the chain is broken and you, along with everyone else in the chain, are affected. With several people in the average chain, the chain can dominate transactions in England and Wales. A lot of juggling has to go on between solicitors to ensure that exchange of contracts and completion happens at the same time on all properties in a chain.

Chains – especially long ones – can easily be broken because there is more of a chance of complications arising. The shorter the chain you're involved in, the better. It might not seem important when you find an enthusiastic buyer who is prepared to pay the asking price for your home, but if the buyer is the first in a long and complicated chain, you could be asking for trouble.

If at all possible, opt for someone who isn't part of a chain, such as a first-time buyer. They may have more trouble financing their purchase than a homeowner – although this doesn't always follow – but this is likely to be the only potential hiccup. If you have several interested buyers to choose between, someone who is buying their first home – or anyone else not involved in a chain – should be top of the list.

Buyers you want

Just as you need to avoid certain prospective buyers, others you want to be looking to attract. These are buyers who've gone to the trouble of arranging their finances in advance, aren't tied up in complicated chains and want to move as quickly as possible (if this happens to suit you too). Below, I run through what to look for in a buyer.

Cash is king

Any reasonable offer made by someone who can afford your property is worth considering, but the most desirable buyer is one who has the cash ready to buy your home. He doesn't need to get a mortgage beforehand, nor does he have to sell a property before he can buy yours. He has the cash – whether it is from investments, an inheritance, or other source – and he is ready to make an offer.

Cash buyers can move quickly because they don't have to wait for money to come through from a lender or for their home to be sold. They may also be more prepared to pay close to the asking price if they really want your home, as they have funds at their disposal.

First-time buyers

If you're selling a studio, one-bedroom flat, or small house, your property may be suitable for a first-time buyer – an attractive option for a seller. First-time buyers aren't caught up in complicated chains because they aren't selling a property (see the section 'Buyers in chains' for information on why a chain is a bad thing).

Pay particular attention to a first-time buyer's finances. With property prices rocketing in the early 2000s, many first-time buyers have been priced out of the market. They can only afford to purchase a property with help from parents and family or by borrowing many times their income. Ask for evidence that a mortgage lender has agreed in principle to lending them the money, subject to survey.

Because first-time buyers are new to the house buying process, they may not be aware of the order in which things are done. Ensure that your agent keeps an eye on them so they know when to send what to the solicitor. If you aren't using an agent, be sure to do this yourself.

Buyers between homes

Some people choose to sell their home and move into rented accommodation while they look for another. Maybe they made this decision because of a booming housing market; they want to get the best price for their home but don't want to buy another until prices fall. Or they may be considering moving to a new area and want to rent before committing to a permanent move. Either way, these buyers have cash in the bank, so are perfect candidates for a quick sale.

Landlords

The growth of the buy-to-let market means an increasing number of people are setting themselves up as landlords. It's good news if a buyer intends to rent your home to tenants, particularly if he already owns several properties: He probably has a good relationship with his lender, so arranging financing shouldn't be a problem. And because he won't be living in the property, he won't have to sell his own home – speeding up the process.

If you're dealing with a professional landlord with scores of properties, he is likely to be hard-nosed about the price he pays. He is running a business after all and is unlikely to allow emotions to play a part in his decision. Bear this in mind, and don't feel pressurised into accepting a lower price than you're happy with.

Taking Action When You Aren't Getting Any Offers

The nightmare scenario for sellers is when no-one shows an interest in their home. There could be many reasons for this, including a depressed market, an over-priced house, or the rundown property next door. If you find yourself in this unenviable position, work out what's causing a lack of offers before you take action, such as lowering your price. You may discover that price isn't the issue at all.

Give it time. Some top-end or unusual properties can take months to shift. And if the market is slow, you'll struggle to sell your property. Don't panic if your home has been for sale for two weeks and you haven't had a buyer round. These things don't happen overnight, so don't rush into taking remedial action before giving it a chance.

Seeking advice

If your property hasn't sold after several weeks, there may be a problem. Seeing what could be causing a lack of offers can be hard, because you've grown accustomed to your home. What may be a glaring fault to a prospective buyer you may not even notice. If nobody is biting your hand off to purchase your home, you need to find out from others why that is.

Prospective buyers

One of the best sources of feedback is a prospective buyer who viewed your property but didn't make an offer. The agent should give you feedback after viewings. If several buyers make the same complaint – about the caravan in the drive or the poky garden, for example – you can rectify the situation by removing the caravan or thinning out the plants. Recurring complaints need attention if you're going to find a buyer.

Estate agent

If you haven't had any viewings, ask the agent why. She may suggest that the price is too high or that business is slow and you have to be patient. She may also suggest improvements you can make to the property to increase the chances of a sale.

If you're unhappy with your agent's efforts and have given him several weeks to prove his worth, you may want to consider switching agents. Check your contract to see when you can instruct another agent without incurring a penalty or having to pay two lots of commission if the second agent manages to sell your home.

Staying put – for now

If prospective buyers willing to pay close to the asking price are few and far between, you may decide to take your home off the market for now. If you aren't in a hurry to sell, this may be the best plan. Once the market picks up a bit, you can put your home up for sale again. This way you're more likely to get the price you want.

Lowering the price

Sitting tight and waiting for a buyer prepared to offer the asking price isn't always convenient. If you're short of time and need to move quickly, or haven't had any offers in several months, you may have to reduce the price. If the market is quiet and many sellers are reducing their asking price, you're even less likely to get a sale if you don't reduce the price.

Lower the price by a few thousand pounds initially to see whether this generates more interest. If it doesn't, think about reducing it further. Try not to make the mistake of knocking too much off initially because you could end up under-selling your home when doing so is not necessary.

Lowering the price should be your last resort for these reasons. First, buyers who sense desperation try to take advantage and knock the price down further. Second, after the asking price has been reduced, warning bells start to sound. Buyers will wonder what's wrong with your property and think twice about making an offer at all.

Part V
The Legal Process of Buying and Selling

'Fire, theft, subsidence, riot, plague, war, alien landing, but we're not covered for flood damage.'

In this part . . .

*B*ecause a property transaction involves a considerable amount of money, you'll want to make sure that it's all done legally and above board. In the chapters in this part, the not-so-fun issue of conveyancing is dealt with in an easy to understand way.

I also give you some great tips to ensure you don't unwittingly hold up the process and make sure it all goes through as smoothly as possible. There are also separate chapters on the legal process for buying and selling in Scotland. So for all issues legal, roll up, roll up!

Chapter 19

Conveyancing for Buyers and Sellers in England, Wales, and Northern Ireland

*F*inding your dream home or a suitable buyer can feel like a big achievement after all the hard work and effort you've put in to get this far. But it's just the beginning. Once an offer has been accepted, the next step is *conveyancing*: The legal transfer of a property from seller to buyer. Not only do both parties' solicitors have plenty to do to achieve this goal, but the buyer and seller themselves have their own roles to play. If you know what happens, and in what order, it will reduce the chance of you unwittingly holding up the transaction.

A lot can go wrong between an offer being accepted and exchange of contracts – when buyer and seller are legally obliged to go through with the deal – because there is so much work to be done. It is an extremely stressful time. In this chapter, I offer tips to make everything go as smoothly as possible and to reduce the chances of the transaction falling through.

The Offer Has Been Accepted: Let the Conveyancing Begin!

Once buyer and seller have agreed on a price for the property – subject to contract and survey – the conveyancing can begin. This transfers 'good title' – the legal right to possession – from one person to another. A lot of detective work is involved and it can take many weeks to gather all the necessary information. Even though each party's solicitor does the bulk of the work, hold-ups and delays make for an incredibly stressful time.

During conveyancing, several things happen:

- ✔ **You appoint a solicitor or conveyancer to act on your behalf.** Some buyers and sellers prefer to do their own conveyancing in order to avoid paying legal fees. However, it is very risky (see the sidebar 'Do-It-Yourself Conveyancing' later in this chapter). For more details on locating a solicitor or conveyancer, hop to the section 'Finding a Solicitor or Licensed Conveyancer.'

- ✔ **The solicitors get busy.** The seller's solicitor draws up the draft contract, including details of the particulars and conditions of sale and includes a copy of the Home Information Pack (HIP) in England and Wales. In Northern Ireland, the buyer's solicitor conducts the local searches and contacts the Land Registry. The buyer's solicitor also goes through the draft contract and raises any questions he has with the seller's solicitor. Once they come to an agreement, the seller's solicitor can draw up the final contract. For more details on what the solicitors get up to, see the 'Role of the Buyer's Solicitor' and 'The Role of the Seller's Solicitor' later in this chapter.

- ✔ **You make yourself available to answer questions.** If you are the seller, you must complete the seller's questionnaire, if you are the buyer you want to ensure that everything you agreed with the seller is included in the contract. For example, if you agreed to purchase certain fixtures and fittings, these should be included. (For more info on your obligations, see 'The buyer's role' or 'The seller's role', later in this chapter).

- ✔ **When all necessary tasks have been completed and the final contract accepted by both parties, contracts are exchanged.** Now there's no going back, you can celebrate and get busy moving! Go to 'Exchange of Contracts' later in this chapter for details of what happens in the final stages.

Following are things you can do to make the conveyancing go more smoothly:

✔ Find a solicitor before making or accepting an offer – ideally before you start looking for a property or put yours up for sale. Otherwise you may hold everything up while you find one (see 'Finding a Solicitor or Licensed Conveyancer' later in this chapter).

✔ If you're buying and selling a home at the same time, get one solicitor to handle both transactions. This saves you money and lets your solicitor coordinate the sale and purchase so they happen simultaneously. Otherwise, you could end up homeless while you wait for your purchase to go through.

✔ Complete and return the necessary forms and documents to your solicitor as soon as you can. Part of the reason why it can take 12 weeks between an offer being accepted and exchange of contracts is that people sit on documents for days before they return them.

✔ If your solicitor tells you that the other party is dragging her heels, contact her to find out what is causing the delay. And while you're at it, make sure that you aren't responsible for hold ups.

The buyer's role

After your offer has been accepted, you need to do several things to ensure that your purchase goes through as quickly as possible:

✔ Instruct a solicitor

✔ Apply for a mortgage

✔ Commission a survey

I cover these steps in more detail below.

Instructing a solicitor

When you make the decision to purchase a property, you must inform your solicitor of the seller's contact details and those of his solicitor, the address of the property, and the purchase price.

Applying for a mortgage

If you need a mortgage – and let's face it, most people do! – apply without delay. If you have an agreement in principle (which I highly recommend and which you can find out more about in Chapter 2), inform the lender that you have found a property. Complete and return a mortgage application form, along with a cheque for the lender's arrangement fee, if required.

If you haven't found a lender yet, don't delay. The best way of obtaining a mortgage simply and quickly is to use an independent mortgage broker (see Chapter 11 for more details on this). She can help you find the best deal on the market. The broker also supplies the lender's mortgage application form; once you've completed this, return it directly to the lender, along with the fee (if applicable).

The advantage of using a broker, apart from not having to wade through the multitude of available mortgages on the market, is that she can apply pressure to the lender if it seems to be dragging its heels over processing your application.

After you've received a formal written mortgage offer from your lender, pass this onto your solicitor. He will need the formal offer in order to exchange contracts with the seller's solicitor.

Commissioning a survey

Your lender instructs a local surveyor to value the property you intend to buy to ensure that it is worth the money you intend to borrow. Although you have to pay for this valuation, it is wholly for the lender's benefit, ensuring that, if you default on the loan, the lender can recoup its investment by repossessing and selling your home.

The basic valuation doesn't tell you anything about the condition of the property and whether any potential problems exist. To find this out you must commission a survey. There are two types: The one you opt for depends on the condition and age of the property, your own expertise in assessing potential problems, and how much you can afford to spend. Most buyers need no more than a Homebuyer's Report – which is more detailed than a simple valuation and will point out glaring faults. If the surveyor thinks further investigation is necessary, you need to obtain a more detailed report. If the property is very old, however, the likelihood of potential problems is much greater so opt for a full structural survey. (For more details on surveys and cost, see Chapter 9).

The seller's role

If you're selling your home, you're probably also buying one. So in addition to arranging a mortgage and commissioning a survey on your new purchase (see the preceding section), you also have to do several things after you accept an offer from a buyer:

✔ Tell your solicitor that you have accepted an offer on your home.

✔ Find a property to buy yourself, if you haven't done so already.

✔ Apply for a mortgage.

✔ Complete the seller's questionnaire – a list of questions from the buyer's solicitor.

I cover these tasks in more detail in the following sections.

Informing your solicitor that you've accepted an offer

When you accept an offer, you need to inform your solicitor in writing, along with contact details for the buyer and his solicitor, the price you accepted and whether fixtures and fittings are included.

Your solicitor draws up a draft contract using this information and passes this onto the buyer's solicitor who examines it and queries anything he disagrees with or doesn't like the look of.

Finding a house to buy

You may already have made an offer on another property. If so – and that offer has been accepted – congratulations. Many people, however, wait until they have a firm offer on their current home before they begin serious house-hunting. If you're in the latter group, you must go flat out to find one and get an offer accepted. If you don't know what kind of property you want, head to Part II, where you can find lots of detail about all types of housing options. Chapter 9 gives you information on making an offer.

Applying for a mortgage

Unless you make a massive profit on the sale of your home, you probably have to take out a mortgage to buy a new property. Once you know how much you can get for your home, you can work out how much you have to put towards a new property (simply subtract your outstanding mortgage from the amount your old home fetches; contact your lender to find out how much you owe).

The next step is to find out how much you can borrow, which is based on your income. Check to see whether your existing lender can offer you a competitive deal and then check this against the mortgages offered by other lenders. A mortgage broker can direct you to the best deals or you can check for yourself on the Internet to find out whether your lender's offer sounds good. To compare mortgages, try financial Web site Moneysupermarket (www.moneysupermarket.com).

Completing the seller's questionnaire

Your solicitor passes on a standard list of questions from the buyer's solicitor for you to answer. These questions are known as *preliminary enquiries, enquiries before contract*, or simply *the seller's questionnaire.* They're designed to find out more details about your property; for example, you will be asked the following:

- ✔ What is included in the sale

- ✔ What the boundaries of the property are

- ✔ Who is responsible for the upkeep of hedges, fences, or walls

- ✔ Whether there are any guarantees on any structural work that's been done on the property

- ✔ Whether you've had any disputes relating to the property

You must complete and return the questions as soon as possible – or you risk delaying the sale.

 The buyer relies on the answers you give in the seller's questionnaire when deciding whether to purchase your property. You must answer as truthfully as possible; incorrect information provides the buyer with a good case for compensation from you. Or if the buyer finds out you lied before exchange of contracts, he could pull out completely. If you don't know the answer to a question, say so. Don't take a guess. If your guess turns out to be incorrect, you're still held responsible.

Finding a Solicitor or Licensed Conveyancer

If you already have a solicitor that you're happy with, you may think he is the perfect choice to do your conveyancing. But while the legal work involved in transferring a property from seller to buyer is often regarded as one of the more mundane jobs in the legal profession, it is nevertheless a very exact science.

Most lenders insist that you use a qualified solicitor to carry out your conveyancing and that the practice have at least two partners who are members of the Law Society. The rest is down to you, but I suggest you choose a solicitor who specialises in conveyancing. In England and Wales you can use a licensed conveyancer instead of a solicitor. These people offer the same services as a solicitor but are limited to house purchasing.

The buyer and seller must use a different solicitor to ensure that both parties are dealt with completely fairly. Your mortgage lender insists upon this to eliminate the possibility of conflict of interest. If, by some strange twist of fate, you both happen to have the same solicitor, one of you may be able to use a different partner from the same firm. But it may be better for one of you to just retire gracefully and find another solicitor to use for this transaction.

General advice for locating a solicitor

Personal recommendation is the best way to choose a solicitor or licensed conveyancer. If someone you know still speaks highly of the solicitor who helped them with a property purchase, this solicitor is probably all right. Likewise, if someone tells you that he's had a bad experience with a solicitor, you may want to give that solicitor a wide berth.

If you don't have a personal recommendation to go on, you can find a solicitor experienced in conveyancing by contacting the following:

- ✔ The public enquiry line of the Law Society in England and Wales (0870 606 2555). This society can provide you with details of up to three solicitors working in your area. You can also try www.lawsociety.org.uk.

- ✔ Alternatively, try the Council for Licensed Conveyancers (www.theck.gov.uk) or 01245 349599.

- ✔ The National Solicitor's Network provides details of solicitors experienced in conveyancing in England, Wales and Scotland (www.tnsn.com or 0845 389 0381).

- ✔ In Northern Ireland, contact the Law Society of Northern Ireland (028 90 231 614 or www.lawsoc-ni.org).

Your estate agent or mortgage lender may recommend a solicitor or licensed conveyancer to you and may offer a special rate if you use his services. If you're considering following your agent's or lender's advice in this regard, keep the following in mind. You're under no obligation to use this person, and if the agent or lender insists you do, take your business elsewhere. Even if the charges seem attractive, compare them with what other solicitors are charging to make sure that they truly are competitive.

Checking the solicitor out

Find out as much as you can about a solicitor and his practice before instructing him. Although nobody can say for sure how long conveyancing will take, try to get some idea. If the solicitor is extremely vague or off-hand, find somebody else. But if he seems eager, he's more likely to get on with the job. When you contact a solicitor find out about the following:

- ✔ **Who will be dealing with your case on a day-to-day basis.** Quite often it's an office junior. If this is the case, find out how involved your solicitor will be – whether he will be overseeing this person closely, for example.

- ✔ **When your solicitor is away on holiday who will take over his caseload in his absence.** This is good information to have just in case something goes drastically wrong at the last minute.

- ✔ **If you're selling your property, is the solicitor signed up to the Law Society's TransAction Protocol?** If he is, you can save a lot of time because, under this protocol, certain documents automatically accompany the draft contract when it's sent to the buyer's solicitor; he doesn't have to apply for them. These are copies of the title deeds; the property information form, which contains preliminary enquiries answered by the seller; and a fixtures and fittings form, detailing what is included in the sale price. The TransAction Protocol speeds up the tortuously long conveyancing process. If you're in a hurry, choose a solicitor who is signed up with this scheme.

Your aim is to assess how professional and efficient the solicitor is because you'll be dealing with him on a regular basis over the next few weeks and how he does his job directly affects the outcome of your property transaction.

Local isn't always necessary

Select a solicitor who is local to the property you're buying. Such a solicitor should have a good knowledge of the area and any planning restrictions. The other advantage of the local solicitor is that you can speed up the whole process by popping into the office with forms and documents or to sign paperwork rather than relying on the post.

You don't *have* to use a local practice as you won't have much face-to-face contact, if any, with your solicitor. Modern communications mean that conveyancing is carried out over the telephone, by fax, e-mail, and via the post. This is good news if you live in an area where conveyancing is expensive – such as a city – as you will almost certainly get a cheaper deal if you use a solicitor who is based further afield.

Cost isn't everything . . . but it's worth considering

Cost is a major consideration when you choose a solicitor; some homebuyers end up spending hundreds of pounds more on conveyancing than others. You inevitably pay higher charges if you're buying a six-bedroom mansion than if you were purchasing a studio flat, or a leasehold property rather than freehold. But shop around and get a couple of quotes for the work, in writing, before you instruct a solicitor, to ensure that you aren't paying over the odds.

While you don't want to pay too much for your conveyancing, beware of paying too little. The cheapest quote may be attractive, particularly as money is likely to be tight, but this solicitor's charges may be low because he doesn't offer very good service. He may cut corners in order to offer this price or take on more work than he can cope with in order to make up his money. A very expensive solicitor isn't necessarily a better choice. That big, bustling, expensive City firm may be too busy to treat your case as a priority. You could end up pushed right to the bottom of the pile.

As a general rule, if you pay a little more, you're likely to get better service. Avoid the solicitor offering the cheapest quote, as well as the most expensive. A small practice dedicated to conveyancing, with moderate charges, may produce much quicker results for you.

The cost of conveyancing is divided into solicitor's fees and disbursements, both of which are explained in more detail below.

Fees

Both buyer and seller have to pay their solicitor a fee for all the work done liaising with the other party's solicitor, sending out forms and contracts and giving you advice and guidance. Solicitor's fees can cost anything from £500 upwards, depending on the complexity of the case and your individual solicitor.

Some solicitors base their fee on the size of your property; the more expensive the home, the bigger the fee. Other solicitors have a set fee regardless of property size. If you're buying a leasehold property, expect to be charged more than if you're buying a freehold property because of the extra work involved in checking the lease.

Don't rely on a verbal quote over the phone or a rough estimate. Whatever the fee, make sure you get a detailed, fixed quote in writing; then if complications arise, you shouldn't be landed with a huge, unexpected bill upon completion.

Disbursements

In Northern Ireland, the buyer's solicitor incurs a number of costs or disbursements when making various enquiries, known as local searches, on the property. Expect to pay a Land Registry fee, local authority search fee, water authority search fee, and land charges search fee – and there may be others.

You must pay all outstanding charges and fees to the solicitor before completion can take place. Check out Table 19-1 for an example of the breakdown of the actual costs incurred on the purchase of a three-bedroom house in Guildford, Surrey for £240,000; this should give you an idea of the sort of sums you can expect.

Table 19-1	Solicitor's fees, Disbursements and Stamp Duty on a £240,000 Property
Item	*Typical Costs*
Property purchase price	£240,000
Solicitor's fees	£550
VAT on solicitor's fees	£96.25
Stamp duty	£2,400
Bank fee for electronic transfer	£35.25
Mortgage arrangement fee	£1,000
Total cost	**£244,081.50**

The buyer also has to pay stamp duty to his solicitor – at the same time as he pays the solicitor's fees. Your stamp duty bill depends on the value of your property, starting at 1 per cent on properties costing £125,000, rising to 4 per cent on properties of £500,000 or more (for more details, go to Chapter 11).

The Role of the Buyer's Solicitor

If you're buying a property, your solicitor's job is to ensure that there is nothing that can cause you any problems either in the contract or lease (if there is one), or revealed by the local searches. Your solicitor should do the following:

- Check the legal jargon in the title deeds.

- Find out the property's background by checking planning and title searches in the seller's Home Information Pack (HIP).

- Make sure that nothing's in the lease (if it is a leasehold property) that affects your ownership of the property.

- Ensure that the contract is legal.

- Help you renegotiate the price if problems crop up.

Your solicitor doesn't have to take any action until he has received the draft contract, which is drawn up by the seller's solicitor. Before he receives the draft contract, however, he may send out a list of questions to the seller to obtain more information about the property (see 'Completing the seller's questionnaire' earlier in this chapter).

Working through the draft contract

There are two parts to the draft contract your solicitor gets from the seller's solicitor:

- **Particulars of sale:** A description of the property, what fixtures and fittings are included, and details as to whether the property is freehold or leasehold.

- **Conditions of sale:** Details of the proposed completion date and the deposit you have to pay when contracts are exchanged.

The contract may also include a provision for you to purchase certain fittings such as carpets and curtains, if you want to, for an extra sum. A copy of the title deeds usually accompanies the draft contract. Your solicitor needs this so that he can check that the seller actually owns the property and has the right to sell it to you.

Your solicitor works his way through the draft contract and raises any questions he has with the seller's solicitor. He also sends you a copy of the contract. Check this carefully to ensure that everything you agreed with the seller is included. If the seller promised to throw in the carpets, for example, and that's not been noted, inform your solicitor before you sign the contract, or you won't have any comeback.

The draft contract can go back and forth between solicitors for some time.

TECHNICAL STUFF

Understanding the contract: Differences between freehold and leasehold

The contract states whether the property is freehold or leasehold. Freehold is much more straightforward: You own the property and the land it stands on, up to its boundaries. As long as you act within the law, you can do what you like on your property. Most properties in England, Wales, and Northern Ireland are freehold.

Buying a leasehold property is more complicated. There are 2 million such homes so you may end up with one. You don't have the freedom of a freeholder; instead, you're buying the right to live in a property for a fixed number of years – the length of the lease. Leases vary in length. Many have more than 99 years left to run, while some have 999 years left on them. Once the lease has expired, the property reverts to the landlord.

The landlord retains ownership of the building and the land the building stands on during the term of the lease. He imposes an annual service charge for the upkeep of the communal areas and structure of the building, as well as ground rent.

The conveyancing process on a freehold property is much more straightforward than on a leasehold because there are fewer potential problems. Keep in mind, however, that most people buying flats have no choice but to buy leasehold, and in the majority of cases, this doesn't cause a problem. As long as the lease has at least 40 years left to run (mortgage lenders generally won't lend money on shorter leases), and your solicitor has studied it closely to ensure it doesn't include any nasty clauses likely to affect the value of your investment, you should be okay.

Local searches and Land Registry search

If you're buying a property, your solicitor needs to establish that the seller is actually in a position to sell it to you and that there are no conflicting rights to the land that the property is built upon. These may not be immediately obvious because these rights can go back hundreds of years. It is not unheard of for there to be ancient ecclesiastical or common rights to the land, which could affect your rights to the property. Your solicitor's job is to discover whether this is the case by checking the HIP (in England and Wales) or conducting local searches and contacting the Land Registry (in Northern Ireland).

Local searches

If you've set your heart on a cosy cul-de-sac, you'll be devastated if you discover that there are plans for a motorway to run right through it. Local searches are designed to reveal whether such plans are in existence *before* you buy your new home. If something is planned that would be detrimental to your enjoyment of the property, you'll probably be gutted. But at least you can pull out before exchange of contracts so that you won't have to put up with traffic roaring past your living room window.

Local searches reveal the following:

- ✔ Whether the council has plans for a motorway at the end of the road.
- ✔ Whether any planning restrictions affect your ability to renovate or extend the property.
- ✔ Whether planning permission was received for the property before it was built (otherwise the council may insist you have it knocked down).
- ✔ Whether any extensions or conversions in need of planning consent were actually received before building work started.
- ✔ Whether the water drainage system is working as it should be and who owns the drains.
- ✔ Whether the sale includes covenants associated with the property and its land.

The location of the property determines whether other searches are necessary, such as commons searches or coal mining, for example.

Local searches aren't comprehensive – there are plenty of things they don't unearth. They only cover the property itself and the areas immediately next to it, as well as roads. They don't check the surrounding area. Your property may be built on contaminated land, but not all councils keep a detailed register of this so you may not find out. Or if a waste disposal plant or block of flats is planned for the adjoining land, you won't find this out either. If your prospective property is close to vacant land, ask your solicitor to check whether anything is registered against it – such as planning permission for a supermarket.

Your solicitor won't visit the property you're buying, so if you have any concerns about adjoining land, mention them to him so he can investigate further.

The Role of the Seller's Solicitor

The seller's solicitor has a number of tasks to carry out. These include:

- ✔ Drawing up the draft contract
- ✔ Negotiating with the buyer's solicitor over the terms included in the draft contract
- ✔ Drawing up the final contract

✓ Finding out how much you owe your lender

✓ Getting you to sign the transfer deeds ahead of completion

✓ Receiving the purchase price from the buyer's solicitor and releasing the title deeds to the buyer's solicitor

✓ Paying off your mortgage, subtracting his fee and the estate agent's and transferring the remaining cash to you (or your new lender if you're taking out another mortgage)

As soon as you notify your solicitor that you have accepted an offer, he contacts your lender and requests the title deeds to the property. He then prepares a draft contract setting out the terms of the sale.

The draft contract is a starting point and is altered as the solicitors haggle over the terms. The purchase price may also be reduced if the survey throws up unforeseen problems. Both solicitors negotiate the contract to their satisfaction. Once this is done and the buyer's solicitor has checked the local searches (see 'Local searches and Land Registry' for details), the draft contract is sent to you for your approval. If you and the buyer are both happy, you both sign. Contracts are then exchanged, and neither of you can pull out.

Your solicitor will then find out how much you owe your lender. He asks you to sign the transfer deed ahead of completion, when he will receive the rest of the purchase price (minus the deposit that has already been paid) from the buyer's solicitor, usually by electronic transfer. On receipt of this money, the title deeds are released to the buyer's solicitor.

Once your mortgage has been paid off and your solicitor has subtracted his fee and paid the estate agent what she is owed, any money left over is transferred to you (or directly to the lender supplying the mortgage for your new home, if you're buying one).

Dealing with Problems Arising from the Survey: Advice for Buyers

It's not for nothing that moving house is regarded as one of the most stressful things you'll ever do. So much can go wrong that you shouldn't be surprised if you have a hiccup or two along the way. How big these hiccups are, however, and how you deal with them can have an impact on whether your purchase goes through – or not. The following sections explain two types of problems that may come from the survey and give you strategies for overcoming them.

Seller's packs

Home Information Packs (HIPs) require the seller to pay for local authority searches, not the buyer. This is intended to speed up the process – because the searches are done before the property goes on the market.

The seller also has to provide details of works carried out and a copy of the lease (if relevant)

before he puts her property up for sale. An Energy Performance Certificate is also mandatory. HIPs make the process less uncertain for buyers. You'll get the complete picture before you make an offer so you'll know there are no potential nasties. This should increase the chances of the sale going through. See Chapter 16 for more on HIPs.

The property isn't worth what you need to borrow

The mortgage lender's valuation states whether the property is worth what you want to borrow to pay for it. If the surveyor gives the thumbs up, you and the seller can breathe a huge sigh of relief because your mortgage is likely to be approved – unless other problems exist and you're seen as a credit risk (see Chapter 11 for more details on why this might happen).

Sometimes, however, the surveyor doesn't think the property is worth the amount of money you want to borrow on your mortgage; that is, it thinks the property is over-priced. In this case, the lender may agree to lend you as much as it thinks the property is worth and you have to find the remainder. Which is all well and good if you have that sort of money. If you don't, you have a couple of other options:

✔ **Ask the seller whether he will reduce the price:** You're in a strong position because the property is overpriced. If the difference is just a couple of thousand pounds, he may be willing to negotiate. However, you have to be prepared for him to refuse and pull out of the sale altogether.

✔ **Raise the cash by other means:** Use a bridging loan from your lender, take out a personal loan, extend your overdraft, or use a credit card.

Think carefully about whether you can afford to take on this extra debt, because bridging loans in particular can be very expensive.

If your appeal to the seller is turned down and you have no way of raising the extra money, you may have to give up on the property.

The surveyor discovers big problems with the property

If you opted for a Homebuyer's Report or full structural survey (refer to Chapter 9 for a description of these surveys) and the report unveils problems, you have to assess whether you still want to buy the property. Your decision depends on the extent and cost of the work to be done and the willingness of the seller to put things right.

If severe damp or subsidence is found, for example, get a clear idea of the cost of repair by talking to your surveyor, who can give you an estimate of the cost involved in putting it right. Alternatively, you can get quotes from two or three builders. Armed with this information, you're in a strong position to renegotiate the price with the seller.

The seller may decide to get the work done himself *before* you buy the property. In this case, the price remains the same. But you may worry about whether the job gets done properly: You may have to send your surveyor back to check the completed work.

If the job is sizeable, however, the seller may not want to go to the trouble of getting the builders in, which means you will have to get the work done after you move in. In this case, ask for a reduction on the purchase price. To strengthen your case, give the seller a copy of the surveyor's report because he may try to downplay the problem.

Before you make any big decisions about the property based on the survey, try to assess how grave the situation really is. You may want to commission another report to look specifically at the problem, particularly if the surveyor recommends this. Although you may be reluctant to spend the extra cash on an additional survey, doing so can save you in the long run. If the problem is serious, you have the opportunity to pull out before making an expensive mistake.

Your lender will insist that you arrange for any extra investigations to be done if the surveyor recommends them. And if you still want to proceed with the purchase, be prepared for the lender to hold back part of the loan until it's happy that you've rectified the problem.

The Final Contract: Vetting and Signing

After both solicitors approve the draft contract, the seller's solicitor draws up a final contract for buyer and seller to sign. Legal documents tend to be full of complicated jargon and can be hard to understand. Although you may be tempted to leave it all to your solicitor, don't. A lot of money – yours – is at stake, so read the final contract very carefully.

If, after you pore over the contract, there's anything you're still not clear about, ask your solicitor to explain it to you.

When you're satisfied with the contract and all its provisions, sign it and return it to your solicitor. When everyone's in agreement and the contract has been signed by both parties, you're ready for exchange, as explained in the next section.

If you're buying a property, as soon as you sign the contract you must arrange for the deposit – usually 10 per cent of the purchase price, although sometimes lower – to be transferred to your solicitor's account. This is non-refundable and subtracted from the amount you must pay at completion. Solicitors may accept a cheque but most insist that the money is transferred electronically by BACS (Banks Automated Clearing Service), which takes a couple of days, or, if it's urgent, by CHAPS (the Clearing House Automated Payments System), which occurs on the same day. Expect your bank to charge you around £25 for this. Your solicitor forwards the deposit to the seller's solicitor, who holds onto it until completion.

Exchange of Contracts

After both parties sign the final contract (as explained in the preceding section), contracts are exchanged, usually over the telephone. The deal is then legally binding on both sides. Now you can relax, confident that the sale will go through. A completion date is also set (see the next section for information about completion).

Here are some important things to remember about exchange of contracts:

- ✔ **After exchange of contracts, you can't back out without significant penalties.** Make sure that you don't exchange if you're not 100 per cent sure.

- ✔ **If you're selling your home and buying another property, exchange contracts on both properties on the same day (make sure the completion date is the same on both transactions as well).** Otherwise, you could end up homeless if one sale goes through more quickly than the other.

- ✔ **If you're the buyer, as soon as contracts are exchanged, you're responsible for taking out buildings insurance on the property.** The reason is that the sale is binding at this point. Even if, heaven forbid, the property burnt down before completion, you're still legally obliged to go through with the purchase. See Chapter 12 for details about insuring your property.

Arrange buildings insurance before exchange of contracts – you can ask the insurer to cover the property from the date of exchange.

Completion

A completion date is set when contracts are exchanged. On this date, the seller must move out and the buyer takes possession of the keys to the property and moves in. But there is still some work to be done before completion can take place.

Setting the completion date

There are no set guidelines for when completion must take place. On average, it tends to follow exchange by up to four weeks. The date you choose should suit both parties, give you time to book the removal van, notify various utility companies, and pack.

Don't pick the nearest date for completion, particularly if it's a Friday. Although moving just before the weekend seems sensible, it can become problematic. If you have problems with the property, such as a water leak, you'll have to wait until Monday to get someone out to fix it – unless you're prepared to pay exorbitant call-out fees to get someone out over the weekend.

Gathering the rest of the money

If you're buying, you must ensure that the funds are ready to pay to the seller on the day of completion. Your solicitor prepares the mortgage documents and arranges for the loan to be available on completion. If you're putting down any funds yourself in addition to the mortgage, ensure that your solicitor gets this money in time (electronic transfer can usually be done by the same day.) Your solicitor then transfers funds equal to the purchase price to the seller's solicitor.

Preparing the transfer document and other stuff

The seller's solicitor prepares the document to transfer ownership of the property and the seller must sign this. The buyer is sometimes required to sign it as well.

Do-it-yourself conveyancing

If you fancy a challenge – not one I'd recommend – you can have a go at doing your own conveyancing. An increasing number of buyers and sellers are doing this to save themselves solicitor's fees. But think very carefully before taking on such a daunting project. If you have no prior experience of conveyancing or are buying a leasehold property (which can be particularly complicated), I'd steer clear. And if the other party is doing their own conveyancing, I'd think twice. A whole lot of legal problems could arise which neither of you are capable of dealing with.

Conveyancing is complicated, time-consuming, and lots of hassle. If you have a busy full-time job you may not be able to cope. And if you cut corners and mess up, the penalties are severe.

Even if you do your own conveyancing, your mortgage lender is likely to insist that you pay its legal fees for preparing the mortgage deed (usually a lender allows the buyer's solicitor to do this on its behalf). And some lenders won't agree to you doing your own conveyancing at all so check before taking the plunge.

Try not to go on holiday so that you're available to answer any last-minute questions your solicitor may have, sign documents or hand over any money. If you decide to head off to the sun for three weeks and aren't contactable, don't be surprised if problems await you when you return. If you're buying a property where the seller has agreed to do some remedial work, you need to check whether this is done before completion.

Paying up

If you're buying, this is what you have to look forward to on completion day. You pay the balance of what you owe for the property (minus the deposit) to the seller, via your solicitor. You also have to pay your solicitor's fees plus VAT, stamp duty, and other outstanding charges. Your lender will transmit the mortgage funds electronically to the seller's solicitor. Then you get the keys to the property. The tortuous house buying process is over! Congratulations! Crack open the champagne and enjoy your new home.

If you're the seller, here's what you can expect. You receive a completion statement, stating all the outstanding fees and monies that you need to be pay, including the estate agent's fee. This is usually paid out of the money your solicitor receives from the buyer and his lender. Your solicitor pays off any outstanding mortgage you had on your property and gives your agent (if you used one) her fee. He then transfers the balance to you – or, if you're buying another property – puts this money towards that purchase.

Alas, the solicitor's job still isn't finished. He must stamp the transfer (and pay stamp duty) and put the title deeds in the buyer's name and send the deeds to the mortgage lender, if the buyer has taken out a mortgage. For a leasehold property, the solicitor also ensures that the freeholder is informed that the sale has been completed, and the buyer's name is put on the lease.

Chapter 20

The Scottish House-Buying Process

*W*hen you buy a house or flat in Scotland, the legal process is very different from the rest of the UK. Not only is it different; the home buying process in Scotland is also considered far superior to the outdated practice in England, Wales, and Northern Ireland. In Scotland, everything happens much quicker, and gazumping is virtually unheard of because the contract is binding once the seller accepts an offer.

But no system is perfect, and the Scottish way of doing things has its problems. You have to be absolutely sure when you make an offer because you can't pull out. And because you pay hundreds of pounds for a survey before making an offer (it plays a part in deciding how much you bid), you lose that money if your bid is unsuccessful – and then you have to start all over again with another property.

In this chapter, I highlight what you need to bear in mind to achieve a successful purchase in Scotland – the first time you try.

Becoming an Owner-Occupier

Nearly every property in Scotland – whether a house or flat – is sold on an *owner-occupier basis*, which means that you own the property absolutely and can dispose of it as you would a freehold property in England, Wales, or Northern Ireland.

If you're buying a flat, you also need to:

✓ **Watch out for the communal areas, the roof, stairs and hallways.** These are owned equally by the proprietors of the flats in a block or converted house. If you buy a flat, you're responsible for the joint maintenance of these areas. When you view the property, pay close attention to them (your surveyor should check them out as well).

✓ **Remember that you own the external walls of your own flat and are responsible for their maintenance, but the proprietors of the other flats have an interest in this being done because if you neglect this, it could affect the value of the whole building.** Make sure the title deeds spell out how maintenance and repair costs are split between flat owners.

Getting the Order Right: Finance First

As soon as your offer is accepted, you're committed to the purchase so it's important that you have your finances arranged first. Get them agreed in principle *before* you arrange your first viewing; that way, you won't lose out on the dream home you've just found because you couldn't get a mortgage in time to make an offer.

The first thing you must do is check that you can afford to buy a property. The best way of finding a lender prepared to let you have a mortgage is to shop around. To make this easier, use an independent broker (see Chapter 11 for more details on finding a mortgage).

When you arrange for financing so early in the process, you don't need a firm offer because you'll have no idea of the price of the property you're going to buy – you haven't even started looking yet! What you need is an *agreement in principle* where the lender promises to let you borrow a certain amount. With this certificate, you can hunt for a property safe in the knowledge that you can afford to spend a certain amount of cash.

Finding a Solicitor

You will need the help of a solicitor, or an independent qualified conveyancer, fairly early on in the process. (Conveyancers only specialise in *conveyancing* – the legal transfer of property from seller to buyer – unlike solicitors, who can usually handle other aspects of the law in addition to property transfer.)

The solicitor has a much greater role than he does in the rest of the UK. He's involved from the start, informing the seller's solicitor that you're interested in the property, advising you on what price you should offer, and negotiating a deal with the other party. And this is on top of all the conveyancing he does, explained in the later section 'When Your Offer Is Successful'.

Although you can do your own conveyancing, I don't recommend that you do so unless you're *absolutely sure* you know what you're doing.

Most buyers use a solicitor because independent qualified conveyancers are still rare in Scotland – although they are slowly becoming more common.

Personal recommendation is the best way to find a good solicitor. But if you don't have a recommendation to go on, contact the Law Society of Scotland, which has a 'Find a solicitor' search engine. Go to: `www.lawscot.org.uk`. Alternatively, try the SiteFinder directory for a list of solicitors. You can find this in your local solicitors' property centre (see the next section, 'Finding the Property of Your Dreams').

When you look for a solicitor, keep these things in mind:

- ✔ **Solicitors don't charge fixed fees for conveyancing, and prices can vary a great deal.** Be sure to shop around and get two or three quotes for the work. Also find out from the solicitor how much the *disbursements* – known as *outlays* – are likely to cost for the searches he carries out on your behalf; these can be substantial.

  Because you instruct a solicitor at such an early stage, you have no guarantee that your purchase will be successful. So find out what your solicitor charges if it falls through.

- ✔ **You cannot use an English solicitor in Scotland (they're not permitted to practice north of the border).** If you're moving to Scotland, ask your English solicitor to recommend a practice in Scotland.

Buyers tend to make an offer through their solicitor because it's the safest way of doing so. Find a solicitor before you start viewing properties. Then, when you find a property that you want to buy, you'll be ready to move quickly and make an offer.

Finding the Property of Your Dreams

The process of finding a house or flat in Scotland is not dissimilar to the rest of the UK. Properties are advertised in estate agent's windows and brochures, newspapers, and on the Internet (see Chapter 4 for more about these). The difference is that solicitors, as well as agents, sell properties. In fact, the most common way of finding property in Scotland is through a solicitor's property centre.

Solicitors' property centres

Solicitors' property centres tend to be located in shopping centres in major towns and cities, even though they don't actually sell anything, least of all property. All they do is provide information to buyers, with staff able to give only general advice. Properties are displayed and described in the same way as in an estate agent's window, along with the name of the solicitor handling the sale. If you want further information on a property, you must contact the solicitor handling that sale.

Big cities often have several solicitors' property centres at different locations. The Edinburgh Solicitors Property Centre (ESPC), for example, has showrooms in Edinburgh itself, Dunfermline, Kirkcaldy, Stirling, and Falkirk. The ESPC sold a property every five minutes in 2006 and advertises thousands of properties for sale on its Web site and in its showrooms. Go to www.espc.co.uk. The Web site also includes tips on arranging a mortgage or finding a solicitor.

The big advantage of solicitors' property centres is that you can view thousands of properties for sale across the region – not just those on the books of one solicitor, thus saving shoe leather and time. The ESPC, for example, has more than 240 member solicitor firms. The service is free to buyers and you can register online for e-mail alerts should a property that suits your requirements become available. Alternatively, arrange for your local centre to post you its weekly list of properties for sale.

For a list of solicitors' property centres, contact the Law Society of Scotland or visit the Scottish Solicitors Property Centres' Web site (www.sspc.co.uk), where these centres are listed by location.

Estate agents

Agents work in much the same way as they do in England, Wales, and Northern Ireland, and you should bear the same things in mind when dealing with them (refer to Chapter 4). Only use an agent who belongs to the National Association of Estate Agents (NAEA) as this organisation gives you a comeback if you have a complaint against a member (www.naea.co.uk or call 01926 496800).

Agents are legally obliged to treat buyers fairly and not deliberately mislead you, but keep in mind that they act for the seller, not you (the seller pays the agent's commission). So take everything an agent tells you with a large pinch of salt. If you feel that you've been misled, complain in the first instance to the agent involved. If he's part of a chain, contact the head office instead. If the problem isn't resolved or you're still unhappy, contact Citizens Advice Scotland at www.cas.org.uk or on 0131 550 1000. If the agent belongs to the NAEA, complain to this body (call 01926 496800 e-mail info@naea.co.uk).

The agent writes the description of the property, known as the *property particulars,* which include the number and type of rooms, their size, and any other details she feels may be of interest. If you don't understand anything, ask. Chapter 4 has information about property particulars.

Get hold of a copy of *Real Homes*, a fortnightly list of properties for sale compiled by the biggest estate agents in Edinburgh. You can obtain a copy from the office of any agent who contributes to the list.

Newspapers

All the big Scottish papers, such as *The Scotsman* and the *Herald,* have sizeable property sections on certain days of the week. They also have extensive property websites, which they update regularly. You can search through hundreds of properties for sale by price, size, and region on *The Scotsman*'s *and Scotland on Sunday*'s Web site: `http://property.Scotsman.com`.

Don't forget local newspapers. They often carry a good selection of properties for sale in the area you're interested in.

Viewing properties

When you come across a property you like the sound of, you must view it before you even contemplate making an offer (see Chapter 5 for more details on what to look for during a viewing and what questions to ask).

As you view properties, remember that an offer is binding. So if you *think* you want to make one but aren't absolutely sure, go back again and again until your mind is made up – one way or the other.

Make sure that you don't agree to anything or sign any documents before contacting your solicitor (see the next section). Otherwise you could be committing yourself to a purchase before you're in a position to do so.

Found the Property? What to Do Before You Make an Offer

Once you've found a property you want to buy, there are several things you must do before you make an offer because it is binding. Below, I run through the order you should follow to make sure that everything goes smoothly.

Get your solicitor to note interest

Once you find a property you want to buy, your first phone call shouldn't be to family and friends to tell them how excited you are but to your solicitor. Your solicitor's response may be less enthusiastic (he won't, after all, jump up and down at your good news), but he will telephone the seller's solicitor or agent to *note interest* in the property. This means you will get the chance to make an offer.

Complete your mortgage application

After your interest has been noted, you can apply for your mortgage. If you have an agreement in principle from a lender (refer to the earlier section 'Getting the Order Right: Finance First'), request an application form. Complete this without delay and return it to the lender, with a cheque for the arrangement fee (if applicable).

If you haven't got an agreement in principle, there is no time to waste. Contact an independent broker (see Chapter 11 for more on how to find one) to help you locate a home loan. You will have to fill out an application form (as above) and pay the arrangement fee.

The lender arranges for the property to be valued to ensure that it's worth what you're planning to borrow. This valuation isn't a survey and doesn't give any indication of the condition of the property; it simply covers the lender's back, although you have to pay for it. You need to arrange for a survey yourself, as explained in the next section. (You can find additional information on valuations and surveys in Chapter 9.)

Don't make an offer on a property without your lender's approval. Otherwise, you could commit yourself before you have the funds to pay for it.

Survey first, offer later

Unlike in England, Wales, and Northern Ireland, you arrange a survey *before* you make an offer because the offer is binding, *not subject to contract and survey.* If structural faults are discovered after you've made an offer – tough.

I recommend that you pay for a survey. You may be tempted to reduce costs but skipping the survey is not the way to do it. True, there's no guarantee that your offer will be successful, but if you discover serious structural faults only after you have made an offer, you will regret it.

The best way to find a surveyor or valuer is through personal recommendation. But if you don't have a recommendation to go on, and even if you do, make sure that you use one who belongs to a professional body so that you have some comeback if things go wrong. Your surveyor should belong to the Royal Institution of Chartered Surveyors (RICS); look out for the letters ARICS (associate) or FRICS (fellow) after her name. For a list of RICS-registered surveyors in your area, contact RICS Scotland on 0131 225 7078. Alternatively, membership of the Incorporated Society of Valuers and Auctioneers or the Incorporated Association of Architects and Surveyors, is also acceptable.

RICS Scotland publishes a helpful leaflet explaining the different types of surveys available, called *Buying Property? Then you need a survey.* For a free copy, contact RICS Scotland (on 0131 225 7078). You can also read the leaflet on its Web site at www.rics-scotland.org.uk.

The types of survey available are more or less the same as elsewhere in the UK. Most buyers opt for a homebuyer survey and valuation (known as a homebuyer's report elsewhere in the UK) as this is cost-effective – usually from £650 – standardised and compact. It tells you what condition the property is in and how much it is worth. Few buyers bother with a full structural survey – also known as a building survey – which costs between £750 and £1,500 but if the property is very old or unusual, it may be worth considering.

If your survey reveals potential problems, instruct a surveyor to investigate further (it's worth the extra expense). More details on what's involved in each type of survey can be found in Chapter 9.

If you're buying a flat, you're jointly responsible for the upkeep of common parts, such as the hallways and stairs, with the rest of the flat owners in the purpose-built block or converted house. Ask your surveyor to check the whole building – not just your flat. If the building desperately needs redecorating or a new roof, you'll have to pay part of the bill. Be sure you're prepared to do this and can afford it.

Making an Offer

If the survey is satisfactory and your lender is happy with it, it's time to make an offer. Even if the survey has raised problems, you may still be prepared to make a lower offer.

If significant building work is required, get a couple of quotes from builders before you make an offer. Once you know the extent of the problem, you can make an informed decision as to how much you're prepared to pay for the property.

After you make an offer, you can't retract it. If the seller accepts your offer, it's legally binding. So don't make an offer unless you're absolutely sure you want to buy that property – and can do so.

Offering above the asking price: Why you should

In England, Wales, and Northern Ireland, sellers expect bids below the asking price. To allow for this, sellers often set a higher asking price than the property will realistically fetch. But in Scotland, the opposite is the case: bids are invited *above* the asking price. The asking price is also known as The *upset* – the minimum that will be considered.

In a very small number of cases, the price is *fixed*, usually when a builder or developer is selling a property. There is very little chance of negotiation and the first buyer offering the asking price gets the property.

Discuss how much you're going to offer with your solicitor, taking into account the upset, the survey's findings, and what similar properties are fetching in that area. You don't have to follow your solicitor's advice but it may be helpful. Also keep the following in mind:

✔ The seller may have set the asking price low to generate interest among buyers, in which case you could find that the actual purchase price could be as much as 20 or 30 per cent higher. If the housing market is strong, or you're bidding for a popular property, expect to pay significantly more than the upset to secure it.

✔ If several buyers note interest in a property, it will go to sealed bids (see Chapter 10 for more information on how these work). The seller's solicitor sets a deadline by which date bids must be submitted, and you're notified after it has passed as to whether you have won.

Once you've decided how much you're prepared to offer, your solicitor informs the seller's solicitor in writing. This is the first of a number of letters – known as *missives* – that go back and forth between solicitors if your bid is successful. As well as your bid, include the following:

✔ Details of when you want to move in – the *date of entry* – and what fixtures and fittings you want included in the sale. (A list of what the seller is happy to leave behind is included in the *property particulars*, which you should have received before viewing the property; refer to Chapter 4).

✔ A number of *qualifications* or conditions, which enable you to withdraw your offer if the property turns out to be subject to local authority proposals or notices that adversely affect it.

The seller may give a qualified acceptance to your offer – accepting some terms and rejecting others, such as the date of entry. You then discuss with your solicitor whether you're happy to accept the seller's terms. Missives go back and forth until an agreement is reached.

Offering below the asking price: When to consider it

As a general rule, if you offer below the upset, you've got little chance of being successful – except in the following situations:

- ✔ **The property is proving difficult to shift.** Test the water first so you know this to be the case (your solicitor should have a good idea of how the land lies) before making a lower offer.

- ✔ **Your survey has unearthed a lot of problems with the property, and it turns out to be worth less than the upset.** If this is the case, you're justified in offering below the upset. (You certainly don't want to offer more than the property is worth if you're going to face a sizeable repair bill after you move in.)

When Your Offer Is Successful

If your offer is accepted, it's tempting to start celebrating. But you're not quite ready to pop the cork, so keep the champagne on ice for a little longer. Several missives must pass back and forth between your solicitor and the seller's solicitor as all the clauses in your offer are discussed. The aim is to *conclude missives* – a bit like finalising contracts in the rest of the UK – once everything has been agreed. The fixtures and fittings included in the sale will also be finalised, along with the date of entry.

Once missives are concluded, a *bargain* is made – the equivalent of exchanging contracts. The purchase can now be completed in a few days, unlike the four to six weeks it takes in the rest of the UK. You have now entered into a binding contract with the seller. Unless the conveyancing process throws up some complications, you can't back out unless you're prepared to pay thousands of pounds in compensation.

Conclusion of missives can occur quickly, leaving you little time to get your finances arranged. So it's vital that you complete your mortgage application *before* you make an offer. You must also ensure that you have enough cash to cover solicitor's fees, charges for searches, stamp duty, the deposit, and hiring a removal van.

You're responsible for insuring the property once missives are concluded, so be sure to arrange buildings insurance beforehand. This covers the cost of rebuilding the property should it burn to the ground or some other disaster befall it before you have even moved in. Lenders insist upon it. See Chapter 12 for details on arranging insurance.

The conveyancing process begins

Once missives are concluded, your solicitor checks a number of documents to ensure that the property can be legally sold to you and that the local authority doesn't have any plans adversely affecting it. The items he checks include the following:

- ✓ **Title deeds:** The solicitor checks whether he is happy with the title you are being offered. The deed tells him whether the seller actually owns the property and is therefore in a position to sell it, and that there are no problems with rights of way.

- ✓ **A Search:** This is a document provided by the seller detailing the history of the property. It states when each sale occurred and whether there are any outstanding charges on any loans taken out to purchase the property.

- ✓ **Property Enquiry Certificates:** Like local authority searches in the rest of the UK, Property Enquiry Certificates are provided by the seller and list any planning proposals that are in existence that could affect the property.

- ✓ **Building warrants or certificates of completion:** A building warrant is issued to provide permission for the building of the property, and the builder must obtain a certificate of completion once the work has been satisfactorily completed, in line with building regulations.

If your solicitor is happy with the findings of the searches, he drafts a *disposition*, which transfers ownership of the property to you.

If you're taking out a mortgage, you should have completed your application form by this stage. Your solicitor normally acts for the lender as well as you, informing the lender about the title on the property and preparing the *standard security* – the lender's mortgage deed. She also arranges for the loan money to be ready at date of entry and gets you to sign the loan documents.

Make sure that you draw up a will. If you aren't Scottish and purchase a property there to use as your main residence, you acquire Scottish domicile. And if you die without making a will, Scottish law regulates the distribution of the land and buildings you own in Scotland. To avoid any confusion, consult your solicitor about drawing up a will.

Preparing for the date of entry

A couple of weeks before your date of entry, your solicitor sends you a letter telling you how much cash you need to forward to her to complete the transaction. You need to pay the following:

- ✔ **The deposit:** This is the amount you put down when you take out a mortgage. How big the deposit is depends on your savings and your lender's requirements – some require a minimum of 5 or 10 per cent, while others require no deposit at all.

  The bigger your deposit, the better mortgage rate you're likely to get. You could also avoid paying the higher lending charge (see Chapter 11 for more information).

- ✔ **Solicitor's fees:** In addition to the fee you negotiate with your solicitor, you must pay VAT – at 17.5 per cent – on top.

- ✔ **Stamp duty:** Stamp duty is payable on properties costing more than £125,000 and is calculated on a sliding scale. The rates in Scotland are the same as the rest of the UK. No stamp duty is payable on properties costing less than £125,000; one per cent on properties between £125,000 and £250,000; three per cent on properties between £250,000 and £500,000; and four per cent above that. Properties under £150,000 in disadvantaged areas may qualify for exemptions. To see a list of areas that qualify, go to the HM Revenue and Customs Web site at www.hmrc.gov.uk or call 0845 603 0135.

- ✔ **Search and registration charges:** You have to reimburse your solicitor for various charges, such as drawing up the disposition or transfer of ownership from the seller to you. There is also a charge for registering the title in your name.

Completion

This is it – the day you've been waiting for! The date of entry is quite often the same as the date of settlement, when the sale is completed and you can move into your new home. The day before the date of settlement, ensure that you have passed onto the solicitor all the money that you're stumping up including your deposit and his fees and disbursements.

In order to get those all-important keys, your solicitor must transfer funds equivalent to the full purchase price to the seller's solicitor on the date of settlement. In return, your solicitor receives the title deeds, which are sent to your lender to keep for as long as you have that mortgage, the disposition – proving the property has been transferred to you – and the keys.

Your solicitor registers the disposition and standard security in the General Register of Sasines or the Land Registry of Scotland, depending on where the property is, and passes your stamp duty onto the HM Revenue and Customs.

Chapter 21

Selling Your Home in Scotland

. . . .

In This Chapter

▶ Knowing when to notify your solicitor of your intention to sell

▶ Deciding how much to ask for your home and getting the best price

▶ Advertising and showing buyers round

. . . .

The house selling process in Scotland is quite different from the rest of the UK. But if you're selling in Scotland, at least you probably have some idea of what to expect as you will also have bought a property there (unless you inherited your home).

As with buying in Scotland, a solicitor gets involved much earlier on in the selling process than in England, Wales, or Northern Ireland. And unlike the rest of the UK, solicitors offer an integrated service. Not only do they offer legal advice, they also play the role of estate agents in advertising and helping you sell your home. This means you don't have to deal with an agent at all if you don't want to – information which is likely to be music to the ears of many sellers (and buyers)!

The main advantage of the Scottish selling process is that it's far quicker than the process in the rest of the UK. And because neither party can pull out once missives are concluded, you can make an offer on a property yourself, confident that your sale won't fall through. It all makes for less stress – and a better night's sleep!

In this chapter, I offer tips on finding a solicitor and advertising your property. I also look at what to consider when setting the asking price and deciding which offer to accept.

The Preliminaries

The house selling process moves so much quicker in Scotland than in the rest of the UK and the transaction is legally binding much earlier. For these reasons, you must get everything ready *before* you put your property up for sale otherwise you can find yourself accepting an offer before a solicitor has made sure everything is in order.

Finding a solicitor

Just as you need to find a solicitor before you view properties if you're buying in Scotland, you must also instruct a solicitor as soon as you decide to sell. This should be done *before* you put your property on the market because your solicitor has work to do before you can do this.

Personal recommendation is the best way of finding a solicitor. If a friend or relative has had a good experience with one, try to instruct this solicitor as well. Or if you were happy with the solicitor you used to purchase your home and he's available again, use him. Finding a good solicitor can be hit and miss so if you have a head start, take advantage of it.

Because most Scottish properties are sold through solicitors' property centres, you may also want your solicitor to help find a buyer for your home – usually the estate agent's role in the rest of the UK. If so, opt for a solicitor who uses a big property centre so that your home gets plenty of exposure. That way, you could find a buyer more quickly.

If you're buying a property as well as selling one, I suggest you use the same solicitor for both transactions. Not only is this likely to be cheaper, it also saves you the hassle of having to deal with – and chase up – more than one person.

As you look for a solicitor, get quotes, in writing, for fees and charges. If you contact several solicitors, get quotes from all of them. As you choose, however, keep in mind that the cheapest solicitor may not be the best choice. A solicitor who's been recommended to you may be worth a little bit extra. You don't want to end up paying in the long run because you skimped on advice at this stage.

Once you've found a solicitor, he has a number of tasks to complete before you can put your home on the market. These include:

✔ **Checking whether the property is yours to sell in the first place:** The title deeds are your proof of ownership; your mortgage lender usually keeps these safe. Your solicitor applies to borrow this document so that he can check that you have *clean title* – that is, you can sell the property. You may not be able to if you share title with a spouse, friend, or sibling, for example, and need to get that person's permission before you can sell. This can slow things down if you're divorced or separated or in the process of being so.

✔ **Finding out how much you owe on your mortgage:** When you sell your home, you have to repay the outstanding sum on your mortgage. Your solicitor finds out from your lender how much you owe. He takes this money out of the purchase price (which the buyer's solicitor transfers to him on the date of settlement) and repays the lender for you. Knowing what you owe is important so that you can work out how much cash you'll have left over after you clear the balance because the leftover amount is what you can put towards your new home.

✔ **Undertaking various local authority searches:** Your solicitor checks with the local authority on a range of matters, such as your right of way, restrictions, outstanding proposals, and so on.

✔ **Getting you to complete a property information form and fixtures, fittings, and contents form:** The property information form is a standard questionnaire. You have to provide details of boundaries, whether you've had disputes with your neighbours, and other information about your home. As for fixtures, fittings, and contents, you have to decide what is and isn't included in the sale.

Setting the asking price

You can put your property on the market for a fixed price but most sellers go for *offers over.* The asking price – or upset price – is usually the very minimum you expect to get for the property, and bids are invited above this amount.

In setting the asking price, discuss the issue with your solicitor or an agent. They should have a good idea what price similar properties are fetching in your area. Your asking price should be set with this in mind. You don't have to listen to their advice – the ultimate decision is yours. But they should know what they are talking about, so at least consider their advice. Chapter 16 has more advice on setting the asking price.

If you're selling privately, you will have to set the price yourself. Check what similar properties in your area are fetching and price your home accordingly. The alternative is to commission a chartered surveyor to value your home; however, that isn't always that useful because the report doesn't take prevailing market conditions into account.

In England, Wales, and Northern Ireland, most sellers ask two or three estate agents what they should set the asking price at. In Scotland, however, nearly half of buyers ask their solicitors. According to a survey from the Scottish Executive, 48 per cent of sellers sought advice from an agent, while 38 per cent asked a solicitor what she thought they should put their property on the market at. The remainder asked a surveyor or valuer, or simply didn't seek any advice.

Picking Someone to Sell Your Home

You can sell your home yourself, but most people prefer to get somebody else to do it for them. Estate agents sell most property in England, Wales, and Northern Ireland but in Scotland, most sellers use a solicitor.

Whether you use an agent or solicitor to sell your home, read the contract carefully before signing. Pay particular attention to these things (and see Chapter 16 for information on the finer points of contracts):

- **Whether you can cancel the contract and how long the contract runs.** Don't sign any contract that ties you to the agent or solicitor for longer than about eight weeks.

- **How much the solicitor or estate agent is going to charge you.** You should get a complete breakdown of the cost, including extra fees for advertising, if applicable, and VAT. If you aren't happy with the price you're quoted, try negotiating, or if the agent or solicitor won't budge, take your business elsewhere.

Using a solicitor

When you use a solicitor to sell your home, he does your legal work in addition to providing a full estate agency service and dealing with offers from prospective buyers. The only thing he won't do is show buyers round. You can ask him to if you'd rather not do this yourself, but you will have to pay extra.

Solicitors sell property through solicitors' property centres. These are located in most main cities throughout Scotland, and only solicitors can advertise in them. The advantage of selling your property through a solicitor who has access to a property centre is that you get much greater exposure to potential buyers than if you opt for an estate agent.

Your solicitor writes the property particulars – a description of your home and the number and type of rooms – and includes the asking price. Also included are arrangements for viewing the property and your contact details. Prospective buyers contact you, not your solicitor.

Your solicitor pays the property centre a fee for advertising your home, which varies from centre to centre. To give you an idea of the likely cost, the Glasgow Solicitors Property Centre (GSPC) charges from £195 to advertise your home until it is sold. The fee covers advertising in the GSPC Property Guide (a mailing list); an advert on the Web site; and another in the property centre. For more details on the GSPC's services, go to www.gspc.co.uk.

This fee is just the cost of advertising your property. You also have to pay your solicitor commission (usually between 1 per cent and 1.5 per cent of the selling price) if he sells your home. Some solicitors charge a separate conveyancing fee for handling the transfer of property from you to the buyer, and you also have to pay VAT on this.

Using an estate agent

If you opt for an agent to handle your sale, she deals with all aspects of the sale from writing the property particulars, to advertising your home, showing people round (sometimes she charges an extra fee for this), and negotiating. This is ideal for sellers who prefer to keep their distance from prospective buyers. The Office of Fair Trading produces a guide to using an agent to sell your home. Go to www.oft.gov.uk.

Finding the right agent is crucial for a successful sale. Opt for one who is registered with the National Association of Estate Agents (NAEA) or a member of the Royal Institute of Chartered Surveyors (RICS); that way you've got some comeback if you aren't happy. (For more information on what to look for in an estate agent head to Chapter 16).

Expect to pay 1.5 per cent of your property's selling price in commission to the agent who achieves the sale. Make sure that you get these charges in writing before signing a contract so there are no nasty surprises. Some agents charge extra for advertising the property (although how they hope to achieve a sale without this is anyone's guess!) or for a 'For Sale' board. Some agents charge a fixed fee rather than commission. Check what your agent prefers before instructing her. Fees are usually paid on conclusion of missives, so make sure the contract states this.

Try to negotiate lower commission and fees with the agent, particularly if it's a quiet time of year, and she's desperate for the business.

Estate agent's contracts often contain a number of confusing technical terms. Make sure that you fully understand them before you agree to anything. For more details on the most common terms see Chapter 16.

Whatever happens, don't sign over sole selling rights to an agent; this means you have to pay commission even if *you* manage to find a buyer. Also avoid the phrase 'Ready, willing and able purchaser' which means you still have to pay the agent's commission even if you withdraw from the sale, and unconditional missives are not exchanged.

If you use an agent, you will still have to deal with a solicitor when you get to the conveyancing stage. So don't forget that, in addition to the agent's commission, you also have to pay a solicitor for the legal work and searches. For that reason, most people prefer to use a solicitor to sell their home in the first place and be done with it.

Doing it yourself

Some sellers try to save money by selling their home themselves, rather than using a solicitor or agent. This may save you money but it's also time-consuming, stressful, and may ultimately turn into a disaster if you get it wrong. If you have never sold a property before using a solicitor or agent, I don't recommend doing it yourself because you haven't got a clue how things work.

Have you got the time and energy to devote to selling your home? You have to set the asking price, write the property particulars, do the advertising, and handle viewings. You also need to negotiate a purchase price. This is a lot to take on, and if you can't do it properly, it's better not to attempt it at all. I discuss going it alone and selling your home privately in more detail in Chapter 17.

Even if you sell your home yourself, you still need to employ a solicitor to do your conveyancing – unless you fancy an even bigger challenge and want to do it all yourself! But unless you really want your life to be that much more difficult, get a professional to handle the legal side of things.

If you use a solicitor for the conveyancing, give him notice that you're planning on selling your home, just as you would if you were using a solicitor or agent to handle the sale. You must also clarify in advance, in writing, what he is going to charge you for the conveyancing.

Handling Viewings

If you use a solicitor or agent to sell your property, you will still probably end up showing prospective buyers around yourself. Handling your own viewings makes sense because you know more about your home than anyone else and can field questions from interested buyers. Of course, not everyone is comfortable doing this. If you don't want to, your solicitor or agent will do it – although you have to pay extra.

Before you show anyone around your home, make sure you present it in its best light. See Chapter 15 for lots of tips on creating the right first impression for buyers.

The easier you make it for prospective buyers to view your property, the quicker you're likely to find one ready to make you an offer. Accept evening and weekend viewings, even though it will upset your family's routine. And make sure you give the prospective buyer space on second and subsequent viewings. She should already know her way round and may want to measure up. She will appreciate it if you don't breathe down her neck so remain in the background, ready to answer questions if needed.

Receiving Offers

If a buyer is interested in making an offer for your home, his solicitor will *note interest* with your solicitor. This means you have to give him an opportunity to make an offer – in other words, you can't accept an offer from another buyer until you have given him a chance to bid.

When you get only one offer

If only one prospective buyer notes interest, you should wait until he makes an offer. As this should be above the upset, it is likely to be acceptable to you. (If it is below the upset, there may be a reason for this – perhaps the survey reveals lots of problems. You don't have to accept this offer but you may want to negotiate with the buyer until you agree on a price that you're both happy with.) The prospective buyer also includes the date of entry (when he proposes to move in) and what extras, such as carpets and curtains he also wants to buy. Even if you're happy with the price, you may want to negotiate the other details.

Going with sealed bids

If more than one buyer notes interest, it can go to sealed bids – where you're likely to get more than the asking price. Your solicitor sets a deadline by which interested parties must submit their bid for your property. They don't know what the other buyers are offering (hence, this is sometimes referred to as *bidding blind*).

The deadline for bids should be far enough ahead to give buyers time to arrange a survey and mortgage. Once the deadline has passed, your solicitor or agent tells you what the bids are. As well as a price, the buyer includes a proposed entry date and whether she wants any of your fixtures and fittings. Take all these factors into consideration when considering offers.

The advantage of sealed bids is that the offer process isn't long and drawn out. You know that by a certain time on a certain day you will have some serious offers on the table.

When you work with sealed bids, keep these points in mind:

- ✔ You get to choose which bid to accept – or you can reject all of them. The highest bid is usually successful, but not always – particularly if the bidder has some unacceptable conditions. You may choose a lower bid if the buyer can move quickly and has picked an entry date in line with your expectations. Or you may be tempted by the offer from the buyer who wants to buy your carpets, because that means you can buy new ones for your new home.

- ✔ If none of the offers are as high as you'd hoped, you can ask all the bidders to improve their offers; there's no guarantee any of them will though. Remember that it's unethical to ask one bidder to increase her offer without giving the others an opportunity to do the same.

- ✔ A buyer usually only gets the chance to make one bid so he is under pressure to make sure it is a good one. If your property generates a lot of competition, one of the buyers may bid a lot more than the upset in order to secure the property. This is excellent news for you.

Entering the Home Straight

Once you have decided to accept an offer, your solicitor or agent informs the successful buyer's solicitor over the telephone and then follows this up with a formal qualified acceptance, saying which terms in the offer you accept and which ones you don't. Your solicitor also contacts unsuccessful buyers.

The exchange of missives

The buyer's offer isn't set in stone at this stage. Even though your solicitor has informed the buyer's solicitor that you've accepted the offer, you and the buyer can still negotiate the fine points through your solicitors, who send letters backwards and forwards to hammer out an agreement. This is known as *exchange of missives*.

The buyer's solicitor responds with his comments to your proposed changes and your solicitor responds to the buyer's solicitor's response, and so on, until both parties are happy. This usually takes days rather than weeks.

Both you and the buyer can pull out of the deal while missives are being exchanged. You don't have to pay compensation if you pull out.

Conclusion of missives: No going back

When both of you are happy with the contract, missives are *concluded* and the contract is legally binding on both sides. If either party pulls out after this, considerable compensation must be paid to the other party. So make sure that you know what you're getting into before this stage.

If you use an agent, he now passes details of the successful offer onto your solicitor. The agent's work is done, and he's usually paid at this stage; it is now down to your solicitor to do the conveyancing. By now, you know what the date of entry is (usually a month after the sale is concluded) – the date by which you vacate the property and give your solicitor the keys. The buyer can then move in.

Completing the Sale

Once missives are concluded, your solicitor must send the title deeds to the buyer's solicitor. The buyer's solicitor checks these to ensure that the deed is in your name and that you can sell the property. If all is correct, she prepares the disposition – the document transferring your home to the buyer.

Your solicitor also informs your lender that missives have been concluded and asks for a redemption statement detailing the outstanding balance on your mortgage. He arranges for this to be paid on completion. At this stage, he also prepares the discharge document and gets the lender to sign it before the date of entry. He also searches the Registers to ensure nothing untoward is noted against you or the property.

Your solicitor adjusts the terms of the disposition, if necessary, once he receives it from the buyer's solicitor, and you have to sign it. On the date of entry, your solicitor delivers the keys to the buyer's solicitor and the signed disposition – in return for the money to buy your property. Your solicitor deducts his fee and the outstanding mortgage. The remainder of the cash is transferred to your account, and the transaction is complete. You can now go house hunting yourself – if you haven't started already.

Part VI
The Part of Tens

'An interesting feature of the house, Mr Wimbell, but whether it's a strong selling point I'm not sure.'

In this part . . .

This just wouldn't be a *For Dummies* book without the Part of Tens. Here you'll find short bursts of information on everything from what a first-time homeowner needs to know, to selling your home, to dealing with estate agents. So if you're looking for a lot of information, but don't have much time, you've come to the right part.

Chapter 22

Ten Things for a First-Time Homeowner to Do

In This Chapter

▶ Enjoying your first foray into the property market

▶ Must-have expenditures and money-saving suggestions

▶ Fun things to do as a new homeowner

*B*ecoming a property owner for the first time can be extremely daunting. While it's very exciting – nothing beats walking into your new home the first time after you take possession of the keys – it's also a huge responsibility. In this chapter, I give you ten tips to bear in mind so that you can enjoy buying your first property and, at the same time, meet your financial obligations.

Budget for the Mortgage

Many first-time buyers fall into the trap of thinking that, once they manage to persuade a lender to give them a mortgage, they don't have to worry about the financial side of things any longer. But a mortgage is a big financial commitment, and you must ensure that you can meet your monthly payments, on time, every month. If you fall behind with your repayments, your home is in danger of being repossessed. Budgeting to ensure that you can pay your mortgage may sound boring, but I can't stress enough how important it is. And if you aren't very sensible with money, now's the time to teach yourself good habits.

Grab a piece of paper and divide it into two columns. On the left-hand side, write down your incomings – how much money you get each month from your employment and any benefits or maintenance payments. Then on the right-hand side make a note of your outgoings. Put your mortgage repayment first on this list, followed by insurance payments, utility bills, council tax, and so on. If your outgoings are much greater than the money you've got coming in, you have to reduce them. Start cutting from the bottom of the list.

Buy Everything – within Limits

The most exciting thing about a new home is that it's the perfect excuse for spending lots of cash on new stuff. New sofas, new chairs, new television, new curtains and carpets, new shower curtain – the list is endless. While buying new things for your new home can be great fun, I advise a modicum of caution. Don't spend money that you don't have. Yes, getting credit is easy, but you have to pay it back at some stage. By all means have fun. Buy that impractical cream sofa your mother will disapprove of because it isn't a sensible colour. But don't spend so much that you can't afford to go out for the next year while you pay it all back.

Get Insurance!

Insurance is a necessity, not an option. Money may be too tight to mention once you've bought your new home and paid the stamp duty and the solicitor. You may also be planning a trip to your local furniture store. The last thing on your mind is likely to be insurance. Indeed, you may think you can cut costs by taking out cover at a later date when you're flush. But skimping on insurance is false economy. What if you never get round to it or the worst happens – you get burgled or lose your job – before you have a chance to?

Lenders insist you take out buildings insurance before they let you have a mortgage, so you can't avoid this one. But what about contents insurance? Can you afford to replace all your belongings if your home is destroyed by a fire? Probably not. Or what if you have an accident and can no longer do your job? Could you afford to pay your mortgage? If the answer is no, you need some form of mortgage payment protection or critical illness cover. You may think you're saving money by not taking out insurance, but it covers the unknown – and you never know when you might need it. For details on the types of cover available, see Chapter 12.

Switch Utility Providers to Slash Your Bills

Fuel bills can be expensive, but short of wearing chunky knitted jumpers around your home and going to the pub instead of heating your sitting-room, you have to put up with them. Well, to a certain extent. Deregulation of the gas and electricity industries means you can shop around for a cheaper deal – you don't need to stick with the provider you inherit when you move in.

Take gas, electricity, and water meter readings as soon as you move in and contact the relevant suppliers to tell them what these are. (Remember, you may not have a water meter; if you don't, reading a water meter obviously is not possible.) Next, find out whether you can get a cheaper gas, electricity or water deal from another supplier. This is a simple process. A number of websites allow you to compare costs. If you find a cheaper provider, the process of changing is also straightforward. Try Energywatch, the gas and electricity watchdog (www.energywatch.org.uk) or www.saveonyour bills.co.uk. To compare phone and digital TV costs, try www.uswitch. com or telephone 0845 601 2856.

Introduce Yourself to the Neighbours

The newspapers are full of stories about neighbours from hell. One way of minimising the likelihood of ending up with one or two of these is to get off on the right foot. So even as you move your stuff into your new home, be on the lookout for the neighbours. Then pop round and introduce yourself within a day or two of moving in. Be sure to pick a good time. Early evening is usually better than first thing in the morning or late at night. Be polite, friendly, and not too pushy. You don't want to come across as a right pain otherwise your neighbours will avoid you when they see you coming.

If you're planning a housewarming party, invite the neighbours. You may not particularly like them, they may not be your kind of people, and they probably won't come. But if you don't ask them along, you risk alienating them for good. Keep them on your side in case you ever have to borrow that cup of sugar!

Throw a Housewarming Party

Everyone who moves into a new place – whether they are renting or buying – is expected to throw a party, so you may as well bite the bullet and set a date.

Although you probably want to get your new place perfect and decorated to your taste before you ask anyone round, having the housewarming *before* you do the place up makes more sense. How are you going to relax if your guests are swigging red wine while standing on your new pristine white rugs? The 1970s-style swirly floral carpet with the brown background that the previous owners left behind may not be to your taste, but if you leave it in the sitting-room for the party you'll have as good a time as your guests. And if it makes you feel better, you can always tell them that your new carpet is on order.

Learn to Operate the Washing Machine

This is it. No more trips down the launderette, sitting for hours watching your smalls whizz round the drier. Although you still have to do your own laundry, you get to do it in your own machine. Read the operating instructions very carefully before shrinking your best knitwear or dyeing your favourite white shirt a delicate shade of pink.

Accept that Dinner Party Conversations Will Never Be the Same Again

Before you got your foot on the property ladder, you probably never 'got' those conversations that people with their own homes always seem to have about house prices. But as soon as you buy your own home, you instantly get it. Dinner parties will never be the same again as you boast about how much your flat, in an edgy part of town, has doubled in value since you bought it. Or you may take an unhealthy interest in what the Bank of England plans to do to interest rates. You'll find these topics, which you previously viewed as dull as ditch water, to be endlessly fascinating and you won't be able to get enough of them.

Stop Worrying about Fluctuating Property Prices

When you invest a large chunk of your hard-earned cash in property, you start obsessing about how much it's worth. Was the property a good investment, demonstrated by a rise in the value of your home? Or have you made a big mistake because your home is now worth less than you paid for it (that is, you've fallen into negative equity)?

Property prices move up and down, it's a fact of life. Over the long term, they are more likely to go up; and that's what you should be bothered about if you are concerned about making money. But primarily your home is where you live rather than a way of making a quick buck. View any appreciation in value as a welcome extra, not your main motivation for buying the property in the first place. And if you plan to stay in the property for years, the inevitable short-term fluctuations in the price shouldn't bother you one bit. It's certainly not worth losing any sleep over.

Go Mad Decorating

When you live in rented accommodation, the amount of decorating you can do is usually very limited. If the landlord has any sense, he simply won't allow you to do any at all. Or you may think spending the time or money isn't worth it because you'll be on your way within six months and someone else will benefit from your hard work.

But when you have your own place, you take a different view of decorating. You don't have to ask anyone for permission before you start. You don't have to temper your tastes or opt for neutral colours. You can paint or wallpaper your walls exactly how you want. If pink walls with green spots have always been your dream, you can have them. And it's not money down the drain because you are – hopefully – improving your property. Remember, though that if you have bought a listed property there may be restrictions on what decorating you can do. See Chapter 8 for more details.

Chapter 23

Ten Ways to Sell Your Home

· ·

In This Chapter

▶ Ensuring that you sell your home as quickly as possible

▶ Making sure you get the best price for it

· ·

Selling your home can be a stressful time as there is so much to think about; from getting it clean, tidy and in good repair, to setting the asking price and deciding whether to use an estate agent to sell it or not. By the time you have decided to sell your home, you probably don't want to hang around for months waiting to find a buyer. Most people want to sell up quickly because they have a new place in mind that they are keen to buy themselves. In this chapter, I give you ten tips to make sure that you sell your home quickly – and get the best price for it.

Maintain Kerb Appeal

First impressions are vitally important when it comes to selling your home. And these start from when the buyer pulls up outside and sees it for the first time (see Chapter 15). If the front gate is hanging off its hinges, there's a burnt out car in the street and an old mattress on the front lawn, it's unlikely that he'll like what he sees. Indeed, there is a very good chance he won't even bother ringing the doorbell. He'll be back in that car quicker than you can say 'kerb appeal'.

If you want to sell your home *and* get a good price for it, you must ensure that it looks clean and inviting from the street. Trim your hedges, cut the grass, weed the flowerbeds, paint the walls, fences, and front door, and ensure that the gate shuts properly. Don't let rubbish blight the property, and even clear your windowsills of clutter – vases of freshly cut flowers are the only things the prospective buyer should see. If it takes several months to sell your home, do regular checks on the kerb appeal to ensure that it doesn't slip during this time.

Keep the Interior Spick and Span

Inside is just as important as outside so ensure that you give your home a thorough clean before showing any prospective buyers round. Keep clutter to a minimum. This covers all those knick-knacks you couldn't be without but which just distract potential buyers. Your aim is to get your home as neutral as possible so that the prospective buyer can imagine himself living in it, with his stuff. And if he can't see beyond the hundreds of fluffy toys stacked up on the bed or your collection of milk bottle tops, you can bet he won't be making you an offer.

Attend to Minor Repairs

When you are getting your property ready to sell, you must check every room with a critical eye (Chapter 15) before you invite a single potential buyer through the door. While cleaning is vital, routine repairs are equally important. Prospective buyers will notice cupboards hanging off their hinges and may well try to open kitchen drawers so if they are stuck or come away in their hands, it won't create a good impression.

Familiarity is going to be your main problem here. It can be hard spotting what needs doing when you've come to live with certain faults. If a light fitting is broken, for example, you might have got used to using a lamp instead. But buyers have a knack of spotting every fault so it's up to you to finish the tiling in the bathroom or fix the leaky washer on the kitchen tap. This helps buyers see the bigger picture, rather than focusing on minor faults which, believe me, will really stand out.

Set a Reasonable Price

While it may be tempting to ask for a sum beyond your wildest dreams there's a danger you'll put off potential buyers if it is way too high. In England, Wales and Northern Ireland, sellers expect to be knocked down on the asking price so tend to set it slightly higher than you'd be happy accepting to allow for this (Chapter 16 has more advice on this or see Chapter 17 if you are selling your home without an agent). In Scotland the situation is different – the asking price is the minimum the seller will accept so buyers are invited to offer over this (see Chapter 21 for details).

Wherever you live, seek advice before setting the asking price (from your estate agent, solicitor or surveyor) as to how much your home could fetch and check out what similar properties in the area are going for. Whatever you ask for, it helps to have an idea in your mind of the absolute minimum you would be happy to accept. Don't tell prospective buyers what this is but bear it in mind when considering offers and don't accept less than this.

Be Flexible on the Price

It's a fact of life that you don't always get what you ask for – and this is particularly true when it comes to selling property. Buyers like to haggle. Sellers should accept this is the case and prepare to negotiate (see Chapter 18). But remember, you hold all the cards as you have the last word. Don't be badgered into accepting a lower price if you aren't happy doing so.

In some instances a lower offer is justified such as if the survey throws up a lot of problems with the property that the buyer will have to put right. But if he is just trying it on and you aren't desperate to move, feel free to refuse to entertain an insultingly low offer with him. If the market is quiet and properties are taking ages to shift, buyers tend to get a bit cheekier. I suggest you don't stand for any of their nonsense.

Be Prepared to Include Your Curtains and Carpets

Flexibility is key. You may intend to take all the contents of your home with you when you move out, particularly if you are rather attached to them, but if your carpets and curtains look so fantastic *in situ* the buyer may be keen to hang onto them and persuade you to leave them behind. She may even be prepared to pay you handsomely for them. If this is the case, it may really be worth considering her offer. Just think about the hassle you'll save yourself – no pulling up carpets and taking down curtains. It's far easier – and a lot more fun – to buy brand new ones once you move into your new place.

Hide Your Pets

Fido and Fluffy are no doubt exceptionally cute and well behaved but while you may adore them, not everyone loves pets (see Chapter 15). And if they are less than exceptionally well-behaved, you'll have to get them out of the way before viewings – a bite on the leg of the prospective buyer isn't the memory you want her to leave your home with. There's also a chance that a prospective buyer is allergic to cats or dogs.

Stick cats and dogs in the garden if possible or arrange for a neighbour to look after them while you are showing a potential buyer round your home. It's also important to get rid of traces of them. Smelly litter trays, dirty food plates on the floor, cat or dog hairs everywhere, and those peculiar smells that animals seem to leave behind. A good spray such as Febreze liberally sprayed on curtains and furniture before prospective buyers come through the door, will mask most of the unwelcome odours.

Use the Internet

More people are selling their own homes rather than employing an estate agent to do it (or a solicitor in Scotland) – and the Internet is making it far easier to do this (see Chapter 17). A number of Web sites have sprung up enabling sellers to advertise their property for a lot less money than an estate agent charges in commission. And as these Web sites expand, and more buyers hear about them, the chances of achieving a successful sale through this medium are growing.

One advantage of the Internet is that you can use several photos to advertise your property instead of relying on the single outside shot most estate agents use in their property particulars. Some Web sites even allow sellers to offer prospective buyers an interactive tour, so they can look round your home without actually making an appointment to come and see it. This'll cut out the timewasters and ensure that those that do make an appointment to view are serious about buying.

Keep Track of Your Estate Agent's Progress

Even if you decide to use an agent to sell your home (see Chapter 16), this doesn't mean you can wash your hands of all responsibility and leave all the work to her. You have responsibilities too, from ensuring that the property is clean and tidy for viewings to checking that the agent is doing all she can to sell your home. Updates and feedback are the very least you can expect, particularly soon after a viewing. If a potential buyer decides he doesn't want to make an offer, you want to know why. Is the price too high, the house too dirty, the neighbours too off-putting or did it simply not meet his requirements? Only once you know the answers can you address any problems that may have arisen during the viewing.

Give your agent enough time to sell your home (six to eight weeks is more than adequate). If a buyer hasn't been found during that time, consider switching to another agent. But make sure the contract you sign allows you to do this without paying a penalty.

Find a Cash Buyer

If you want to sell your home as quickly as possible with the least chance of things going wrong, you need to find a cash buyer. This is usually someone who has already sold her home, is renting and has the money ready to buy another property. She isn't stuck in a complicated chain because she doesn't need to sell her home to be able to afford to buy yours. And she is more likely to be focused and know what she wants.

 It is always a good idea to establish the financial situation of a potential buyer when they view your home (see Chapter 18). First-time buyers are also usually attractive to sellers as they aren't in a chain either although you need to ensure that they have the finances in place to proceed with a purchase. Anyone in a long and complicated chain with several people caught up in it should be avoided unless you are really desperate to get a sale and this buyer is the only one to have made you an offer. But prepare yourself for holdups along the way and possible heartbreak in the end.

Chapter 24

Ten Tips on Dealing with Estate Agents

In This Chapter

▶ Suggestions to help buyers get the most from their estate agents

▶ Recommendations to help sellers avoid common pitfalls

The one thing most people hate about buying or selling property is dealing with estate agents. In some cases, their bad reputation is fully justified, yet estate agents remain the most common channel for buying or selling property in England, Wales, and Northern Ireland. (In Scotland, solicitors are used more commonly than estate agents to sell property, as explained in Chapter 20.) Because you will probably end up using an agent, in this chapter I offer ten suggestions on how to deal with them to make the experience as painless as possible.

Tips for Buyers

If you want to make your property hunting less stressful and time-consuming it's worth using an estate agent. You don't have to pay anything to use an agent so register with as many as possible to increase your chances of finding the right property as soon as possible. But bear a few things in mind when dealing with agents.

Ignore the bull!

Estate agents are salesmen, and when you're in sales, exaggeration is the name of the game. As long as you remember this and take most things that an estate agent says with a hefty pinch of salt, you shouldn't go far wrong.

Although the estate agent works for the seller, who pays the agent's commission (see Chapter 16), he is legally obligated not to mislead you, the buyer. Of course, the line is very fine between being economical with the truth and being deliberately misleading: You must be on your guard and read between the lines. A 'cosy' flat in agent-speak may be more accurately described as 'poky'. So be sure to check out for yourself any claims the estate agent makes.

Refuse the agent's finance

When you use an estate agent's services to buy a home, you may find that he asks you whether you want help finding a mortgage as well. A number of estate agents now have finance arms, which offer mortgages. I'd give this financing a miss. At best, you'll be offered the most competitive deal out of a very limited sample, so how on earth is this going to be the best one on the market? As a rule, the best place to obtain a mortgage is from an independent mortgage broker who has access to all the deals on the market so he can pick out the best one for you (see Chapter 11 for information on finding a broker).

Consider the agent's legal or surveyor recommendations

As well as handling financing, most estate agents can also recommend solicitors or surveyors who can offer you a cheaper price for handling your legal work or surveying the property than you would get from a solicitor or surveyor you find in Yellow Pages. The agent is likely to put a lot of work their way, so prices should be competitive. You must still ensure that the solicitor belongs to the relevant Law Society, just as you would if you found the solicitor by other means. Surveyors should belong to the Royal Institution of Chartered Surveyors. This will ensure that you have some comeback in case anything goes wrong.

To ensure that you're getting a good price for your legal work or the survey, get a quote from the solicitor or surveyor recommended by your estate agent. Compare this with prices charged by other solicitors or surveyors as you may find a cheaper deal elsewhere. If this is the case you'd be mad not to go for it, as you're not obliged to use any solicitor or surveyor recommended by the estate agent.

Make friends with your agent

You don't need to go down the pub with an agent or invite him round for dinner. But if you're looking to buy a property, you need to get the agent on your side. There is a lot of competition out there for the best properties, so you want your agent to instantly think of you when a new one fitting your criteria comes onto his books. Getting the first call and being the first to see the property and the first to make an offer could give you a crucial head start.

The best way of getting an agent on your side is to prove your seriousness about buying a property. Organise your finances in advance (be sure to let your agent know) and respond quickly when an agent rings and suggests a property you might be interested in. By arranging to view a property as soon as possible, and turning up on time, you give the impression that you're serious.

Tips for Sellers

If you're selling your property, you could try selling it privately but it is much easier to use an agent. Choose your agent carefully though, and read the small print on the contract before signing. Other tips to bear in mind are included in this section.

Don't let the agent set the asking price too high

Agents are generally paid a percentage of the purchase price in commission for achieving a successful sale (see Chapter 16 for details). Because a higher asking price means a greater reward for your agent, she may try to encourage you to put your home on the market for much more than you think the property is realistically worth. But a greatly over-priced property isn't likely to get many, if any, offers; it may even deter prospective buyers from arranging a viewing in the first place. If you set the asking price too high, what is likely to happen is that, at the end of three or four months of not getting any offers, you'll have to reduce the price anyway. Then, not only will you have wasted your time, but buyers will also be inclined to think something is wrong with your home and may try to knock you down even further.

When setting the asking price, ask two or three agents for their opinion as to how much your property could fetch. Opt for the average – and don't forget to ensure that the price of your home is in line with what similar properties in the area are fetching at that time.

Shop around for an agent

The best way to choose tradesmen, professionals – such as solicitors and accountants – and mortgage brokers is by personal recommendation. The same is true of estate agents. However, if you don't have a personal recommendation to go on, you will have to find an agent yourself. The best way to do this is to shop around and do some research. Who are the biggest agents in your area? Who sells properties similar to yours? Whose branches always seem bustling? Who places the biggest adverts in the local paper?

After you narrow your list down to two or three agents, invite each of them to your home and ask them what they think it could fetch. And then, before you finally settle on one, remember that the agent you choose should be one you personally like and can see yourself working with. If you come across one who meets all your requirements, you've found your agent.

Give your agent a chance

You can easily become impatient if your home isn't selling, particularly if you're itching to make an offer on another property. In this situation, you may blame the estate agent for not finding a buyer for your home. But keep in mind that your agent may not be at fault.

Sometimes property can be slow to sell. Maybe the housing market is very quiet right now, so no properties – including yours – are selling. Or your home may be very unusual, or an acquired taste, in which case you can reasonably expect finding the right buyer to take longer. Maybe your home isn't selling quickly because it needs a lot of renovation or the price is too high. Whatever the reason, every agent deserves a chance. You can generally give your agent around six to eight weeks to sell your home. If, by that time, you haven't had any viewings or firm offers, then you may want to switch agents.

Try not to harass your agent from the beginning. If you do, you're more likely to get his back up and make his job even more difficult. If you aren't getting feedback from viewings, by all means find out why this is the case, but if your property has been on the market for two weeks and nobody has been round to view it yet, it's too soon to get worked up about it. Try to relax.

Listen to your agent's advice

When it comes to your home, you may know best. But when it comes to *selling* your property, your estate agent (or solicitor in Scotland) is the expert. Selling property is really the agent's domain, and sometimes – not to put too fine a point on it – you need to shut up and listen.

Agents can offer advice on all sorts of aspects of the sale. An agent can direct you as to what work is needed to get your property ready for sale, what the asking price should be, and whether you should accept an offer below that price. Listen to this advice. You don't have to take it, but you may hear something that proves useful to you.

Give the agent a key

If you're like most people, you may prefer your agent to handle viewings. If this is the case, you can make life much easier for the agent – and ensure that you don't hold up a potential sale – by giving the agent a key. With a key, your agent can come and go during the day with potential buyers, while you're at work or doing something else – an arrangement that will cause minimum disruption to your life.

Not wanting to leave your key with a relative stranger is certainly understandable, but if you use a reputable firm of agents you can be relatively confident that your belongings will be safe. After all, your agent has too much money riding on this deal to risk it for the sake of a bit of petty theft.

Don't stick with a useless agent

Although you want to give your agent a chance, there's no point flogging a dead horse. If you've given your agent several weeks and she still isn't producing the goods, it's time to move on. You owe her nothing, certainly not any loyalty, and as long as your contract is worded in such a way that you can get out of it (see Chapter 16 for what to look for in an estate agent's contract), find another agent to sell your home. If you stay with this agent any longer in the hope that she will come good, you're likely to be wasting your time – during which time another agent may have found you a buyer.

Appendix

Resources

● ●

*O*ver the next few pages I list some of the main organisations referred to throughout this book. You may want to contact some of them for more information on specific aspects of buying or selling your home.

Professional and Trade Organisations

Below are the contact details for a range of professional and trade organisations that you may need to contact for information when buying or selling your property:

Association of British Insurers (ABI): The trade association for the UK insurance industry, the ABI represents around 400 companies. Contact: 020 7600 3333 or visit www.abi.org.uk.

Association of Relocation Agents (ARA): The professional body for the relocation industry in the UK and Ireland, ARA can provide you with details of local members. Call 08700 737475 or visit its Web site at www.arp-relocation.com.

British Association of Removers (BAR): The trade association of the removals industry can provide details of three members in your area. Contact: 01923 699 480 or visit its Web site at www.bar.co.uk.

Citizens Advice Bureau (CAB): The CAB offers free, confidential, and independent advice on a range of financial issues to those living in England and Wales. Find your nearest CAB at www.citizensadvice.org.uk. For **Citizens Advice Northern Ireland**, go to www.citizensadvice.co.uk. For **Citizens Advice Scotland,** visit www.cas.org.uk.

Council for Licensed Conveyancers (CLC): The CLC publishes a list of licensed conveyancers across the country. Contact: 01245 349599 or visit its Web site at www.theclc.gov.uk.

Council of Mortgage Lenders (CML): The CML is the trade association for UK mortgage lenders and promotes good lending practice. Call 020 7438 8956 or www.cml.org.uk.

Council for Registered Gas Installers (CORGI): The National Watchdog for gas safety in the UK can suggest a CORGI-registered installer local to you. Call 0800 915 0485 or visit its Web site at www.corgi-gas.com.

English Heritage: English Heritage aims to help people understand and appreciate why historic buildings matter. Visit www.english-heritage.org/uk. In Northern Ireland, try the **Environment and Heritage Service in Northern Ireland** (www.ehsni.gov.uk); in Scotland, try **Historic Scotland's** Web site www.historic-scotland.gov.uk. In Wales, go to www.cadw.co.uk.

Federation of Master Builders (FMB): The largest trade organisation in the UK for the construction industry is a good place to start when looking for a builder. Call 020 7242 7583 for details of FMB members in your area or visit its Web site at www.fmb.org.uk.

Guild of Master Craftsmen: Membership of the Guild is recognition of a company's skill and integrity. Call 01273 477374 or visit www.thegmcgroup.com for more information.

Institute of Plumbing and Heating Engineering: The UK's professional body for plumbers can help you find a local registered plumber. Telephone 01708 472791 or visit its Web site at www.iphe.org.uk.

Law Society of England and Wales: The Law Society provides advice on choosing and using a solicitor in England and Wales. For information, contact the Society by phone (020 7242 1222) or visit its Web site at www.lawsociety.org.uk.

Law Society of Northern Ireland: For more information on choosing and using a solicitor in Northern Ireland, contact the Society by phone (028 90 231 614) or visit www.lawsoc-ni.org.

Law Society of Scotland: For more information on choosing and using a solicitor in Scotland, contact the Society on 0131 226 7411 or visit www.lawscot.org.uk.

National Association of Estate Agents (NAEA): The NAEA has become the leading professional body for residential estate agents in the UK over the past 40 years. It represents estate agents and property professionals and aims to improve professionalism and accountability in the industry. There are over 10,000 NAEA members nationwide. If you use a NAEA member when you buy or sell a property, you can be assured of certain standards. Members are bound by a Code of Practice and adhere to professional Rules of Conduct. For more information, call 01926 496800 or visit NAEA online at www.naea.co.uk.

National Guild of Removers and Storers: The guild provides details of removal men in your area. Call 01494 792279 or visit its Web site at www.ngrs.co.uk.

National House Building Council (NHBC): The NHBC is the regulatory body for the building industry. The advantage of using an NHBC-registered builder is that NHBC inspectors carry out checks during the building process to satisfy themselves that the property conforms to NHBC standards. You can telephone NHBC on 01494 735363 or visit the Web site at www.nhbc.co.uk.

National Inspection Council for Electrical Installation Contracting (NICEIC): The NICEIC is a voluntary regulatory body and charitable organisation, which aims to protect the public from unsafe or unsound electrical work. Call 0870 013 0382 or visit its Web site at www.niceic.com.

Ombudsman for Estate Agents (OEA): The OEA Scheme is devised to address disputes between estate agents who are members and the public. Consumers can register complaints if they feel that their legal rights have been infringed or their estate agent has not complied with the OEA Code of Practice. Telephone 01722 333306 or visit the OEA's Web site at www.oea.co.uk.

Royal Institute of British Architects (RIBA): RIBA has a database of architects in the UK and can put you in contact with a member near you. Members are subject to the Code of Professional Conduct, and RIBA can offer practical assistance if they fall foul of this Code. Contact RIBA at www.ribafind.org.

Royal Institution of Chartered Surveyors (RICS): RICS is a global professional body representing, regulating, and promoting chartered surveyors. If you are looking for a surveyor, contact RICS for your nearest member. You can reach RICS on the phone (0870 333 1600) between 8:30 a.m. and 5:30 p.m., Monday to Friday. You can also visit the RICS Web site at www.rics.org. For RICS Scotland, call 0131 225 7078 or visit the Web site www.rics-scotland.org.uk.

Society for the Protection of Ancient Buildings (SPAB): This national pressure group fights to save old buildings from decay, demolition and damage. It offers advice, educates and campaigns. For more details on conservation, call 020 7377 1644 or go to www.spab.org.uk.

Government Agencies

You may need to contact a handful of government agencies directly. Here are the details:

Department for Children, Schools, and Families: The Web site provides performance tables for schools across the country, which can be useful when deciding where you want to move. Visit www.dfes.gov.uk.

Environment Agency: Information on air, land, and water quality is all provided on the Environment Agency's Web site, so it's a good place to start when investigating a local area. Visit its Web site at www.environment-agency.gov.uk.

Office for Standards in Education (OFSTED): OFSTED offers a useful Web site for doing more research about schools in a particular locality. Go to www.ofsted.gov.uk.

Scottish Executive: The devolved government for Scotland is responsible for the day-to-day concerns of those living in Scotland. For more information, call the enquiry line on 084577 741741 or visit its Web site at www.scotland.gov.uk.

Further Information

The Internet has many useful sites offering invaluable information for those buying or selling their home. Below, I include some of the sites I find most useful: I recommend that you check them out as well.

Bricks and Brass: Information on buying, maintaining, and renovating a period house is available on this helpful Web site. Owners are guided through the renovation process room by room, with plenty of invaluable tips and advice. Visit www.bricksandbrass.co.uk.

Buildstore: This is a useful and comprehensive Web site for the self-builder or renovator. There is a facility to enable you to search for land that has already received planning permission, specialist mortgages, and plenty of advice and tips. Check out the Web site at www.buildstore.co.uk.

Moneysupermarket: Moneysupermarket offers a comprehensive service allowing users to compare the cost of a range of financial products from mortgages, credit cards, and personal loans to home insurance and life cover. Visit the Web site at www.moneysupermarket.com.

Self Build ABC: Self Build ABC offers lots of advice and practical tips on self-build and what you need to consider before taking the plunge. Visit www.selfbuildabc.co.uk.

Up My Street: Up My Street provides all the local information about an area that you could possibly need to know, from details of local schools and crime statistics, right down to the most widely read newspapers in the postal district. Just type a potential property's postcode in at www.upmystreet.com.

Credit Reference Agencies

Everyone has a credit file, which mortgage lenders check when deciding whether to let you have a mortgage or not. Your credit file contains details of your debts, and basically shows whether you're a good risk or not. If you've missed payments on a personal loan or previous mortgage, for example, this will be recorded. It's worth getting a copy of your file *before* you apply for a mortgage to check all's in order (errors do crop up but they can be rectified). Enclose a cheque for £2 when writing to Equifax or Experian for a copy of your credit file.

Equifax PLC
Credit File Advice Centre
PO Box 1140
Bradford, BD1 5US
Phone: 0870 0100 583
Web site: www.equifax.com

Experian Ltd
Consumer Help Service
PO Box 8000
Nottingham, NG1 5GX
Phone: 0870 241 6212
Web site: www.experian.co.uk

Index

• *G* •

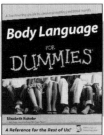

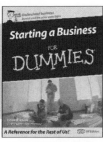

FOR DUMMIES®

Do Anything. Just Add Dummies

HOBBIES

Poker
FOR DUMMIES

978-0-7645-5232-8

Knitting
FOR DUMMIES

978-0-7645-5395-0

Drawing
FOR DUMMIES

978-0-7645-5476-6

Also available:

Art For Dummies
(978-0-7645-5104-8)

Aromatherapy For Dummies
(978-0-7645-5171-0)

Bridge For Dummies
(978-0-471-92426-5)

Card Games For Dummies
(978-0-7645-9910-1)

Chess For Dummies
(978-0-7645-8404-6)

Improving Your Memory
For Dummies
(978-0-7645-5435-3)

Massage For Dummies
(978-0-7645-5172-7)

Meditation For Dummies
(978-0-471-77774-8)

Photography For Dummies
(978-0-7645-4116-2)

Quilting For Dummies
(978-0-7645-9799-2)

EDUCATION

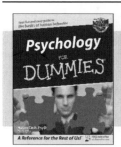

Psychology
FOR DUMMIES

978-0-7645-5434-6

The Koran
FOR DUMMIES

978-0-7645-5581-7

Anatomy & Physiology
FOR DUMMIES

978-0-7645-5422-3

Also available:

Algebra For Dummies
(978-0-7645-5325-7)

Astronomy For Dummies
(978-0-7645-8465-7)

Buddhism For Dummies
(978-0-7645-5359-2)

Calculus For Dummies
(978-0-7645-2498-1)

Cooking Basics For Dummies
(978-0-7645-7206-7)

Forensics For Dummies
(978-0-7645-5580-0)

Islam For Dummies
(978-0-7645-5503-9)

Philosophy For Dummies
(978-0-7645-5153-6)

Religion For Dummies
(978-0-7645-5264-9)

Trigonometry For Dummies
(978-0-7645-6903-6)

PETS

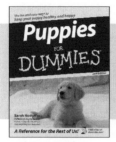

Puppies
FOR DUMMIES

978-0-470-03717-1

Dog Training
FOR DUMMIES

978-0-7645-8418-3

Cats
FOR DUMMIES

978-0-7645-5275-5

Also available:

Aquariums For Dummies
(978-0-7645-5156-7)

Birds For Dummies
(978-0-7645-5139-0)

Dogs For Dummies
(978-0-7645-5274-8)

Ferrets For Dummies
(978-0-7645-5259-5)

Golden Retrievers
For Dummies
(978-0-7645-5267-0)

Horses For Dummies
(978-0-7645-9797-8)

Jack Russell Terriers
For Dummies
(978-0-7645-5268-7)

Labrador Retrievers
For Dummies
(978-0-7645-5281-6)

Puppies Raising & Training
Diary For Dummies
(978-0-7645-0876-9)

FOR DUMMIES®

The easy way to get more done and have more fun

LANGUAGES

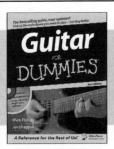

978-0-7645-5193-2

978-0-7645-5193-2

978-0-7645-5196-3

Also available:

Chinese For Dummies
(978-0-471-78897-3)

Chinese Phrases
For Dummies
(978-0-7645-8477-0)

French Phrases For Dummies
(978-0-7645-7202-9)

German For Dummies
(978-0-7645-5195-6)

Hebrew For Dummies
(978-0-7645-5489-6)

Italian Phrases For Dummies
(978-0-7645-7203-6)

Japanese For Dummies
(978-0-7645-5429-2)

Latin For Dummies
(978-0-7645-5431-5)

Spanish Phrases
For Dummies
(978-0-7645-7204-3)

Spanish Verbs For Dummies
(978-0-471-76872-2)

MUSIC AND FILM

978-0-7645-9904-0

978-0-7645-2476-9

978-0-7645-5105-5

Also available:

Bass Guitar For Dummies
(978-0-7645-2487-5)

Blues For Dummies
(978-0-7645-5080-5)

Classical Music For Dummies
(978-0-7645-5009-6)

Drums For Dummies
(978-0-471-79411-0)

Jazz For Dummies
(978-0-471-76844-9)

Opera For Dummies
(978-0-7645-5010-2)

Rock Guitar For Dummies
(978-0-7645-5356-1)

Screenwriting For Dummies
(978-0-7645-5486-5)

Singing For Dummies
(978-0-7645-2475-2)

Songwriting For Dummies
(978-0-7645-5404-9)

HEALTH, SPORTS & FITNESS

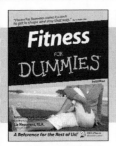

978-0-7645-7851-9

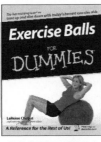

978-0-7645-5623-4

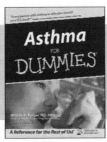

978-0-7645-4233-6

Also available:

Controlling Cholesterol
For Dummies
(978-0-7645-5440-7)

Diabetes For Dummies
(978-0-470-05810-7)

High Blood Pressure
For Dummies
(978-0-7645-5424-7)

Martial Arts For Dummies
(978-0-7645-5358-5)

Menopause FD
(978-0-470-061008)

Pilates For Dummies
(978-0-7645-5397-4)

Weight Training
For Dummies
(978-0-471-76845-6)

Yoga For Dummies
(978-0-7645-5117-8)

Available wherever books are sold. For more information or to order direct go to www.wiley.com or call 0800 243407 (Non UK call +44 1243 843296)

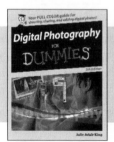

Printed and bound by CPI Group (UK) Ltd, Croydon, CR0 4YY